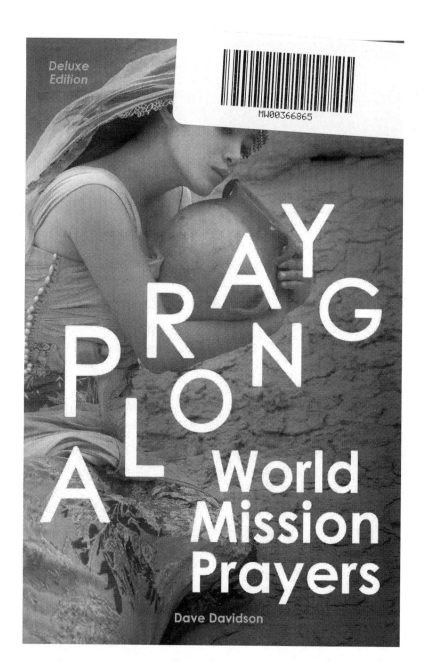

Deluxe
Edition

MW00366865

PRAY
ALONG
World
Mission
Prayers

Dave Davidson

Pray Along

World Mission Prayers Deluxe Edition
365 Powerful & Effective Pray Along Prayers
For All The Peoples & Nations Of The World

Written, compiled, created, designed,
photographed, & published by Dave Davidson
© 2001, 2016, 2018 Dave Davidson

(Photography for most country categories by Unsplash & Pixabay)

Key prayer contributors include Dan Davidson, George Verwer,
Joan Davidson, Bill Drake & Todd Morr.

Scripture taken from the Holy Bible, NEW INTERNATIONAL VERSION®,
NIV® Copyright © 1973, 1978, 1984, 2011 by Biblica, Inc.® Used by permission.
All rights reserved worldwide.

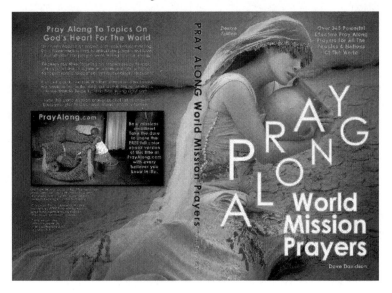

PrayAlong.com

Foreword

Lord, teach me to pray unceasingly.
1 Thessalonians 5:17 & Luke 11:1

Once ten people attended a church prayer meeting. Only three were willing to articulate prayers out loud, but at least ten people were willing to pray along.

Redeem the time focusing on prayers ready to rock. Are you willing to agree in prayer and "Pray Along" to topics rarely relegated, yet resoundingly relevant?

If so, let's rock and roll! It's that simple and profound. We could read, write, and talk about prayer all day... Make time to Surge Up and Pray Along right now.

May this world mission prayer bucket list of prayers bless you, glorify God, and impact eternity forever.
Dave Davidson

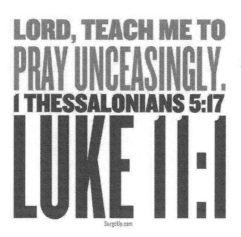

(More about prayer in Afterword Recap in back of book.)

Topic Contents – Pray Along

10-40 Window

A
Abortion
Acts 13 Breakthrough
Adoption
Afghanistan
Africa
AIDS & Epidemics
Air & Sea Ministries
Albania
Algeria
Andorra
Angola
Animalists
Answered Prayers
Antigua and Barbuda
Arabian Peninsula
Argentina
Armenia
Aruba
Asia
Atheists
Australia
Austria
Azerbaijan
B
Bahamas, The
Bahrain
Bangladesh
Baptism
Barbados
Belarus
Belgium
Belize
Benin
Bhutan
Bibleless People
Bolivia
Bosnia and Herzegovina
Botswana
Brazil
B.O.B.
Brokenness
Brunei
Buddhists
Bulgaria
Burkina Faso

Burundi
Business
C
Cabo Verde
Cambodia
Cameroon
Canada
Caribbean Countries
Catholics
Celebrities
Central African Republic
Central Asia
Chad
Children
Chile
China
Church
Church Planting
Closed & Communist Countries
Clothing
Colombia
Commitment & Calling
Comoros
Congo, Democratic Republic of the
Congo, Republic of the
Continents
Costa Rica
Cote d'Ivoire
Crime
Croatia
Cuba
Cults & Cons
Curacao
Cyprus
Czechia
D
Dalits
Deacons
Deliverance
Denmark
Disasters & Tragedies
Discernment
Disciple Makers
Discipleship
Disease & Illness
Djibouti
Doers of the Word
Dominica

4 PRAY ALONG World Mission Prayers

Liechtenstein Luxembourg
Monaco
Literature
Lithuania
Long Term Missions
M
Macau
Macedonia
Madagascar
Malawi
Malaysia
Maldives Malta Marshall
Islands
Mali
Marriage
Martyrdom
Martyrs
Mauritania
Mauritius Micronesia
Montenegro
Media
Medical Needs
Mega Cities
Mexico
Middle East
Military
Miscarriage & Infant Loss
Mission Agencies
Mission Mobilization
Mission Supporters
Missionaries
Missionary Kids
Missionary Needs
Moldova
Mongolia
Morocco
Mourning & Grieving
Mozambique
Muslims
Myanmar
N
Namibia
Nations
Nauru
Nepal
Netherlands
New Age
New Years
New Zealand

Nicaragua
Niger
Nigeria
North Africa
North Korea
Norway
O
Obedience
Oman
Orphans
P
Pakistan
Palau
Palestinian Territories
Panama
Papua New Guinea
Paraguay
Pastors
People Groups
Persecuted & Tortured
Personal Evangelism
Peru
Philippines
Pioneer Ministries
Poland
Poor & Oppressed
Portugal
Praise
Pray Along
Prayer Bucket List
Prayer in Church
Prayer Ministries
Prisoners & Injustice
Prison Ministry
Purity
Q
Qatar
R
Race of Faith
Race Reconciliation
Ramadan
Refugees
Revival & Repentance
Romania
Russia
Rwanda
S
Saint Kitts & Nevis, Saint Lucia

Saint Vincent and the Grenadines
Samoa
San Marino
Sanctity of Life
Sao Tome and Principe
Satanic Conspiracies
Saudi Arabia
Scripture Prayers
Scripture Songs
Senders
Sending Churches
Senegal
Serbia & Montenegro
Seychelles
Shelter
Short Term Missions
Sierra Leone
Sin & Temptation
Singapore
Sint Maarten
Slave Children
Slovenia
Solomon Islands
Somalia
South Africa
South East Asia
South Korea
South Sudan
Spain
Sphere Of Influence
Spiritual Gifts
Spiritual Warfare
Sri Lanka
Starvation
Stewardship
Strongholds
Sudan
Suffering
Suicide
Suriname
Sweden
Switzerland
Syria
T
Taiwan
Tajikistan
Tanzania
Teenagers

Tentmakers
Thailand
Thanksgiving
Third World
Those Who Have Heard
Those Who Have Not Heard
Timor Leste
Togo & Tonga
Tribal Groups
Trinidad and Tobago
Tunisia
Turkey
Turkmenistan
Tuvalu
U
Uganda
Ukraine
United Arab Emirates
United Kingdom
USA
Uruguay
Uzbekistan
V
Vanuatu
Venezuela
Vietnam
Vision
Walking in the Spirit
War
Widows
Willingness
Wolves in Sheep's Clothing
Women
World
World Leaders
Worship
Y
Yemen
You
Youth Ministry
Z
Zambia
Zimbabwe
Afterword Recap
Contributor Bios
Book Dares

10-40 Window

He looked up at the window and called out, "Who is on my side?
2 Kings 9:32

Lord, we pray for some of the least evangelized nations
of the world, which geographically make up 10/40 window:

Afghanistan, Albania, Algeria, Azerbaijan, Bahrain,
Bangladesh, Benin, Bhutan, Brunei, Burkina Faso,
Cambodia, Chad, China (PRC), China (Taiwan),
Djibouti, Egypt, Eritrea, Ethiopia, Gambia, Guinea,
Guinea-Bissau, India, Indonesia, Iran, Iraq, Israel,
Japan, Jordan, Kazakhstan, Korea, Kuwait,
Kyrgyzstan, Laos, Lebanon, Libya, Malaysia,
Maldives, Mali, Mauritania, Mongolia, Morocco,
Myanmar (Burma), Nepal, Niger, Nigeria, Oman,
Pakistan, Qatar, Saudi Arabia, Senegal, Somalia,
Sri Lanka, Sudan, Syria, Tajikistan, Thailand, Tibet,
Tunisia, Turkey, Turkmenistan, United Arab
Emirates, Uzbekistan, Vietnam, Western
Sahara, Yemen and more!

Lord forever lay on our hearts the 10/40 Window, the rectangular-shaped area extending from West Africa to East Asia, from ten degrees south to forty degrees north of the equator. May this area somehow inspire, in some way challenge, and always motive us for the rest of our lives.

Father in heaven we pray for the 4 billion people who live here, including 90 percent of the world's poorest of the poor. Lord our hearts break for the estimated that 1.6 billion of these people who have never had the chance to hear the Gospel of Jesus Christ - not even once!

Lord the fact that the core seat of every major non-Christian religion (Islam, Buddhism, Hinduism, Animism, Atheism, and Sikhism) is headquartered in the 10/40 Window is no coincidence. There is no excuse for us to not at least respond in regular prayer for these lost nations. Use us over and over to reach these various peoples You love so dearly. Lord have mercy on the countries represented in the 10/40 Window, witnessing the Christian Gospel means risking lives to the point of facing certain death. Truly, the 10/40 Window remains the darkest and most inhospitable territory to the cause of Christ as the greatest remaining stronghold of Satan on the planet. Lord change this staggering fact.

Father we lift up the two-thirds of the world's population, 95% of the people are unevangelized and the 90% of the poorest of the poor, averaging $250 per family annually. We ask You to protect and come along side up those persecuted in 43 of the 50 worst countries in the world.

What shall we do about how illiteracy is widespread? We cry out to You Lord how terrorist organizations and child prostitution run rampant in many of these nations. Horrific abuse of women and children remains unchecked. Toddlers are trained to be Jihad soldiers. Have mercy!

Dave Davidson

Abortion

For you created my inmost being; you knit me together in my mother's womb.
Psalm 139:13

Holy God, we intercede on behalf of those contemplating abortion. Plant in their hearts an insatiable love for life and urge to protect the lives of the precious unborn. For the doctors and nurses who have taken oaths to protect life, may they know and live the grace of repentance, serving others as true-life protectors and agents of healing.

For parents who have lost a child to abortion and whose hearts are closed to the mercy of God, I pray that they might know and experience the power of repentance, confession and the healing embrace of You, God, O merciful and loving eternal Father.

We pray for those overwhelmed

by grief and remorse at the loss of their child to abortion, that Jesus the shepherd, so rich in mercy and compassion, will heal their broken hearts. Give all those involved discernment and forgiveness. Lord, we pray for countries like Latvia who have had more abortions annually than live births. May more countries, leaders, believers and non-believers honor the unborn in the womb. Dave Davidson

Acts 13 Breakthrough

*'Set apart Barnabas and Saul for the work
to which I have called them.'*
Acts 13:2-4

Our God and Father, we thank you for these mega
motivating words in Acts 13. We pray in obedience
in Matthew Chapter 9 that You would send forth
laborers and workers into the harvest, locally and
across the world just like You sent out Paul and
Barnabus. O Lord, O Lord, send out 200,000 more
missionaries! Give church leaders the vision to follow
the Acts 13 example. Lord, we believe in faith that by
sending key people others will then step forward on
the local level and make up more than the difference.
Father God, make this an international breakthrough!

Raise up the intercessors,

the mission mobilizers and the senders to make the
great commission a reality, that the church might
be planted among every peoples.

George Verwer

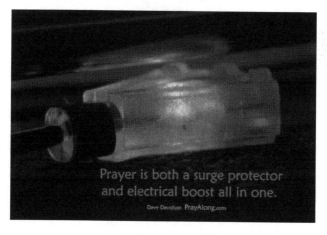

Prayer is both a surge protector
and electrical boost all in one.

Dave Davidson PrayAlong.com

Adoption

He predestined us for adoption to sonship through Jesus Christ, in accordance with his pleasure and will.
Ephesians 1:5

God, you do love adoption. You've adopted us into your family, giving us all rights and privileges of family. We are heirs and co-heirs with Jesus of all your treasures. We pray today for those seeking to adopt a child. Many children in the world do not have mothers and fathers. Many men and women do not have children. God, bring them together. Create the perfect match. Provide resources. Provide perfect timing. Give endurance and emotional strength through the grinding details. Give wisdom for them to anticipate ahead how to prepare practically for the coming change. Strengthen their marriage ahead of this coming gift. Heal any past disappointment. Parental love is nature. Adoptive parental love has to be SUPERnatural. Give a miracle of love and bonding. May nothing stand in the way of you accomplishing a completion of this match – child to parent. In Jesus!

Mark Herringshaw

Afghanistan

Arise, shine, for your light has come...
Isaiah 60:1

Lord Jesus, we give You all glory and honor and praise,
for You have healed the brokenhearted, proclaimed liberty
to the captives and set free those who were oppressed in
Afghanistan! We thank You for the American and coalition
forces who have been the instruments in Your hand to
bring freedom and peace to the Afghan people, and we ask
You to pour out a double portion of grace upon the
families of those in the military or civilian population who
lost their lives or suffered injuries in the process. Now we
ask, Lord, that you be Afghanistan's rock and fortress; and
for Your name's sake, lead the Afghan people and guide
them to establish You as the foundation upon which to
build their new nation. People of Afghanistan, arise, shine;
for your light has come! And the glory of the Lord is risen
upon you. We thank You, Lord, that You have released
a spirit of unity among the many ethnic groups in
Afghanistan, and the people have come together under
one government and one president. We bind the spirits of
division and religion and say that you shall no longer
cause war, oppression, or strife in this nation!

Lord, fill those in authority with Your righteousness that the people may rejoice. Cause the government leaders to take up the whole armor of God. Stir up the citizens to pray for those in authority that they may lead quiet and peaceable lives. We thank You for granting freedom to the Afghan women, including the right to vote and go to school. Lord, Your people humble themselves and pray that You will forgive the sins of the Afghan people and heal their land. As the nation obeys Your voice, Oh Lord, bless the produce of their ground, increase their herds and cattle and flocks. Bless their basket and kneading bowl, their storehouses and all to which they set their hand.

Grant the Afghan people plenty of goods, and open the heavens to give rain to the land in its season. Heal the effects of years of war, and restore the land to the lushness You first created. Bring commerce, industry, entrepreneurship and agriculture to the nation and replace the production of opium with righteous and bountiful sources of income. Jehovah Jireh, establish a sound, stable and prosperous economy, and cause it to expand to the surrounding nations. Grant Your shalom in all its fullness to the people of Afghanistan! Amen.

Prayer from ChavdaMinistries.org

Lord as the Islamic Republic of Afghanistan does not allow conversion from Islam conversion is seen as apostasy and brings shame on the convert's family and community. Please Lord bring change to take place within the country. We pray for openness to religions outside of Islam.
PrayAlong.com

Thank God that Christian relief agencies also manifest the love of God through meeting the nation's immense physical needs. Humble us Lord that many workers have died as martyrs. Amid the great persecution, there are perhaps several thousand believers in Afghanistan today!
PrayAlong.com

Grab the book Pray Along Afghanistan at PrayAlong.com

Africa

It has always been my ambition to preach the gospel where Christ was not known, so that I would not be building on someone else's foundation.
Romans 15:20

We ask Lord, that You will raise up true believers in Algeria to be a light among its people. Soften the president of Egypt's heart toward Christians so churches will be allowed to reopen.

Despite restrictions,

may Mauritanian believers find freedom in Jesus Christ. Rise up spiritual leaders for Equatorial Guinea. Through the work of those who have counted the cost to follow Christ, may many come to know You Lord in Morocco. Have the church cling to Biblical teaching to be a light to Nigeria. May Somalian Christians continue to walk in truth. May the Body of Christ take root and multiply in Tunisia. Bless the Christians in the Comoro Islands who continue to meet in secret despite laws restricting such gatherings. Dave Davidson

AIDS & Epidemics

Jesus went throughout Galilee, teaching in their synagogues,
preaching the good news of the kingdom, and healing
every disease and sickness among the people.
Matthew 4:23

Loving God, you see yourself in those who are vulnerable,
and make your home with the poor and weak of this
world; warm our hearts with the fire of your Spirit,
and help us to accept the challenges of AIDS.

Protect the healthy, calm the frightened,

give courage to those in pain, comfort the dying,
console the bereaved, and strengthen those who
care for the sick. National Catholic AIDS Network
Lord, grant us a balanced compassion and extended
stamina to minister to all those with AIDS.

Humble us all Lord as we seek You in this.

George Verwer

**Lord nearly 8 million African children have been orphaned and at least one
million are infected. Six young people are infected with the AIDS virus
every minute. Show your compassionate mercy to those suffering.**

Air & Sea Ministries

I have been constantly on the move... in danger at sea...
2 Corinthians 11:26

We lift up the 1000 missionary pilots, mechanics and support personnel. May more technically skilled and spiritually equipped servants join them. Thank You Lord, for MAF, JAARS, NTM and ministries like it pioneering the gospel. Supply resources to these strategic ministries.

Keep them safe in your hands Lord.

Bless Operation Mobilisation's ship ministry of literature distribution, encouraging and equipping local churches, evangelism, discipleship training and intercultural exposure through the MV DOULOS and MV LOGOS II. Bless YWAM's Mercy Ships, MV Anastasis and the MV Good Samaritan with their discipling programs, Christian aid and mobile medical work. Thank You for all boat related ministries in South America, through Belgian canals, in southwest France, New Zealand, Korea, Singapore, Indonesia, the Greek islands and Pacific Ocean fleets.

Uphold the spiritual health,

growth and safety of all involved. Stimulate world vision, local evangelism and holy living in ports and airstrips of call and reach the 10 million seamen, seafarers and fishermen around the world. Dave Davidson

Albania

*I will send you rain in its season, and the ground
will yield its crops and the trees their fruit.*
Leviticus 26:4

We pray for unselfish vision in Albanian leaders
and for peaceful alliances for a common purpose among
the political opponents. Lord we pray for continual
economic grow. We pray against the spirit of poverty.
Bestow lucrative partnerships with other nations.
We pray for rain and wisdom for the agricultural sector.
Father we thank you for peace across Albania.
We speak against the rise of organized crime.
May your word find its way into more and
more homes and transform the nation.

Adapted from PrayerRelay.com

Andorra

Lift up your heads, O you gates! Lift up, you everlasting doors!
And the King of glory shall come in. Who is this King of glory?
The Lord of hosts, He is the King of glory.
Psalms 24:9-10

Lord open the hearts of landlocked Principality
of Andorra, as one of the smallest states in Europe,
nestled high in the Pyrenees Mountains
between French and Spanish borders.

Reach the 10 million tourists

who visit each year drawn by the winter sports,
summer climate, and duty-free goods.
Dave Davidson

Angola

"There is the sound of war in the camp."
Exodus 32:17

Father, as we pray for Angola, we pray
for reconciliation through Christ's love after
40 years of civil war. We also pray for the safe
removal of millions of landmines still killing
and maiming many, especially children.

Lord of the harvest, we pray for desperately needed
Christian workers to hear Your call to serve. Father,
we pray for loving partnerships between foreign
agencies and Angolan ministries to lead the way
forward. We also pray for mission agencies that are
surrounded by need and are requiring wisdom
and resources. Lord, we pray for Bible distribution
initiatives and translation efforts... prayer.africa/angola

Animalists

For since the creation of the world God's invisible qualities—
his eternal power and divine nature—have been clearly seen,
being understood from what has been made,
so that men are without excuse.
Romans 1:20

True and faithful God,

have mercy on those who choose to believe that You don't exist. Thank You for extending Your kindness and patience to men and women who once opposed Christ. Hand out wisdom Father and pour out mercy to those who mock You. Lord, for those who by some ancestral tradition believe in the superstition of magic  and powers of animals and false spirits, we ask that You reveal the ministry of Your true Holy Spirit. For the hundreds of people groups in China who perform rituals with animals, bring them to Jesus! We pray that creation itself would be evidence to believe in You, God, as the Creator. Dave Davidson

_____
_____
_____
_____
_____
_____

Answered Prayer

*So we fasted and petitioned our God about this,
and he answered our prayer.*
Ezra 8:23

Lord, we thank you for the privilege to be able to
speak to you in prayer. We thank You for Your
precious promises in Your Word. Thank You for
answering our prayers according to Your will. We
give you praise and glory for the many prayers that
You are answering today throughout the world. May
the prayers of those intercessors glorify You Lord.
We ask for perseverance in our prayer walk as
we wait for Your perfect will to be revealed.

We thank You for Your perfect timing.

We praise You for being a faithful God who always
keeps His promises. You are a true and just all loving
Father. Help us to know You always listen. Reinforce
in our hearts the importance of praying continually
to You. Know our hearts, Father God. Dave Davidson

Antigua & Barbuda

Coral and jasper are not worthy of mention;
the price of wisdom is beyond rubies.
Job 28:18

We pray for complacent Christians to be mobilized
to love the victims of substance abuse in their
communities. We pray for Godly wisdom as leaders
seek solutions to money-laundering issues and for
local Christian radio stations to edify believers
and evangelize the unreached.

adapted from Prayercast.com

Arabian Peninsula

*See, I am doing a new thing! Now it springs up;
do you not perceive it? I am making a way in the
desert and streams in the wasteland.*
Isaiah 43:19

Lord, no region of the world has been so resistant to
the gospel as the countries of Bahrain, Kuwait, Iman,
Saudi Arabia, Qatar and the U.A. E. until now.
We beseech You to move in the hearts of Christians
worldwide for workers to this Christian desert field.
Lord, solve the challenges that face mission strategists
when considering the vast sums of
money going to propagate Islam.
Like the battle of Jericho, Lord, be glorified, be
honored and take the victory! Father, grow Your
church amid the lost Arab people groups of
Yemeni, Hijazi, Saudi, Bedouin, Omani, Bahraini,
Egyptian and the Sudanese Arabs. Lord, bring
a spiritual harvest among the Socotran, Mahra,
Persian, Urdu, Somali, Begali, Southern Baluch
and the Pathan people groups. Dave Davidson

Argentina

They plot injustice and say, "We have devised a perfect plan!"
Surely the human mind and heart are cunning.
Psalm 64:6

God of life, you put in human beings
the imprint of your image and likeness
and made us to participate with you in your creation.
Forgive our incapacity to respect and protect life in all
its forms. God of justice, you call us to travel this
path which is the only route leading to true peace.
Forgive our daily acts of injustice which condemn
many, many persons to death by hunger, exclusion
and war, and lead us to the abyss of endless violence.
God, incarnate in history, forgive us because we
imprison you in our dogmas, limiting you to our
religious institutions
and crucifying you alongside
the vulnerable of our time.
O God, strengthen us in our
daily work for a world
more just, accepting
differences, built on diversity.

Renew our commitment to peace with justice,
a commitment which denounces the arrogance
of those who believe that they are powerful and own
the lives of all the rest. Give us a vision to banish
violence in all its forms. Establish as the foundation
of our lives, and the lives of our people, respect,
equality, truth and justice.

Bishop Nelly Ritchie, Buenos Aires, Argentina

Armenia

*The grass withers and the flowers fall,
but the word of our God endures forever.*
Isaiah 40:8

Thanksgiving and glory - We will give
You always. You give nourishment - To the
flowers of the valley, and to the birds in the
sky. We always enjoy Your graces, Dear
Father, Beneficent God. Glory to You, forever.

Kohootyun yev park Kezee meeshd dank
Too vor tashdee dzagheegeen Yev yergeenkee
trchooneen Snoont goodas adeneen. Shnorhnert,
ov Hayr, Geh vayelenk har, Asdvadz parerar,
Park kez antatar. Amen.
Armenian Prayer of Thanksgiving

Aruba

*...creation itself will be liberated from its bondage to decay
and brought into the freedom and glory of the children of God.*
Romans 8:21

Thank You God that the majority of people living
in Aruba identify as being Christians or Catholic,
so we ask for discernment and wisdom with handling
division in the church. With a history of gold rushes
and the lovely white sand beaches may the attraction
of Aruba itself now be recognized by people serving
God. Deliver people from addiction bondage and
strengthen them during broken family challenges.

Bring the measure of morality and a righteous
standard as part of the healing and recognition
of Jesus as savior to locals and tourists.
Dave Davidson

Asia

This went on for two years, so that all the Jews and Greeks who lived in the province of Asia heard the word of the Lord.
Acts 19:10

সারা বিশ্বের জন্য প্রার্ থন্য করষ্শিন্। প্রবিটা মান্ুশের জন্য প্রার্ থন্য করষ্শিন্ We pray for the war-affected people in the world, especially for the children in different countries around the world. We pray for the Marawi people in the Philippines who are caught in the middle of a war between their government and ISIS-related parties. Peace in Palestine is inevitable. The question is, how do we make it happen today? Amen. িওিওিওংলাশ্বেশের ওিবির জন্য প্রার্ থন্য করষ্শিন্ ত্রিাং সি পবরিাশ্বরর জন্য প্রার্ থন্য করষ্শিন্

Pray for the peace of Bangladesh. Pray for all of our family. Road accidents are one of the great problems of Bangladesh. Every day, an average of eight people are killed and more than double this number are seriously wounded.

We pray for the families and departed souls, and that accidents would be reduced. Please pray for our MCC offices in Bogra, Dhaka and Mimensingh. May our work together in food security, education, public heath training, and peacebuilding bring more resilient communities. We pray for the well-being of MCC national staff, service workers and our families. Amen.

আমাশ্বের সিার পবরিাশ্বরর জন্য প্রার্ থন্যা করশ্বিন্। We pray for those suffering from political violence. During general elections, people are impacted by the political party's conflicts. In Bangladesh, elections will happen in 2019, but the politicking has already begun. We pray for our people who are suffering from climate change, especially poor people. Amen. হে হৈর আমাশ্বের প্রশ্বিযশ্বকর সিান্শ্বের জন্য আবে থিাটে ও সুষ্ঠিযা টোান্ কর। God please bless our children and give them good health. প্রশ্বিযক মান্ুশ্বের জন্য প্রার্ থন্যা করশ্বিন্। We pray for everyone. Amen.

Mary Lou Klassen

Lord break our hearts for Asia as many estimate
70% of children alive today live in Asian countries.

Atheists

...help me overcome my unbelief.
Mark 9:24

Dear Lord point atheists in the right direction eve n though they are convinced they're right, and even if secret doubts, and pride probably gets in the way. God do what we can't do, and conquer even the most stubborn heart. We ask you God to convict him of his sin and his pride and convince him of his need for Christ. May we be a witness to him—a witness to Christ's peace and joy. Lord though some may argue with what we say, but they can't

argue with the reality of a life that's been transformed by Christ. May atheists face honestly the consequences of his atheism. If God doesn't exist (as he claims), then he has no hope of life after death. Nor does he have anyone to turn to when he needs guidance, or when life turns against him. He is like those of whom the Bible speaks, "without hope and without God in the world" (Ephesians. 2:12). Most of all, we urge You Lord to help atheists examine Jesus Christ honestly and openly, as He is found in the Gospels of the New Testament.

Adapted from advice by Billy Graham

Australia

Restore us to yourself, Lord, that we may return;
renew our days as of old.
Lamentations 5:21

Lord and God of this Great South Land,
today we thank you for
this ancient, harsh but beautiful country.

God of the Outback, God of the Cities.
we thank you for
blessing Australia with
rich resources and prosperity,
for freedom of worship,
sound government and
a quality of life that
enjoys sport and open beaches.

Save us from greed and
the material gods of this age
that leave nations dry,
withered and short of mercy.
Open our hearts to
the disadvantaged and
to those who seek asylum.

Bring justice and compassion.
Help us to bridge the gap between
the indigenous people and
the settlers of this land.

We thank you Lord
for those who came before our time to
pioneer and plant the Christian faith.
Save us from living on the faith of our fathers,
and this generation from drifting
away from you and our national heritage.

Renew the church.
Bless good government and
move our nation towards
the fullness of your Kingdom.
We pray in Jesus name.

Lord our God
today we acknowledge you
as the Great Spirit of this land
that rests under the Southern Cross.
We thank you for
this ancient land with
its unique animals, birds and flowers.

Help us to enjoy not only
its beauty and antiquity
but the potential and
responsibility we share
as a young nation in Asia.

Bless all Australians
serving you here and
in other countries,
especially those standing
with the poor and disadvantaged.

Lord restrain the arrogant
and the evils of secularism and corruption.
Help us to embrace pro-life values,
to cherish our children,
the bond of marriage and to pursue
freedom and fairness for all.

Save the church from compromise.
Empower it by your Spirit
to declare Jesus
as Saviour and Lord.
Renew us with
the courage of the prophets.
Rekindle your holy love in us
so that with a love for you,
for people and our country.
we shine as clear advocates of
justice and peace.
This we pray in Jesus name.
Amen. Rev Ted (EA) Curnow

Austria

The land yields its harvest; God, our God, blesses us.
Psalm 67:6

LORD, we pray for Austria, a nation of culture, music, art, and beautiful scenery. We just want to thank You Lord, for the grass roots 24/7 prayer movement that You are raising up among the Youth in Austria, both the Roman Catholic and Pentecostal Protestant groups. May the youth of Austria embrace Jesus as Savior and LORD. Pour out Your Spirit, LORD, the former and the latter rain, like You prophesied by the prophet Joel, on Austria's sons and daughters! Also, we just want to thank You for the Fred Lambert Ministries and others of kindred spirit who are committed to filling Austria with the knowledge of Your glory!

Clothed in Your armor we take our stand with the Austrian Church, releasing prayer reinforcement from many lands. We proclaim Austrians are being drawn by the Holy Spirit into a genuine relationship with Jesus Christ…that nominal Christians are coming home to a personal relationship with Jesus, as Savior and LORD. We ask You, LORD, to raise up hosts of Bible-believing pastors, who will raise up disciples, and empower all Believers with a bold witness for Jesus Christ. LORD of the Harvest, fill the shell of religion in this nation with Your Living Presence to combat the forces of suicide, abortion, and alcoholism. Thank You for sending the Holy Spirit who is moving with power in the Lutheran and Reformed Churches. Renew them with revival fires, and empower them to unite with other members of the Body of Christ that together they might evangelize their homeland. As the Body of Jesus, we unite and pull down the antichrist spirits that have restricted the rights and privileges of smaller Christian organizations/ministries.

We proclaim: the Gospel of Jesus Christ will prevail, bringing favor and good understanding to the children of the Most High God, and unbelievers will be drawn to their message of Hope and a Future.

Reveal Yourself to Austria, the heart of Europe, LORD! We pray Spiritual revival and renewal in Austria, in the name of Jesus!

Word Ministries Prayers That Avail Much

Azerbaijan

For he will command his angels concerning you to guard you in all your ways;
Psalm 91:11

God of the angel armies bring the end to restrictions on worshipping Jesus in unregistered churches in Azerbaijan, which is located between Russia and Iran. With over 80% practicing Muslims confusing Christianity with Russian imperialism, please protect Christ followers often harassed and heavily fined by all sorts of government officials.

Guide and lead any foreign proselytizing and missionary efforts to reach the people groups living in Azerbaijan including the 600,000 displaced in the Armenian-Azeri territorial dispute over the Nagorno-Karabakh.

Dave Davidson

Bahamas

I will destroy your witchcraft and you will no longer cast spells.
Micah 5:12

May the beautiful backdrop of shallow seas
with 2,400 reefs encapsulate a spiritual desire
to follow Jesus Christ in depth.

With a quarter of the economy effected by illegal
Haitian refugees, press upon the hearts of believers
to somehow reach them with resurrection
power over voodoo practices.

Just as the Bahamas use their own currency, multiply
the blessings of this wealthy Caribbean country with
a constant one-of-a-kind authentic ownership
in Christian testimony.

Dave Davidson

Bahrain

Your kingdom is divided and given to the Medes and Persians.
Daniel 5:28

Thank God the island of Bahrain is the most open country in the Gulf region and for the Christian-run hospital and school for more than 100 years (the first western-style hospital and school in the entire Gulf). Thank God bookstores are also allowed to provide Bibles and Christian teaching openly to the public. Lord use the tourist hotspot Bahrain, at the center of the Gulf, linked by a causeway bridge to the most closed Gulf country, Saudi Arabia. Lord reach the many Saudis who come to Bahrain's freer atmosphere for holiday and weekend breaks, as well as visitors from other nearby nations like Qatar and Kuwait.

We pray that the Lord Jesus would send out more laborers to impact Bahrainis and tourists for Christ. Praise God that the church is awakening and that expatriate churches are catching the vision of making disciples. There is a renewed devotion for prayer and witnessing in Bahrain.

Encouragingly, there is also an increasing hunger for the Word of God and a willingness to hear the hope of the gospel. May the Lord work among Bahraini believers desperate for more of Him. May He build up His Church to be a united and powerful voice in this divided land, a land with divisions we pray for the political tensions.

Lord show Your sovereignty whenever protests inspired by Arab uprising in the region, placed a greater strain on the tensions between authorities and opposition, and between Sunni and Shia communities. May leaders and people of influence pursue the best conditions for all citizens of Bahrain. adapted from awm-pioneers.org

_____

_____

_____

_____

_____

_____

_____

_____

_____

Bangladesh

I will bless her with abundant provisions;
her poor I will satisfy with food.
Psalm 132:15

Dear God, bless the growing congregations that
continually contend with the challenge of provisions
for poverty and the despair of long-term effects of
being so prone to monsoon related natural disasters.
Meanwhile we ask for clean water, equipped mission
workers, and ministered to widows.

May mobile medical ministry clinics meet physical,
emotional, and spiritual needs of Bangladesh.
Never let us forget the need to pray
for this prayer-worthy place!
Dave Davidson

Baptism

And this water symbolizes baptism that now saves you also—
not the removal of dirt from the body but the pledge of a clear
conscience toward God. It saves you by the
resurrection of Jesus Christ.
1 Peter 3:21

Dear Lord and heavenly Father, I praise and thank You with my whole being that I was baptized into the body of Christ when I was born into the family of God – and thank You for the wonderful opportunity to declare my new-found faith in Christ and my new life in Him through going down into the waters of baptism as an outward sign of death – and coming up out of the waters – as an outward sign of the inward change that took place in me at my rebirth.

I pray that my baptism may be a true outward declaration to the world of my inwards change of heart and status in Christ – Who lifted me out of the miry clay and has seated me together with Christ in heavenly placed.

Lord may my water baptism truly demonstrate to the world the beautiful spiritual baptism that took place the moment I first believed -when I trusted Christ as Savior and was born again by the power of the Holy Spirit – Who baptized me into the body of Christ.

Just as the children of Israel who went through the Red Sea were baptized into Moses – and just as I was baptized into Christ when I trusted in the blood of Jesus for my redemption – I pray that going down into the baptismal waters may demonstrate to all that I have been crucified in Christ and died to the old life with Him on the cross.

Just as the children of Israel came up out on the other
side of the Red Sea - so also may this water baptism
demonstrate to all concerned that I also have risen-up
into newness of life in Christ Jesus my Lord.
Praise You in the Holy name of Jesus, Amen.

Thank You Father that I am born again and that You
have saved me form sin and death, through Christ
Jesus my Lord - that I have been born from
above in spirit and truth.

Lord I just want to thank You for the wonderful
things that took place the moment that I trusted in
Jesus as Savior. Thank You that You transferred me
from the kingdom of darkness into the kingdom of
Your dear Son. Thank You that I am accepted in
Christ Jesus, Your beloved Son and have been clothed
in His righteousness – thank You that I have become a
child of God and been made a joint-heir with Jesus
and thank You that in Him I am seated in heavenly
places and that I have become eternally secure,
having been given eternal life – by faith
in Jesus Christ my Savior.

Thank You also for the understanding that the moment that I was born again, Your Holy Spirit baptized me, once and forever, into the body of Christ – that he placed me eternally, into that body of believers that is called the Church. Thank You for this precious baptism into Christ and may I learn to grow in grace and in a knowledge Him Who loved me and

gave Himself for me.

Fill me day by day with Your Spirit – lead and guide me in the days that lie ahead and thank You that in Christ I am saved by grace alone, through faith alone in Christ alone and that He did it all and it is finished, in Jesus name I pray, Amen. Knowing-Jesus.com

Barbados

*They search the sources of the rivers
and bring hidden things to light.*
Job 28:11

Creator God, how could we possibly
not thank You for the earth you have given to us!
With joy we praise you for the high mountains and
their trees, for the rushing waters of Caribbean rivers
which give the breath of inspiration and the joy of
fruitfulness, for the forests so luxuriant in foliage,
the glorious tall trees and the abundance of temperate
climes. Still more, we praise You for the wisdom for
living, and the commitment which our dignified and
courageous ancestors taught us, the neighbors in
whom we became acquainted with You.

Caribbean Conference of Churches

Belarus

But those who suffer he delivers in their suffering;
he speaks to them in their affliction.
Job 36:15

Oh Lord, we thank you for these wondrous countries
where priests, pastors, and lay people gave up their
lives during communist times. For the long history of
Christianity in these lands and those who work for
democracy and openness in government.

We especially give
thanks to all those
who help to
alleviate the
suffering of people
due to the conflict
in Ukraine and
who try to

counteract and overcome divisions.

We pray for your guidance as these nations work to
reconfigure political and economic structures and for
compassion and integrity for all peoples in these
nations with such diverse ethnic histories. We ask that
you especially watch over the large number of people
who now live in poverty and are unemployed, and
also those who suffer from alcoholism, HIV
and AIDS, tuberculosis, and other
life-threatening diseases.

We also lift up those trying to revitalize churches after
decades of official atheism and also those in Belarus
and Ukraine who suffer from the continued effects
of the Chernobyl nuclear disaster. Bread.org

Belgium

Do not seek revenge or bear a grudge against anyone among your people, but love your neighbor as yourself. I am the Lord.
Leviticus 19:18

Lord God, please raise up more Belgian Christian leaders. Father, we ask that You give the people of Belgium a vision for what You want to do there. Savior and Lord, please rescue the marriages of Belgium and make your people an example of grace. Heavenly Father give Your people in Belgium a hunger and a thirst for Your Word.

Make the Bible come alive for each believer. We ask, God, that Christians in Belgium would be examples of righteous and upright living and would strive to pay taxes honestly and not to work in "zwart". Please, Jesus, help Belgian Christians be quick to forgive others, not holding grudges.

Lord of the Harvest, please raise up many Belgians and others who will labor in the spiritual harvest of Belgium. adapted from zendingsbode.org

Belize

For them I sanctify myself, that they too may be truly sanctified.
John 17:19

Almighty and Eternal God, who through Jesus Christ
has revealed Your Glory to all nations, please protect and
preserve Belize, our beloved country. God of might,
wisdom and justice, please assist our Belizean government
and people with your Holy Spirit of counsel and fortitude.

Let your light of Your divine wisdom direct their plans
and endeavours so that with Your help we may attain
our just objectives. With Your guidance, may all our
endeavours tend to peace, social justice, liberty, national
happiness, the increase of industry, sobriety
and useful knowledge.

We pray, O God of Mercy, for all of us that we may
be blessed in the knowledge and sanctified in the
observance of Your most holy law, that we may be
preserved in union and in peace which the world
itself cannot give. And, after enjoying the blessings of
this life, please admit us, dear Lord, to that eternal
reward that You have prepared for those who love You.

National Prayer of Belize

Benin

The Lord is a refuge for the oppressed,
a stronghold in times of trouble.
Psalm 9:9

Father, we thank you for the people of Benin. Thank you for creating them and blessing them with so many resources. Thank you for enabling them to create a safe haven for so many Togo refugees.

Lord Jesus, we pray for righteous leaders who will be good stewards of the country, that they will not search for personal gain, but that they will sincerely look after the people of Benin.

Father we ask that You will break the stronghold of Voodoo and release the people of Benin from the fear of Voodoo. Lord we ask that you will touch their lives, especially the people in the Northern parts where they have been fighting over land for decades against tribes from Burkina Faso. Lord, please change their hearts so that may be content with what they have.

Lord, thank you that the people of Benin may have political freedom to honor Your name in public. We pray that it will be lasting and that their testimonies will touch many hearts and bring glory to Your name.

prayer.africa/benin

Bhutan

*For since the creation of the world God's invisible qualities
—his eternal power and divine nature—have been clearly seen,
being understood from what has been made, so that
people are without excuse.*
Romans 1:20

Lord our hearts break for the 75% of people in Bhutan
who are Drukpa Kaygu Buddhists believing there
is no God and no soul. May Romans 1:20 and the
revelation of creation be part of the evidence in
a newfound faith in Jesus Christ. May they see evil
for what it is yet have no fear of evil spirits that can
be rebuked in the name above all names, Jesus.

We lift of their hard to pronounce key villages
by name... Bumthang Dzongkhag, Chhukha
Dzongkhag, Dagana Dzongkhag, Gasa Dzongkhag,
Haa Dzongkhag, Lhuentse Dzongkhag, Mongar
Dzongkhag, Paro Dzongkhag, Pema Gatshel
Dzongkhag, Punakha Dzongkhag, Samdrup Jongkhar
Dzongkhag, Samtse Dzongkhag, Sarpang
Dzongkhag, Thimphu City, Thimphu Dzongkhag,
Trashi Yangtse Dzongkhag, Trashigang Dzongkhag,
Trongsa Dzongkhag, Tsirang Dzongkha, Wangdue
Phodrang Dzongkhag and Zhemgang Dzongkhag.

Dave Davidson

Bibleless People

There are all sorts of languages in the world,
yet none of them is without meaning. If I do not grasp
the meaning of what someone is saying, I am a foreigner
to the speaker, and he is a foreigner to me.
1 Corinthians 14:10, 11

Lord we pray for those people groups who do not have a bible translated in their own language. We pray dear God that they may hear. "How can they believe in the one of whom they have not heard?" (Romans 10:14) We pray Lord they may believe. "But the message they heard was of no value to them, because those who heard did not combine it with faith." (Hebrews 4:2) Father bring them Your Holy Word. Have them read or have it read to them, that they may have the Bible in their own language. "These words were written in the script of each province and in the language of each people." (Esther 8:9) "Blessed is the one who reads the words of this prophecy, and blessed are those who hear it read and take to heart what is written in it." (Revelation 1:3) May the result be indigenous churches using the Scriptures. "All Scripture is God-breathed and is useful for teaching, rebuking, correcting and training in righteousness." (2 Timothy 3:16) "So that all nations might believe and obey Him." (Romans 16:26)

Jesus we pray for the stamina

and continued health of translators, co-translators, their families and their children. May furloughs, administrative duties, and other urgent tasks not interfere. We pray about school issues, family duties and for financial resources to support the work. Dear God in heaven we pray for final decisions on key terms to be acceptable to all concerned. Jesus we pray for involvement and consensus of denominations on wording, writing, and printing. This includes reconciliation of alphabets and alternate wordings, due to dialect differences. We also pray for authorizations and approvals by church authorities and governments where required.

Jesus we pray for translations

being done in secret to protect lives of those involved and their families. We pray for survival from hurricanes, earthquakes and safety of manuscripts. Dear God we pray against wars and insurrections that render it impossible to continue the work. Father God we pray against the outbreak of persecution against the mother-tongue workers involved. May those involved in the translation not fall into sin that nullifies their efforts. We pray against subversive political forces that make it impossible to live

and work in villages. We ask for protection against theft and destruction of computers, printers, homes and translation centers.

We pray against technical failures of computers, storage discs, copiers, printers, and service items. We ask You God for readers to be available to give community acceptability of the translation and for trained consultants.

We ask for accuracy

of typesetters, often working in a language they do not understand, for proofreaders, that they may catch and correct errors that would mar the translation and for printers, that inking, pagination, binding, may result in clear, useable, durable books. We pray for all aspects of publishing, printing and fulfillment of bibles!

adapted from Wycliffe.com

Bolivia

Are God's consolations not enough for you,
words spoken gently to you?
Job 15:11

O God, from Bolivian soil,

The Bolivian people implore you to listen to their voice,
feel their sadness and see the tears of your people, which
are also your tears. So many bodies without any life left
have fallen in the streets, in the roads and in the fields,
leaving behind pain and sorrow within the Bolivian
family. In those moments in which their hearts are
mourning from such suffering, give them consolation.

Do not allow them to relinquish their self-control,
but give them a vision so they can see with their own eyes
the way they ought to go, so they can reach life by the path
of justice. Hear, O God, the voices of the multitudes who
march in the streets and highways crying for justice,
tired of so much misery, the lack of work, corruption and
violence; tired of so much authoritarianism by the people
in power, who take decisions without consulting the
people and who are guided by their own stingy interests;

tired that the natural resources that you have given for the well-being of all the people are once more being used to benefit the economic interests of the large transnational corporations.

Hear the voice of the Bolivians
and give them discernment and strength
so that they can respond to hatred with love,to injustice
with righteousness, to apathy with commitment to their
people, to individualism with solidarity,
to violence with peace.

Hear their voice and inspire within their hearts (and within ours) the knowledge of peace, the strength of justice, the joy of being close to one another. Guide them to walk with the crowds on the way of peace with the signs of justice. O God, hear their voice and grant to them (and us) your eternal peace.

Gustavo Loza and Mirela Armand Ugon,
Cochabamba, Bolivia

Bosnia & Herzegovina

As we have heard, so we have seen in the city of the Lord Almighty, in the city of our God: God makes her secure forever.
Psalm 48:8

Lord we agree in prayer over the song, "God of This City" by Bluetree, declaring it over these major cities in Bosnia: Sarajevo, Banja Luka, Tuzla, Zenica, Bijeljina, Mostar, Prijedor and Brčko.

Pray4Bosnia.com

Botswana

He is the one we proclaim, admonishing and teaching everyone with all wisdom, so that we may present everyone fully mature in Christ. **Colossians 1:28**

We pray for mature beliefs free from tribal or animistic thinking. Lord, we ask that You establish more Biblical training for indigenous Church leaders so that the full Gospel of Jesus Christ can be preached in all the churches, without being mixed with animistic beliefs. Please help congregations to work together, Lord.

We also pray that the youth will choose abstinence to cleanse their nation of HIV/AIDS. Father, we ask that You will show Yourself as a Dad to more than 100,000 AIDS orphans. We pray, Lord, that people will make use of services providing ARV's in order to prolong their lives. Father, will You please bring an end to the stigma toward HIV/AIDS sufferers. prayer.africa/botswana

Brazil

In all your detestable practices and your prostitution you did not remember the days of your youth, when you were naked and bare, kicking about in your blood.
Ezekiel 16:22

Father God bless the over 195 million in Brazil as the fifth most populous country of which approximately 30% are under 18 years of age. Reduce the rise of child prostitution by foreign tourists in places like Rio de Janeiro, Recife and Fortaleza. Lord have mercy in how teenagers murdered in Brazil has more than doubled in the last 20 years with about 28 per day. God guide the 3 million children and adolescents who remain out of school. Ease maternal mortality rates and curb cocaine consumption protecting children exposed to drug-related violence, weapons smuggling, and financial extortion crimes.
Dave Davidson

B.O.B.

Therefore, since we have such a hope, we are very bold.
2 Corinthians 3:12

B-urden: Lord stir my heart by the spiritual lostness all around. Give me the desire to see people saved. Spark a burning passion for the unreached peoples of the world to hear the gospel. I yearn for the salvation of people without Christ. I long for friends and loved ones to know You Lord, to earnestly desire for the gospel to go to the ends of the earth. God move my heart. Give me a burden for the souls of people and Your compassionate heart for the lost.

O-pportunity: Make me a witness for Christ. Open doors to share my testimony and faith with others. Give me opportunities to share the good news. Specifically, Lord make opportunity for those I know don't know You. Open my eyes to recognize those opportunities when they come. I pray that the Holy Spirit would prepare hearts before me paving the way of a fearless faith filled journey.

B-oldness: Keep me far from any fear sharing my faith. Boost my boldness in evangelism. Increase courage to share Your gospel when those opportunities come. I pray for the "perfect love" that casts out fear and a not ashamed of the gospel attitude. Open my mouth to share Your love with others. As opposition to Christianity increases, may I hold fast to the gospel and be faithful to proclaim it. Give me strength as I go out with Your message.

Todd Benkert & Dave Davidson

Brokenness

My servants will sing out of the joy of their hearts, but you will cry out from anguish of heart and wail in brokenness of spirit.
Isaiah 65:14

Oh God and father, we thank you for your holy word, like a two-edged sword. It penetrates the very inner being of our heart and attitude. We come in brokenness and surrender. Realizing we have failed, realizing at times we have not worn the whole armor.

We've left the shield of faith to one side and let the sword of the spirit back in the closet, and we come to you somehow to recommit our lives, to be your men, to be your women, to go where you want us to go, to do what you want us to do, and Lord, even as we received this, we're still vulnerable. We're still very human. We may not even know what to say to one another throughout this thing because there's been a strong word to our hearts, but oh Lord, enable us not to be hearers of the word, but doers.
For we ask this in Jesus' name, Amen.
George Verwer

Brunei

Therefore, among God's churches we boast about your perseverance and faith in all the persecutions and trials you are enduring. **2 Thessalonians 1:4**

God almighty in a place, local newspapers in Brunei often publish reports of converts to Islam receiving gifts and financial support while Christians are not allowed to evangelize at all, be the heaven inspired equalizer. Despite such unfair odds in human terms, God grant Your people wisdom and brave boldness in sharing Jesus. May the underground believers endure persecution if their faith in Christ is exposed.

Strengthen the faith of the secret believer trying to somehow reach the Malay Muslims, who if they turn to Christ face strict punishment under Sharia law.

Dave Davidson

Buddhists

*Pray also for me, that whenever I open my mouth,
words may be given me so that I will fearlessly
make known the mystery of the gospel...*
Ephesians 6:19

God thanks for loving Buddhists. Each of these 350 million
souls are precious in your sight. From the saffron-robed
monk to the Tibetan twirling a prayer wheel, You know
and love each one. Free them, Father, from trying to save
themselves. May they know, instead, the gift of salvation
by faith. We long for them to depend not on karma, but on
Christ. Break through their belief that "all is suffering"
with the reality that Jesus suffered for them.

Help them to realize that desire is not the root of all evil,
but that you desire that none should perish. May they
abandon the Eightfold Path and embrace Jesus, the way,
the truth, and the life (John 14:6). Break strongholds of
idolatry and indifference, and bring them to You Lord.
Replace their stone hearts by pouring out Your Spirit in
them that they may follow your laws. (Ezekiel 36:26-27).

We trust You, Lord, for great things.

Caryn M. Pederson – Pioneers

Bulgaria

Fear the Lord, you his holy people,
for those who fear him lack nothing.
Psalm 34:9

May Jesus be revealed as Lord of Lords.
Have Your will and way abide in Bulgaria.
Grant government a holy fear of His name to burn
in the hearts of politicians. Dim racial discrimination
and brighten the freedom of speaking the Word
of God in all media. Give power in battling
corruption, abuses, and addictions.

Dave Davidson

Burkina Faso

But we said to him, 'We are honest men; we are not spies.
Genesis 42:31

Father, as Burkina Faso means "land of honest men"
we pray for true believers to biblically deal with
extreme poverty issues overcoming a dependence
mentality. Break strongholds of occult influences
to be broken and strictly subordinate to the lovely

mighty name of Jesus.

We thank You Lord some Muslim groups are
responding to the gospel despite idolatry, fetishism,
and secret society tendencies. Ignite the indigenous
church to continue to grow embracing God's word
and as a missions-sending body. Stir a strong
grassroots movement that places missions above
church agendas. Father, we pray for wisdom for
Christian leaders responsible against temptations
in handling large amounts of aid and money.

Dave Davidson

Business

*Unless the LORD builds the house, the builders labor
in vain. Unless the LORD watches over the city,
the guards stand watch in vain.* **Psalm 127:1**

Lord, I know that unless the Lord builds that house,
its builders labor in vain. Watch over all I do in my work
today Lord and I pray for all those whom my life will
touch today, through this work into which

You have placed me.

May I be a worthy worker, who has You as the director of
my business and the one that oversees all my activities and
transactions. Give me wisdom today in all the decisions
I may need to make. I pray that I may demonstrate honesty
and integrity in all my dealings - whether it is my
relationship with people or my dealings with financial
matters and the material side of my work.

Lord I know that without You I can do nothing but also
You have promised that I can do all things through Christ
who strengthens me- and so Lord, I rely on You to bless
my business as You see fit. I pray Lord that my business
may thrive with You at the helm – but I ask that it will not
become a burden and that in all things You will lead and
direct my business path – May You be glorified in my
business dealings, I pray in Jesus name, Amen.

Loving Lord I kneel humbly before You seeking Your grace and guidance for my future life and witness. Times have become increasingly difficult, but You are my Lord and Savior and I only want to do that which is pleasing to You and honoring to Your name.

Give me I pray patience and perseverance, insight and integrity in my work environment and business dealings, knowing that this world is a place that is increasingly discarding the unchangeable principles of Scripture and the godly traits of honesty, sincerity and integrity. Lord I pray that I may maintain all that is good and righteous in my position of employment and not compromise the standard that You desire for my life.

Give me wisdom as I face the daily challenges in my place of occupation

and I pray that I may conduct all my activities with honesty, integrity and fairness. I pray Your blessing on all I do and may my life and witness be such that You are not discredited, but rather that Your name may be glorified in all I do, in Jesus name I pray.

Knowing-Jesus.com

Cabo Verde

This only have I found: God created mankind upright,
but they have gone in search of many schemes.
Ecclesiastes 7:29

As you have created and designed Lord...
Cabo Verde (Greek for "Islands of the Fortunate")
is a collection of 10 islands, off the coast of Senegal,
in West Africa. Lord bless this area long with the
Canary Islands, Madeira and the Azores, part of the
area called Macaronesia. Praise God it is one of the
most developed and democratic countries in Africa.

Lord protect Cabo Verdeans from frequent draughts
upon agriculture and health concerns like Zika Virus
warnings. Since 90% of citizens still identify with the
Roman Catholic Church from being founded as
a Portuguese colony, church goers often have
influences with African traditional religion as well.
We pray for bible-based theology discernment
to flourish even more than tourism.

Dave Davidson

Cambodia

And this is my prayer: that your love may abound more and more in knowledge and depth of insight.
Philippians 1:9

God raise up Cambodian men of honor and character to lead the young Church in Cambodia. We pray against the spirit of idolatry and ancestor worship that binds the Khmer people in darkness. May tens of thousands of Cambodians follow Christ and that mission worker will abound. Reach the ethnic Chinese living in the city center.

Reach the Phnom Penh chasing after material wealth. Send Christian counselors for the millions in this country who suffer from Post Traumatic Stress Disorder. Bless marriages that husbands would love their wives as Christ loves the church. Abolish forces of spiritual darkness that cause so many young girls and boys to be abused every day. Let the local Church rise up to battle this horrible reality.

May missionaries not lose heart.

Grant Your mission vision for this place and these people. Over the social physiological phenomenon that many see church and/or religion only as a way to gain authority, money, healthcare, food, without any sort of saving relationship with Christ. Balance the perception out. Plant a church-planting movement in Cambodia so newsworthy that

Paul and Apollos would long to write all about.

May Muslims and fetishists open up to God's Word. In the name of Jesus Christ we pray. Amen.

Dave Davidson

Cameroon

Surely the idolatrous commotion on the hills and mountains is a deception; surely in the Lord our God is the salvation of Israel.
Jeremiah 3:23

Lord Jesus, we pray that You will bring an end to widely held tribal spiritist traditions among Christians in Cameroon. Father, let Your light shine as to overcome all darkness, deception and syncretism. We ask that You will establish a moral government system that will provide for clean water, food, and health needs of the people. Father, we also pray for a gentle transfer of spiritual leadership from Western organizations to national believers.

Lord, we pray that You will establish effective Christian discipling in churches and by youth and children's agencies. May Your blessing be upon the Bible study programmes and Christian camps that are being held for young people in Cameroon. May these children become fruit-bearers to the glory of Your Name.

Lord Jesus, we pray for the leadership of the churches, that pastors will have integrity and teach in ways that honour You.

prayer.africa/Cameroon

Canada

*Let all the earth fear the Lord;
let all the people of the world revere him.*
Psalm 33:8

Let all of Canada fear the Lord. Let all the inhabitants of this great dominion stand in awe of Him. Blessed is the nation whose God is the Lord, and the people whom He has chosen as His own inheritance. (Psalm 33:8, 12)

We pray that the Prime Minister will seek Your wisdom and counsel in all his actions on behalf of this country and in his personal and private life. (Psalm 89:21)

Lord, act in Your own displeasure toward those who would strike terror into the earth. (Ezekiel 32:22-25; Psalm 7:11-16) Root out and bring terrorists to justice. Please show mercy, expose and thwart terrorist schemes. Grant wisdom, discernment and protection to all in authority working to prevent terrorist attacks.

We pray that You would give Your wisdom to those who would preside in our courts of justice. Let all judges and those who work in our court system seek to preserve justice in a fair and impartial way according to Your statutes. (Proverbs 2:6-8)

Grant wisdom and courage to all those who serve in our Parliament and all elected officials across this country. Let them not be distracted from governing by the lure of money, power or fame. Encourage them to always stand for what is right and to faithfully serve those who have put their trust in them.
(Ecclesiastes 8:1-5)

Let those who serve our country in the military not rely solely upon the strength of their weapons and intelligence, but first turn to You, Lord, the source of all wisdom and strength. Raise up men and women of faith among all ranks of the military and give them opportunity to witness to their fellow soldiers.
(Matthew 8:5-12)

We agree with You, Jesus, that the Church will be one, as You are one with the Father. Heal any divisions that exist between pastors and their congregations, and between denominations. Let our nation see the Body of Christ united in love for one another and toward those whom You have come to save. (John 17:21)

Lord, return the state of marriage to a place of honour in our country. We praise You for sturdy marriages that model Your commitment to the Church. Let hope and healing now come to those marriages that are strained and breaking. (Hebrews 13:4)

Father, let our earthly fathers look to You as the ultimate spiritual head of the family, and serve their families by carrying the responsibility for the physical, emotional and spiritual well-being of their wives and children. Bring absentee fathers to a faith and radical life-change. Let Your character be clearly seen in the lives of all fathers. (Ephesians 6:4)

We ask you Lord, to refresh mothers in the honour of fulfilling the glory of motherhood. Strengthen them with grace, wisdom, and love in serving their husbands and children. Let mothers would reflect Your own love and nurturing nature. (Proverbs 31:25-26, 28)

Thank You that You are father to the fatherless and husband to the widow. Restore our broken families with Your wholeness and let them turn to You for all spiritual, emotional and physical needs. (Psalm 146:8-9)

We pray that our children will come to know You as Lord and Saviour early in their lifetime. We pray that they would participate fully in establishing your kingdom here on earth. (Mark 10:14)

We agree with Your word, Lord, that You are instructing our children and great will be their peace in the land. (Isaiah 54:13)

Let the unborn be protected. We affirm their personhood and we honour them as unborn citizens. Rescue them from the atrocity and violent death by abortion. Convict of transgression, forgive and heal those who repent of committing abortion. (Psalm 72:12, 14)

Help us to be a nation that desires purity and avoids debauchery, pornography, perversion, drunkenness, drug use and gambling. (1 Corinthians 6:9-20; Titus 2:12)

Lord, we implore you to make our schools a place where our children can learn in physical, emotional and spiritual safety. Give them godly teachers who encourage them and are dedicated to them. Give them the support systems at home and at school that would enable them to achieve great things in Your Name. (Luke 6:40)

Strengthen and encourage those in the media who are willing to stand for Your truth and practice honest, fair and accurate reporting. Convert or remove those who would use the media to put forth their own selfish agendas and proclaim their lies and distortions. Give discernment to all who know and love You to be able to sift through the untruths and rely on Your steadfast Word. (Proverbs 4:24-26)

We praise and thank You that you give us the arts as a way to worship and glorify Your Name. Let godly men and women now come forth in the arts and entertainment fields who will seek to share your gospel message through their creative endeavours. (Proverbs 14:34)

Lord, bring genuine reconciliation to the races of this nation. Remove long held prejudices, hatreds and hurts and replace them with Your healing love and fellowship. Bring peace, friendship and equal opportunity to all peoples and cultures. (Ephesians 2:14-16)

Thank You that You do not forget prisoners and those who are homeless and needy. Stir up Your heart of compassion in each of us and send Your Spirit to guide us as we reach out to those less fortunate. (Psalm 107:41)

Restore our abandoned inner cities to communities of safety, prosperity and hope. Save and encourage those caught in cycles of poverty, sickness, addiction, brokenness and despair. (Isaiah 58:12)

Lord, grant the people of Canada Sabbath rest. Thank You that there remains therefore a rest for the people of God. Help all be diligent to enter that rest, lest anyone fall into disobedience. (Hebrews 4:9-11)

Lord, let all exhausted labourers in our land come to You, find salvation, and find rest for their souls. For Your yoke is easy and Your burden is light. Comfort those in jail and prison, Lord. (Matthew 11:18-30)

Lord, bring the Word of God to bear on the hearts and minds of those who make public policy in Canada. (Psalm 19:7-11; John 8:31,32) Continue to grant opportunity for a Biblical worldview and principles into the public discourse. (Ephesians 3:10)

Shield and deliver our nation from occultism, New Age cults, false religions and secret societies. (Isaiah 1:29; 2:6)

In mercy, reveal Yourself to those who do not even seek after You, those who have turned away, those who are ignorant of their own need for Your saving grace in their lives. (Romans 10:20; Isaiah 65:1)

Reverse the trends of humanism and socialism in our nation. (1 Chronicles 12:32; Isaiah 59:15)

Grace and enable us, Lord, to travail until the fullness of Jesus Christ is birthed in this next generation of Canadians. (Galatians 4:19)

Send forth more consecrated individuals to

proclaim the Gospel
of Jesus Christ to every nation.
Bring in the harvest, Lord.
(Acts 1:8; 4:33)

Lord, help us to live our lives so that all are prepared to give an account to Almighty God. (Hebrews 9:27)

Now to Him who is able to keep us from falling, and to present us faultless before the presence of His glory with exceeding joy, to the only wise God our Saviour, be glory and majesty, dominion and power, both now and forever. Amen. (Jude 1:24-25)

CanadaInPrayer.com

Caribbean Countries

Let them give glory to the LORD and proclaim his praise in the islands.
Isaiah 42:12

Thank You for the beautiful Caribbean countries, Lord. We ask for your blessing on the over 300 denominations and spiritual influences just in Jamaica alone. Lord, we pray for revival. Allow these groups to work together for the coordination of the missions' message. In the Caribbean

We pray for a greater missions vision.

We pray that Bible schools, churches and seminaries will be a rich source of spiritual growth and a missions' revival would rise up amongst the Caribbean people groups. Father, turn these people away from exotic lifestyles and wicked influences to Your kingdom. Shine Your light in these dark areas where people live for pleasure and have false ideologies of governments. We pray for leadership training with ministry to young people and Christian literature ministries. Dave Davidson

Lord, save Fiji, save Fiji; save these people, O Lord; have mercy upon Fiji; save Fiji!
John Hunt, a missionary to the Fiji Islands, said on his death bed

Catholics

For there is one God and one mediator
between God and mankind, the man Christ Jesus.
1 Timothy 2:5

Dear Jesus, help us to spread Your fragrance everywhere we go. Flood our souls with Your spirit and life. Penetrate and possess our whole being,

so utterly, that our lives may only be a radiance of Yours. Shine through us, and be so in us, that every soul we come in contact with may feel Your presence in our soul. Let them look up and see no longer us, but only Jesus! Stay with us, and then we shall begin to shine as You shine; so to shine as to

be a light to others.

The light O Jesus will be all from You, none of it will be ours; It will be You, shining on others through us. Let us thus praise You without preaching, not by words but by our example, by the catching force, the sympathetic influence of what we do, the evident fullness of the love our hearts bear to You. Mother Teresa

May Catholics skip priests and Mary to pray directly to the one mediator between God and man, Christ Jesus.
Dave Davidson

Celebrities

*If you show special attention to the man wearing fine clothes
and say, "Here's a good seat for you," but say to the poor man,
"You stand there" or "Sit on the floor by my feet," have
you not discriminated among yourselves and become
judges with evil thoughts?*
James 2:3,4

Father God the tabloids and social media feeds
remind us who the famous important are every day,
yet You are very creator of us all. We pray for
celebrities, star athletes, and power people of
influence, and statue to make You their confident
testimony of redeeming salvation. Use their vast
territory of presence as an example of what not to fall
into if they are indeed lost in the ways of the world.
Humble on the Hollywood liberal elites
who attempt brainwashing with ungodly agendas.
Dave Davidson

Central African Republic

But you are a chosen people, a royal priesthood, a holy nation…
1 Peter 2:9

Father as we come before You to pray for CAR,
we pray against the greed and against the hunger for
power that is evident in rebel groups and government.

We pray that you will dismantle the anti-Balaka
group that are walking around with machetes, killing
Muslims. You know that they themselves have
suffered loss from militant Islamists, but we pray that
You will enable them to forgive their trespassers.
Please help them to see that it is mostly
innocent people which they are killing.

We pray for the Christians in CAR who have gone out
of their way to protect the Muslims; especially some
priest putting their lives in danger to house the
Muslims in their churches. We pray, Lord, that the
Muslim refugees who are hiding in the Churches will
have an encounter with You. We pray that the
testimony of the priests and the believers will
enlighten their hearts to see that You are the only
God. In Jesus mighty name we pray. Amen.

prayer.africa/central-african-republic

Central Asia

I gave them the words you gave me.
John 17:8

Holy God, raise up more servants to distribute
Christian literature to the people of Azerbaijan.
We lift up Tajikistan and its past of suffering, corruption,
civil war, and poverty. We pray to You, sovereign Lord,
about the growth of Islam. Protect Christians and give
them boldness to distribute more Bibles and Christian
training materials. Thank You God for the ministry of
the JESUS film in Turkmenistan! We pray for more
souls to be won! We pray for Uzbekistan Christians to
continue worshiping and reaching out to others, despite
government threats. We ask You Lord, for discipleship and
training for Uzbekistan's believers, that they may grow
strong in the Lord continuing to be a light
to those in darkness.
Dave Davidson

Chad

But he lifted the needy out of their affliction
and increased their families like flocks.
Psalm 107:41

Father, we pray for the Church in Chad to be both
burdened and equipped for evangelism among an
increasing Muslim majority. Lord, we ask that You
strengthen pioneer missionaries to persevere in difficult
places in order to reach the unreached. We also pray
for integrity and honesty to rule the nation and
displace government corruption.

Lord God, will You please provide medical care and
services to the people of Chad as the Republic of Chad
has the fifth highest death rate in the world.

Lord, as there are more unreached peoples in Chad than
in any other African country, we confess that they are not
unknown to You. Please reveal Yourself to them through
your Holy Spirit and by Your Word so that they too
may come to a clearer knowledge of Jesus Christ...
prayer.africa/chad

Children

*'Arise, cry out in the night as the watches of the night begin:
pour out your heart like water in the presence of the Lord.
Lift up your hands to him for the lives of your children,
who faint from hunger at the head of every street.'*
Lamentations 2:19

Father God thank You for loving and caring for Your children.
Thank You for being a Father to the Fatherless.
Lord God, there are millions of children throughout the
world who are hungry, hopeless and hurting. Touch them
all today in Your sovereign loving way. Reach them
through the love of others who know You and trust You.
Lord, there are so many children who are sick and
malnourished throughout the world.

We lift our hearts to You, Lord, on behalf of these children.

Lord, we thank You that children are easily receptive to
your good news. We ask that many more would reach out
in this fruitful harvest time in a way they can come to
know Your love. We pray for ministries that focus on the
various needs of children. We pray for those who feed and
clothe children, who give medical care and who teach
youth the love of Jesus in Christian schools. We lift these
children up, to You, God of Grace. We pray for children in
slavery, in abusive labor situations and continual poverty.
Lord, provide for children who live on the streets without
family. We pray for these millions of children of different
ages, people groups, countries, cities and rural areas
throughout the world. Lord, You know each child.
Intervene in their lives and help them in their search
for food, for hope and for salvation.

Dave Davidson

Lord reach the over 100 million street children in the world with no or minimal family, many in Latin America.

Holy Spirit help me live today like an adopted son/daughter of the Creator of the universe. Full of hope, courage, joy, contentment, peace,

...everything that is true

of me in my identity as a child of God.

Todd Morr

Chile

*"I will make you into a great nation, and I will bless you;
I will make your name great, and you will be a blessing."*
Genesis 12:2

Lord bless the less-reached peoples and the
ethnic indigenous and immigrant minorities in Chile.
Multiply ministry to the Mapuche. Create faith in the
Rapa Nui Polynesian people. Attract the gospel to
Chile's many visitors of Peruvians, Ecuadorians and
Bolivians facing discrimination and injustice.
Evangelize the Jews of Santiago. Reach Romani
(Gypsies) often neglected by society. Mobilize
university students to be a bright and bold witness.
Dave Davidson

_____
_____
_____
_____

China

He is the atoning sacrifice for our sins, and not only
for ours but also for the sins of the whole world.
1 John 2:2

Father God, we pray for China's tremendous population to come to Christ in droves. May missions' organizations and churches accept the challenge of adopting the various people groups. Thank You Lord, for the increase of evangelicals the past 20 years. We pray for the Han Chinese, with their eight main languages and 600 dialects. Lord, take authority over the spiritual principalities and powers that are keeping the many people groups bound.

Thwart the communist regime's goal for elimination of all religious groups. Lord, rise up qualified linguists. Strengthen, encourage, and protect Christians in China.

Soften the hearts of devout **muslims, animalists, buddhists and stoic atheists.**

May the doors of China fly open to missionaries! Lord, rise up prayer teams who will break up the soil through worship and intercession. Anoint the Gospel as it goes forth via radio. Dave Davidson

Lord open Tibet closed to the gospel occupied by Chinese forces. There's only 200 Christians among a population of 5 million Tibetans

Shall not the eternal interests

of one-fifth of our race stir up the deepest sympathies of
our nature with the most strenuous effort of our blood-
bought powers; shall not the low wail of helpless misery
arising from one-half of the heathen world pierce our
sluggish ear and rouse us, spirit, soul and body,

to one mighty, continued, unconquerable effort for China's salvation;

that strong in God's strength and in the power of His
might, we may snatch the prey from the hand of the
mighty; that we may pluck these brands from the
everlasting burning, and rescue these captives
from the thralldom of sin and Satan; to grace the
triumph of our Sovereign King, and to shine
forth forever as stars in His diadem.

J. Hudson Tayor founder for the China Inland Mission

_____

_____

_____

_____

Take 8 minutes to Pray Along for China. Download 10/40 Window Prayer Bucket List titles about China at PrayAlong.com and share.

Andrew Murray once said, "The man who mobilizes the Christian church to pray will make the greatest contribution to world evangelization in history."

Get in on the action with a click by sharing FREE Pray Along ebook links with world mission prayer theme social media memes.

Church

*So the churches were strengthened
in the faith and grew daily in numbers.*
Acts 16:5

Mighty and Merciful Father, we pray for our local church,
the collective temple of your Holy Spirit. We ask with boldness
and humility, according to your Word, that the gates of Hell
would not stand against it. May we be faithful subjects of your
Kingdom in matters great and small. Make the church healthy
and fearless in examining the condition of our hearts,
minds and spirits since sin hinders Your blessing.

We ask that you make us passionate, powerful servants that
strive to practice your presence and bring glory to Your name.
Grant us a spirit of selfless submission to those in leadership.
Give them accountability for their spiritual leadership.

Lead us to repent and refrain from all sin, gossip and politics
that tear down the body, and give your enemies opportunities to
blaspheme. Instead, give us a tender spirit that shares the truth
in love in accordance with the Scriptures.

Most Holy Lord, we pray that our church would accomplish the
biblical purposes for which it was founded. We ask that we
would be a worshipping church, loving and glorifying
Your name in spirit and in truth.
Make us an evangelizing church seeking to reach the lost across
the street and around the world and inviting them to meet your
Son. Make us a discipling church, teaching and training your
children to live in the power of the Spirit in obedience with Your
Word. Make us a fellowshipping church, that we would share
with each other not only the Gospel of Christ, but our very lives
as well. We ask that we would be a ministering church, who
looks within and without to meet physical and spiritual needs in
Jesus' name. As we accomplish these purposes, we pray that you
would bless us with abundant growth, both numeric and
spiritual. In Jesus Name and for His Sake… Amen. Walt Collins

Church Planting

I will build my church.
Matthew 16:18

Lord, we believe You will establish Your church
among lost people groups all over the world. Use Your word to
bring people to Christ. Build Your church throughout the world!
George Verwer

So far, I am not able to win souls. I have shared
the gospel to many people, but people did not accept by
faith. Please pray for me, so that I may win souls. I will
not give up. My children are not feeling well. The local
people look down on us, and that may be the reason they
did not accept the gospel. Until the church is planted,

I will not give up.

anonymous Last Frontiers missionary

Closed & Communist Countries

I am sending you to them to open their eyes and turn them from darkness to light, and from the power of Satan to God, so that they may receive forgiveness of sins and a place among those who are sanctified by faith in me.
Acts 26:17-18

Lord, thank You for the fall of the Iron Curtain
and the opening of Albania to the gospel.
Thanks for so many great breakthroughs!

We prayerfully expect more!

Open the floodgates of Your grace to Cuba and North
Korea. As the temple veil was torn Lord, expand the
opening of Your love in closed countries and
all those effected by Communism.
Dave Davidson

Father, thank You for Your power that is greater than any
adversity or adversary Satan may send to destroy us.
John Hagee

Father, help us to stay continually full of the Spirit
and to be endued with power that our lives will
be a spiritual light to the world.
Pastor Kenneth Andrews

Clothing

I needed clothes and you clothed me, I was sick and you looked after me, I was in prison and you came to visit me.
Mathew 25:36

Dear God, You are an excellent provider of warm clothes and blankets to those in need. Keep the cold toes of littles ones warm next winter. Thanks for shoes to protect our feet, also for hats, helmets and head gear keeping workers safe. Thank You for the generosity of urban clothing charities and churches who take ownership of clothing their community. Oh Lord provide for the displaced refugee. Keep the homeless bundled up. Offer the oppressed lovingkindness through the helping hand of me. Answers these prayers in tangible ways.

Dave Davidson

Colombia

Blessed are the peacemakers,
for they will be called children of God.
Matthew 5:9

We pray for the peacemakers in Colombia, the churches,
and all people who in countless ways seek to right the
wrongs, heal the wounded and sick, speak the truth, and
protect the vulnerable. We give thanks for those who are
empowered by their faith to be peacemakers. We ask that
you would protect them from all harm and danger. God,
give us strength as we seek to be voices for peace in
Colombia, strengthen our efforts to bring forth words of
truth, compassion and peace that we receive from our
Colombian brothers and sisters. Bring us all to do justice,
to love kindness, and to walk humbly in your ways,
through Christ our Lord. Amen.

Lutheran Work Relief

Commitment & Calling

...make your calling and election sure...
2 Peter 1:10

Open my eyes that I might see a vision of lost humanity. Open my ears that I might hear the voiceless hurting ones. Open my hands that I might touch the nails of godly sympathy. Open my heart that I might feel the spear of selfless love. And if I should take the name of Christ and all my talk of sacrifice and yet not touch the ones He died for; and if I could speak with angels' tongues, sing the best songs that could be sung and yet, not love then I deny the faith I said I'd die for. And if I should pray in Jesus' name, gather with saints, worship and pray, but not let it move me into action; and if I should study, get degrees, doctrinalise theologies, but never feel any compassion,

what is my faith Oh Lord...

And if I say I'm a Christian, but not willing to obey then by my lips, and by my life I take your name in vain.

Bill Drake from the song "Open My Eyes" BillDrake.com

Comoros

Consequently, you are no longer foreigners and strangers, but fellow citizens with God's people and also members of his household.
Ephesians 2:19

May the three volcanic islands between Madagascar and Mozambique that make up Comoros erupt with an outpouring of God's presence and Holy Spirt conviction to the gospel. God give Christian foreigners boldness to proclaim Christ, regardless of the proselytization consequences legally being expelled from the country. Lord comfort the very few who do come to Christ face largely due to discrimination from the Muslim majority (98%) and are pressured not to practice their faith.

Dave Davidson

Congo Republic

As you go, proclaim this message:
'The kingdom of heaven has come near.'
Matthew 10:7

Lord Jesus, we pray
for the people of Congo Republic.
We pray for a pure Gospel to be proclaimed
that is devoid of syncretism and heresy.
Father, will You please enable your Church to
recapture the vision for evangelism of the entire
country. We specifically pray for an expansion of
ministries that equip youth to decisively impact the
nation for Christ. Lord God, we intercede on behalf of
those who are less reached in central and northern
areas of the Congo. Father, there where the people are
thinly populated, we ask for Your Holy Spirit to move
and touch the hearts of the people. We also pray that
Christian resources will be effectively used and
the Bible translated into more languages.
In the name of Jesus we pray. Amen.
prayer.africa/congo-republic

Continents

And pray in the Spirit on all occasions
with all kinds of prayers and requests.
Ephesians 6:18

Lord God we cover the entire globe now in prayer for
every country, continent and province. As areas come
to mind we declare them to You and whatever is not
specifically listed in this book Lord we lift it up to You
now! Intercede with Your Spirit and lay on our hearts
Your burden for delivering the lost. George Verwer

The God of love will then prepare his messengers
and make a way into the polar regions, into the deepest
recesses of America, and into the interior parts of
Africa; yea, into the heart of China and Japan, with the
countries adjoining to them. And their sound will then go
forth into all lands, and their voice to the ends of the earth.
John Wesley

Costa Rica

*May he give you the desire of your heart
and make all your plans succeed.*
Psalm 20:4

Lord magnify your name with Missions in Cost Rica
with cooperation and fellowship among missionaries
and missions agencies so that their efforts are used to
their fullest potential. Guide them to succeed in
effectively discipling new converts all the while
healing riffs of theology within denominations and
congregations. Reax rigid legalism. Rejuvenate
a renewing for righteous morality.
Dave Davidson

Cote d'Ivoire

Until I come, devote yourself to the public reading of Scripture, to preaching and to teaching.
1 Timothy 4:13

Rev up revival in a revolution of love among the people of Côte d'Ivoire. Forward the gospel to go gangbusters penetrating into the unevangelized sectors of a predominantly Muslim northern area. Boost basic understanding and desire to dive into Scripture truths with discerning theology among all the believers. Jehovah Jireh the Provider graciously supply all of the needs of indigenous missionaries.

Dave Davidson

Crime

Though I walk in the midst of trouble, you preserve my life;
you stretch out your hand against the anger of my foes,
with your right hand you save me.
Psalm 138:7

Merciful God, we reach out in prayer to the millions of
victims of crime every year. We pray for those who have
suffered loss in their life, damage with emotions, physical
pain and possessions. Lord, we pray for the difficult
process and challenge to forgive someone who has
caused devastation through violent crimes.

We pray for these wrongdoers to repent and turn from
their wicked ways. Restore the victims of crime and
encourage them with the promises found in Your word.
For the scarred children, for the battered wives and for
those who suffer from mental, physical, emotional and
spiritual abuse, Lord, we ask that You reveal Your
peaceful presence to them in a personal way today.
Give them evidence that You are a God of hope,
restoration, reconciliation and redemption.

Dave Davidson

Croatia

Hatred stirs up conflict, but love covers over all wrongs.
Proverbs 10:12

May powerful and effective prayers for Croatia bounce back and forth to heaven like the Eastern Europe boomerang shaped gateway country it is.

Give Croatia lasting reconciliation among Bosnians, Serbs, and Croats after centuries-long rivalries and hatred towards one another. May they be full of grace upon grace from God for the body of Christ to unite across denominational lines impacting a perpetually traumatized society. We pray for spiritual breakthroughs among drug addicts in desperate need of hope. Just as the architecture, scenery, and hospitality make Croatia welcoming, may the gospel also pull people towards Christ in a fragrance of forgiveness. Dave Davidson

Cuba

*May there be peace within your walls
and security within your citadels.*
Psalm 122:7

Pray for the people of Cuba.

We thank you Lord that Cubans worship you in
houses, farms and sheds despite old empty church
buildings. Pray that each of its 11 million citizens
will know God's supernatural love for them.

Father provide for their spiritual, physical,
emotional and financial needs. Grant grace to
government of Cuba. We ask that Your will God
will be done on earth as it is in heaven as Cubans
experience increased personal security and stability.
We lift up the pastors of the churches of Cuba.

Dave Davidson

Cults & Cons

See to it that no one takes you captive through hollow and deceptive philosophy, which depends on human tradition and the basic principles of this world rather than on Christ.
Colossians 2:8

Lord, we know we cannot put any group of people in a box and assume that they all believe one way, but so many Jehovah's Witnesses take key components of Your gospel about the deity of Jesus and twist it, Lord, just enough to where Satan gains the victory and the true theology of your plans for us. Lord, we pray for people, who are on the borderline of living and understanding the true meanings of Your words, Lord, and at the same time may be deceived, brainwashed or naïve about Your complete and sovereign truth. Lord, we pray for the people in this sect that think they are doing good by spreading distorted truth. Reveal to them Your true message, Lord, and allow them to be set free from satanic grips of deception.

Lord, we should take example of how the Mormon missionary's work is dedicated and how their message spreads to truly deceives millions of people.

Lord, we pray for those that need more clarity in Your truth. Spread Your gospel faster than any cult message. Squander the efforts of those that would deceive others with false teachings. We pray for these people who claim to seek the truth and base it on a feeling of certainty. Lord, we pray that their feelings would not be the basis of their faith. Convict them with Your Holy Spirit. Merciful Lord, bring them into a clarity of Your truth and Your simple gospel message, Lord, without the extra volume of the Bible, without the deception of Joseph Smith and false prophets, without the phony boloney theology!
Dave Davidson

Curacao

How good and pleasant it is when God's
people live together in unity!
Psalm 133:1

Bless Curacao with the unity of love among believers.
Fan into flame vibrant, growing churches to permeate
the island. Increase production of Christian literature
in the Papiemento language. Waft faith in the saving
grace of the gospel through local podcasts. May the
bitter oranges exclusive to the island be a reminder to
have authentic refreshing relationships with a soul
quenching living Christ among nominal Christians.
Dave Davidson

_____
_____
_____
_____
_____
_____
_____
_____

Cyprus

*Your statutes are my heritage forever;
they are the joy of my heart.*
Psalm 119:111

I pray for the old folks who have seen such rapid
change in such a short time, as Cyprus has shot out
the medieval village life organized around the
Orthodox Church, into a strange world with
fascinating and confusing alternatives.
I pray for the children who will not know the
supportive village family life and deep heritage of
Greek identity, consolidated in three centuries of
survival under oppressive Turkish Muslim rule.

I pray that the winds of change will clarify the new
options of the old gospel lying within the very fabric
of their society, but accepted and often dismissed as
commonplace. I pray that the words of Jesus will
come alive and become personal as my Cyprus
friends read the New Testament in their modern
language... I pray that change will free them to
reclaim Christ. adapted from Orville Boyd Jenkins

Czechia & Slovakia

We have spoken freely to you, Corinthians,
and opened wide our hearts to you.
2 Corinthians 6:11

The apostle Paul wrote his letter to the Corinthians
to encourage them. May we have the same hope as
the Corinthian church as we pray for the church of
God and for all people according to their needs.
Eternal God, we thank you for calling us by name.

In you we live and move and grow. Send down your
Spirit so that we may know Jesus and bear witness to
our life and unity in him. May we know the mind of
Christ in order to speak God's wisdom everywhere.
We pray for the churches in Chechia and Slovakia
and for all churches which are experiencing
growth or struggle, reconciliation or conflict.
We pray for those who have no home, no land,
no food, no work, no medicine, no peace.
adapted from Week of Prayer for Christian Unity 2005, Slovakia

Dalits

I will restore you to health and heal your wounds,'
declares the LORD, 'because you are called an outcast...
Jeremiah 30:17

Outcast God,

Born into poverty in an occupied land,
Living alongside the marginalized and the oppressed.
Dying between criminals to the jeers of the crowd,
Open our eyes, that we who seek to follow you may
recognize your face in the faces of those who are
reviled. Open our ears, that we who seek to hear your
word, may recognize your love in the stories which
are often drowned out. Open our hearts, that we who
seek your way of life may be bold in witnessing
to your longing for justice and peace.

Abundant God,

Those of us with plenty can observe the lives
of those with nothing at the click of a switch.
At the push of a button, we can close down
the images which frighten or revolt us,
silence the stories which disturb and unnerve us.

Give us compassionate eyes

to see clearly the world we live in. Move us from fear
to compassion; from willful ignorance to mindful
action, from the complicity of silence to the joyful
sings of solidarity. We ask it in Jesus' name, Amen.

Dalits Prayer of Solidarity

Deacons

... I will not deny my integrity.
Job 27:5

Lord Jesus, you came to serve, not to be served,
Form within us your generous spirit; Fill us with your
love, that we may love the Father as your love him.
Fill us with your compassion, that we may see our
brothers and sisters as you see them. Fill us with your
courage, that we may give our lives in service to the
Church as you gave your life for her. Fill us with that
Spirit which will make us preachers of your Word,
ministers of your Sacrifice, servants of your Bride,
friends of the poor, and the voice of the forgotten.

Transform us through your Holy Spirit so that we
may transform the world into Your Kingdom of
justice and faith. Amen. Fr. Benedict D. O'Cinnsealaigh

Come to my assistance my Lord and my God, that
I may do for You all that you ask. Strengthen me in
adversity and do not let me succumb to my feelings
of worthlessness. Help me to feel in my heart all that
You speak to me, and help me to understand.

May I be to others what they need: a body to work when others cannot; a heart to love those who are forgotten; a shoulder to console those whose soul is in need; a smile to brighten the most somber of Your children; a mouth to proclaim Your love.

Let me be to You, as a brush is to a painter, worthless without You, but capable of transforming the human heart by the power of Your mercy. Send me, my Lord if you need me, to touch others as You would touch them, to hold them as You would, to love them as only You can. Make my heart like Yours, that I may forgive everything and love beyond my own human frailty. Come live within me, that I may die to myself so You may fill my very being. Let me serve others as You would serve them, that in doing so I may serve You. Do not let me fail, oh Lord, or lead Your people astray. Allow me to live in Your presence today, that tomorrow I may die in Your hands and may You raise me one day that I may touch your face and live in Your glory. Greg Kandra

Deliverance

I look for your deliverance, LORD.
Genesis 45:7

Let us pray. Our God and father, we thank you then in Your providence. Lord, Your ways are past finding out. You have something to say to us about, about China, about India. More than that, about yourself, about this great spiritual warfare into which we have been called. We thank you for all you've done through this great institute over the years. We thank you for so many hundreds that have gone out to the harvest fields and we would just pray,

Oh God, do it again.

Do it again. Oh Lord. We don't want to live on past tradition what we yearn to see, a mighty, fresh new move of Your Holy Spirit in our heart and in our lives. We give you the praise and the glory for the Great Work of world evangelism that at least half the people in the world today have heard the gospel in some way or form and we do come with hearts of praise and adoration and Thanksgiving and yet lord, we come humbled and we come broken knowing there is so much yet to do. Realizing the unbelievable population explosion that takes place all around us and pray that all God, you would grip our hearts and our minds may be penetrated by your word and by the facts about which is actually happening in the world today. You have a spiritual sensitivity. Deliver us from any biases and prejudices, and that includes me, that truly we may obey you tonight.
For we pray in Jesus' name, Amen. George Verwer

Denmark

*Again, truly I tell you that if two of you on earth
agree about anything they ask for, it will be done
for them by my Father in heaven.*
Matthew 18:19

Lord we echo in agreement the hundreds of prayer
requests blogged about at PrayForDenmark.com

Disasters & Tragedies

*For he has rescued us from the dominion of darkness
and brought us into the kingdom of the Son he loves,
in whom we have redemption, the forgiveness of sins.*
Colossians 1;13,14

Lord God, You demonstrate your awesome power through
the natural events of Your Creation. Help us to fear You in
a godly way in reverence as we witness Your sovereign
strength. We pray for those who are victims of natural
disasters such as hurricanes, earthquakes, tornadoes,
floods, monsoons, typhoons, blizzards, avalanches and
volcanic eruptions. Provide for those who have lost their
homes, their communities and those who have lost family
members. Help coordinate ministry relief efforts to

supply needed food, shelter and clothing.

Lift up those who have experienced tragedies in their
lives. Give them comfort and strength through Your
Spirit. What the devil has meant for evil, Lord, work
together for good in the lives of Your people.

Dan Davidson

Discernment

Let us discern for ourselves what is right;
let us learn together what is good.
Job 34:4

God, we thank you for the power and the reality
of your Holy Spirit and we are trusting you to do
a greater thing in our own lives. Give us wisdom as
we share missions. Give us wisdom as we distribute
powerful missions mobilization literature. We'd pray,
especially for our pastors and the leaders of our
churches who are living in days and phenomenal
tension and pressure. We think of the fiery dart of the
morality that is attacked so many and we thank you
for those that it stood firm against that fiery dark.

We thank you for the way you're using books to teach
people how to stand firm against these fiery darts
which are attempting to bring confusion and
destruction everywhere and slow down the
whole world missions thrust.

Lord, we thank you for the discernment that you are
giving us as we move together as one army in the
name of your son Jesus Christ. Oh God, we will
present our bodies now as a living sacrifice according
to Romans 12:1,2 to go where you want us
to go and to do what you want us to do.
For we pray in Jesus' name, Amen.

George Verwer

Disciple Makers

We loved you so much that we were delighted to share with you not only the gospel of God but our lives as well, because you had become so dear to us.
2 Thessalonians 2:8

Lord, you call us to make disciples and to be a witness as Your Holy Spirit transforms seeking souls into Christians. We want to be part of the discipleship process in more lives around us and

all around the world.

Lord, bring people in our own lives to continually mentor and give us real life examples of authentic Christianity to inspire perseverance in our devotional walk with Jesus. May parents, leaders, teachers and friends realize the importance of discipleship and training of new converts.

Multiply the efforts

of all discipleship ministries. Bless the publishers, schools, families and ministries who disciple. Dave Davidson

Discipleship

Then he said to them all: "Whoever wants to be my disciple must deny themselves and take up their cross daily and follow me."
Luke 9:23

If we had a fraction of the faith in you that you have in us then this world would be transformed, Lord.

If we showed a fraction of the love that you show to us then this world would be transformed, Lord

If we possessed a fraction of the patience that you display with us then this world would be transformed, Lord.

If we shared just a portion of the blessings that we have received from you then this world would be transformed, Lord. If we showed as much trust in others as you have shown in us then this world would be transformed, Lord. If we claimed just a fraction of the power you promised to your Church then this world would be transformed, Lord. Transform us first, Lord, that we might transform this world through your love and your power.

FaithandWorship.com John Birch

God of love,

source of mercy and compassion,
weave your dream for the world
into the fabric of our lives.

Remove the scales from our eyes
and lift the indifference from our hearts,
so that we may see your vision –
a new reign of justice and compassion
that will renew the earth.

Transform our lives,

so that we may accomplish your purpose.

Anoint us with your spirit of love
that we might bring good news to the oppressed,

bind up the brokenhearted,

and proclaim release to the captive.

Give us a new urgency and a new commitment
to feed the hungry, clothe the naked,
shelter the homeless, and visit those who live in isolation.

Help us to reach out to those whom no one else will touch,
to accept the unacceptable, and to embrace the enemy.

Surround us with your love, fill us with your grace,
and strengthen us for your service.

Empower us to respond to the call of Jesus –
to deny ourselves, to take up our crosses and to
follow. Make us your disciples. Amen

Kurt Struckmeyer

Disease & Illness

*Therefore confess your sins to each other
and pray for each other so that you may be healed.
The prayer of a righteous man is powerful and effective.*
James 5:16

Let no bitter root grow which leads to physical ailments. Hebrews 12:15 Deliver hope to the hopeless; teach proper expectation. Proverbs 13:12; Psalm 62:5 Let us obey God Isaiah 1:4-6 We turn to God who gives help and true hope. Psalm 121 Protect us from infection. Psalm 5:11-12 Deliver us through imminent peril. Psalm 57:1

Show them hope through the valley

of the shadow of death. Psalm 23:4 Ease their suffering by teaching them to pray for others. Psalm 119:153; Job 41:7-10 Give them peaceful sleep without fear. Psalm 4:8 Give strong minds with good memory. Psalm 13:2 Grant rapid recoveries which amazes onlookers. Psalm 18:16 Strengthen the weak with Your peace. Psalm 19:32,33, Psalm 29:11 Visit those lonely ones with troubled hearts. Psalm 25:16,17 Steady the elderly, the blind, those with arthritis. Psalm 31:9-10 Keep them alive, even when they cannot eat. Psalm 33:18-22 Brace the legs of the crippled. Psalm 37:23,24 Increase tolerance for pain. Psalm 38:7-10 Place a song in their heart. Psalm 40:3 Teach us to trust You, not doctors. Psalm 56:3,4 Defeat diseases attempting to destroy the body. Isaiah 54:16,17
– PrayAlong.com Scripture Prayers

Djibouti

Commit your way to the Lord; trust in him and he will do this:
Psalm 37:5

Father, we pray for wisdom for Christian workers in Arab-focused ministries. We pray for a new bond of unity amongst them. We bring the Afar people before you, Father, as they are essentially unreached with the Gospel. Please reveal Yourself to them and send people who will provide them with Bibles in their own language.

We pray, Lord, for encouragement and perseverance for those ministering in extremely difficult conditions. We pray that they might stand firm in their commitment to follow Jesus, despite persecution in this 97% Muslim country. Father, we pray for the believers that are jobless, and even illiterate – we pray for effective use of literacy and vocational training programmes. We pray for effective use of the Scriptures in their small group meetings and for the Holy Spirit will work in each life.

We pray that You will raise up strong Christian leaders from among and for the Somali and Afar believers. Lord, we pray for the ethnic minority and expats living in this port city of Djibouti (French, Greek, Pakistani, Senegalese, Indian and others). May they have encounters with real Christian witnesses. Amen. prayer.africa/Djibouti

Doers of the Word

Do not merely listen to the word,
and so deceive yourselves. Do what it says.
James 1:22

Lord, we thank you for speaking to our hearts.
Lord, I thank you for the lives of the men who know
that your gospel must come and work in Your authority,
that somehow more and more men will not be lost. Give us
purity and reality bearing fruit in our lives.

Oh God help us as we look into your holy word,
as we see what your word says, urgently and desperately
on important subjects... Bring us, Lord, during these days,
a spirit of expectation that we may not be just hearers of
the word, but doers that God by your grace.

May we never be the same again because we have met
with You amidst mountains as You grant us faith to
receive what you have for us from your word. Even
though the vessel at this moment might be weak and
stammering and struggling, enable us to see beyond any
human instrument to what you are saying to our hearts.
Oh God. For we pray in the name of Jesus Christ. Amen.

adapted from George Vewer

Dominica

...who have tasted the goodness of the word of God...
Hebrews 6:5

Let us give thanks for all God's goodness
and the wonderful heritage into which we have entered:
For Dominica, our island home, the land of our birth –
For the majesty of our hills, the beauty of our valleys,
the flaming loveliness of our gardens -

For the warmth and brightness of our days and the calm
and peace of our countryside –

For the rich heritage of our people coming from many
races, and yet one in purpose, in achievement, and in
destiny; and for the dignity of labour and the service given
by every citizen of our land – For the high privilege and
responsibility and for bringing us to nationhood –

For our parents, teachers, religious, and other leaders and
all those who in every walk of life are helping to prepare
us for responsible citizenship; and for all those who are
giving voluntary service in the public interest –

For the poets, artists, and thinkers and all who create
in us the vision of a new and better society –

For the Godly heritage, the example of Jesus
Christ and the sacrifice of our fathers in the faith –

Bless, we pray Thee, our President, our Prime Minister,
and other Ministers of State, our Parliament, and all who
are set in authority over us and grant that under them
we may be peacefully and justly governed -

Grant us love and compassion for all those in need and
distress, help us to remove poverty and ignorance from
our land, and grant us prosperity and true wisdom, we
pray –

Forgive us all that is unworthy and evil in our nation's life,
establish us in righteousness, and inspire us to work
for universal brotherhood, we pray –

Guide and bless our nation, we pray, and make us loyal
and dutiful citizens through Jesus Christ our Lord.
AMEN. Hear us we beseech Thee, O God.
Dominica National Prayer

Dominican Republic

*I wait for the Lord more than watchmen wait for the morning,
more than watchmen wait for the morning.*
Psalm 130:6

All loving God, we pray for the Dominican Republic
and those of us who call it our home...

God watch over our children working on the beaches and streets selling sweets and services to tourists for pennies and dimes. Watch over those who walk alone for miles to and from Boca Chica where they work. Keep our children safe from predatory tourists, sexual exploitation, trafficking, gangs, and drug use. Watch over the parents and families who face extreme racism and who live with a lack of documentation, education, and employment.

Watch over our families who are the poorest of the poor... living in the shadows of international wealth, fancy hotels, and expensive restaurants.

We pray for all people of the Dominican Republic to care for one another despite differences in nationality, language, culture, religion, or economic status. God be with the poor, the hungry, and the weary. Open our hearts open our eyes as we walk beside our neighbors. Amen.
Ashley Holst

Drugs & Addictions

Therefore, prepare your minds for action; be self-controlled; set your hope fully on the grace to be given you when Jesus Christ is revealed.
1 Peter 1:13

Lord, we all seem to have some reoccurring habits that can either be sinful or a distraction that keeps us from focusing on Your will in our lives. Lord, redirect the steps of those contemplating self-abuse through chemical addiction and protect them from harm. We pray for those who are under the addictive spell of alcohol, drugs or tobacco. Free these people from their cycle of self-destruction and the lies of satisfaction and false comfort.

Lord give those battling addictions an overcoming victory! Dave Davidson

Father, Your power is sufficient to give us victory in any circumstance of life. I am thankful we are kept by the power of God. Dr. Robert White

Ecuador

Be joyful in hope, patient in affliction, faithful in prayer.
Romans 12:12

Lord, tell us to come and meet you on the water,
call us to unfamiliar places. Challenge us not only to
believe deeply, but to act on those beliefs. Help us to
see fully that you are God. Give us faith like Peter,
to go and meet you in the communities of Ecuador;
to Pijal where hard working families and their
children are rejoicing in new opportunities, to Sua
where your people are still recovering from floods
and earthquakes, to Romerillos where gifts are
growing through microcredit programs. Give us faith
like Peter, faith like our partner FEDICE, to step out
of our comfortable and safe spaces, and go where you
call us, and we will meet you there. Amen

Olga Yan-Pardo

Education & Training

*Others, like seed sown on good soil, hear the word,
accept it, and produce a crop—thirty, sixty or even
a hundred times what was sown.*
Mark 4:20

Lord, bless those in Bible studies and Bible schools.
Create more opportunities for Bible correspondence
classes in countries that are otherwise closed to
discovering the truths of Your word. Multiply the fruits
of over 300 centers sending out evangelical materials.

Promote this through tracts, radio and students.
Prepare the hearts and minds of students taking classes
over short-wave radio, apps, podcasts, and over the
Internet. Help ministries use new technologies for
discipleship. We pray for the training of godly men and
women whether it be through an organized curriculum or
simply an open Bible. Lord, train those who seek to serve
You. Train us to be godly and bless these ministries,
according to Your will. Dave Davidson

Egypt

In that day, there will be an altar to the Lord in the midst of the land of Egypt, and a pillar to the Lord at its border. And it will be a sign and for a witness to the Lord of hosts in the land of Egypt; for they will send them a Savior and a Mighty One, and He will deliver them. Then the Lord will be known to Egypt, and the Egyptians will know the Lord in that day, and will make sacrifice and offering; yes, they will make a vow to the Lord and perform it. And the Lord will strike Egypt, He will strike and heal it; they will return to the Lord, and He will be entreated by them and heal them. Isaiah 19:19-22

God of all creation, on a holiday weekend of family, festivities, shopping and decorating, our tendency to forget the wider world of your care comes all too easily. Forgive us. We recognize that as vast as the universe is to us, you cradle every corner, every person, every grain of sand and every hair on each head in the palm of your hand. We grieve with your beloved children in Egypt brutalized by violence as they gathered for worship. We ask your comfort for those who have experienced horror and death in a sacred space of peace and prayer. Help us, Lord of all, to remember that we our bound to one another, all made in your image, connected and called to love as you love us. Bring overwhelming healing where rivers of hurt have spilled their banks. Bring reconciliation to the whole human family so that crying and death will be no more. Embrace the people of Egypt with your compassion and help us to enfold them with ours. Through Jesus Christ we make our prayer. Amen.

Jill Duffield

El Salvador

He heals the brokenhearted and binds up their wounds.
Psalm 147:3

We pray for hope and healing in El Salvador.
Lord have mercy to El Salvador's youth growing up
without their fathers, due to a brutal civil war from 1981
to 1992. Now, 25 years removed from the conflict, violence
and fear still grip communities controlled by ruthless
gangs. Lord heal today's youth a coming of age in a
culture of hate, suspicion, and violence. Up to 70 percent of
El Salvador's youth are thought to be involved in a gang.

Lord solve the dilemma how as El Salvador becomes
increasingly urban, children are more vulnerable to
poverty, violence, and exploitation. Lord, Psalm 147:3
says that You bind up and heal broken hearts.

We pray that this generation of young Salvadorans,
which knows so much brokenness, will seek You for
answers. Bring peace to the nation struggling to mend.

Watch over those working in the most difficult settings, and instill confidence that their good deeds will not be in vain. Lord sustain World Vision staff members working in the thick of it, supporting children and families to promote peace and reconciliation and opening up opportunities for teens who wouldn't otherwise have a chance in life.

We pray for peace that God would use the various youth empowerment and reconciliation movements to build up a generation torn down by war and fear. God protect workers who risk their safety to bring hope to crippled communities.

adapted from worldvision.org

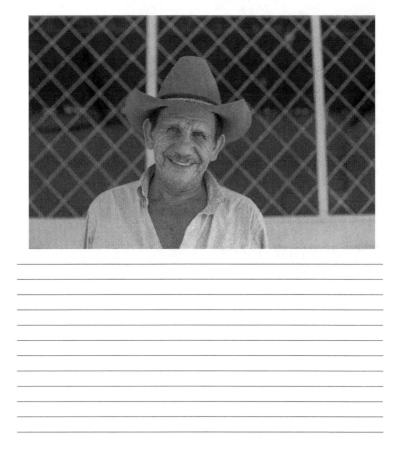

_____
_____
_____
_____
_____
_____
_____
_____
_____
_____
_____
_____

Elderly

Teach us to number our days aright,
that we may gain a heart of wisdom.
Psalm 90:12

Father, we ask for health and safety for the elderly. Help them use their time wisely, sharing their legacy of faith with youth. Improve communication and understanding between generations. Pour out your Holy Spirit upon those who are the caregivers for ailing spouses. Comfort those who have lost family members and help them rejoice in the knowledge of their eventual reunion with their loved ones by trusting in You, dear precious Jesus.

For those elderly who do not yet know Jesus, may they humble themselves and accept the gift of forgiveness and new life in Jesus. Supernaturally reveal the saving power of the gospel to them. Help the elderly not become bitter but learn to forgive. Teach them to give praise and thanks for their lives looking forward to new life in heaven.

Joan Davidson & Susie Paulson

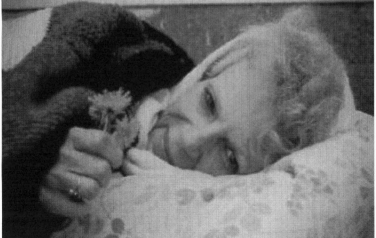

End Times

The end of all things is near. Therefore be clear minded
and self-controlled so that you can pray.
1 Peter 4:7

Yes, Jesus we long for your return

and put our hope fully in You and your promises. Thank
You for Your victory on the cross, from the grave and
towards eternity. With so many denominations, theologies
and theories, Lord, we know this much is true - that You
will return and the world will encounter a very uniquely
glorious and fearfully awesome scene.

We know the prophecies and promises in Daniel,
Revelation and throughout Your word are being fulfilled.
Give us faith, wisdom and discernment in the end times to
glorify You at all costs. May we fearfully and reverently
wait for You Lord and live out obedient lives as disciples
for Jesus until You return or call us home. Use our life,
legacy and testimony to bless others who may
endure the fulfillment of Your end time events.

Dave Davidson

Enemies

On the contrary: "If your enemy is hungry, feed him;
if he is thirsty, give him something to drink. In doing this,
you will heap burning coals on his head."
Romans 12:20

Heavenly Father, You have called us to pray for our enemies and all those that seek to do us harm, and not to heap up unforgiveness or resentments in our heart, and so Lord I want to bring before You all those people in my life who have become enemies of my soul - and to ask for Your grace, favor and forgiveness to be poured out on them - and Lord, I pray that You would convict each one of their need of Jesus as their Savior.

Lord I know that it is not Your will that anyone should perish but that all should come to salvation in Jesus Christ – and so I bring all those people in my life that have sought to do me evil or inflicted harm on me, whether intentionally or unwittingly to Your merciful throne of grace to plead forgiveness and to ask mercy on their souls.

Lord for Your holy names sake, I pray that You would draw close to each. Open their eyes to the truth of the gospel of grace I pray and bring each one into a saving faith on the Lord Jesus and draw them with Your cords of loving forgiveness into Your family, in Jesus name we pray, Amen. Knowing-Jesus.com

Equatorial Guinea

Therefore, among God's churches we boast about your perseverance and faith in all the persecutions and trials you are enduring. **2 Thessalonians 1:4**

Lord, we pray for the government of Equatorial Guinea to seek a Godly plan for developing society in light of great oil wealth. Father, we ask that nominalism and animistic traditions will die as Christ is revealed to the people of Equatorial Guinea. Lord, we also pray for wisdom for missionaries from West and Central Africa in the convoluted socio-political situation of Equatorial Guinea. We pray for Christian immigrant oil workers to boldly share their faith.

We also pray for grace and humility on the part of both expats and nationals in Equatorial Guinea. In Jesus mighty name we pray, Amen. prayer.africa/equatorial-guinea

Eritrea

He delivered us from such a deadly peril, and he will deliver us.
On him we have set our hope that he will deliver us again.
You also must help us by prayer, so that many will give thanks
on our behalf for the blessing granted us through
the prayers of many. **2 Corinthians 1;10-11**

Father, we praise You for the growth of the Eritrean church even among persecution. We pray that You will preserve Your people in Eritrea and grant them freedom from the strong grasp of political and religious oppression.

Lord, we pray for the release of over 3,000 imprisoned and tortured believers. We also pray that You would comfort the bereaved and brokenhearted families who have lost loved ones. Father, we ask for open doors for Christian workers to return to Eritrea. We pray that you will protect the young pastors preaching Your word in Eritrea and grant them the boldness to continue their work.

We also pray for the establishment of peace between Eritrea and Ethiopia. We ask this in the mighty name of Jesus Christ our Lord and Saviour. Amen. prayer.africa/eritrea

Estonia

Make a joyful noise unto the Lord, all ye lands.
Psalms 100:1

As Estonia celebrates 100 years...
Father God, we thank you for blessing this nation.
May your people praise your name.

pray4Eurasia.org

Eswatini

Therefore, rid yourselves of all malice and all deceit,
hypocrisy, envy, and slander of every kind.
1 Peter 2:1

Oh God, Bestower of the Blessings of the Swazi

O Lord our God, bestower of the blessings of the
Swazi ; We give Thee thanks for all our good fortune ;
We offer thanks and praise for our king ;
And for our fair land, its hills and rivers ;

The Blessings be on all rulers of our country ;
Might and power are Thine alone ;
We pray Thee to grant us wisdom without deceit or
malice. Establish and fortify us, Lord Eternal.
National Anthem of Swaziland

Ethiopia

You, Lord, will keep the needy safe
and will protect us forever from the wicked.
Psalm 12:7

Lord, a land
of coffee and grain
of cattle and crops
of pasture and plain
of laughter and love
is thirsty.

O God, comfort your people.
Protect families struggling to get by
protect children losing out on education
protect those seeking water in their travels.

O God, comfort your people.
We pray for Christian Aid and their partners,
with institutions and organizations supporting people
in Ethiopia. Grant them wisdom as they assess need
and bless them as they respond.
O God, comfort your people.

Let your hand rest
upon your people of Ethiopia,
widows and orphans,
aged and children,
strangers and wanderers.
And join us also with them,
protect and strengthen us,
from all evil works keep us apart,
and in all good works unite us.
You are life for our souls.
You are the life of the world.
Amen.
Prayer For Ethiopia

Europe

*In the same way your Father in heaven is not willing
that any of these little ones should be lost.*
Matthew 18:14

We praise You Lord for answered prayer in the collapse
of European Communism, the dismantling of the Iron
Curtain, for breakthroughs in Albania and for Europe's
recent peace without imperial tyrannies. We ask You to
heal the Balkan conflicts with its long history of violence,
ethnic hatreds and convoluted politics. Use the new
freedoms of Europe significantly for church growth.

We praise You for hope in the strength

and confidence of evangelicals, and the emergence of new
church and worship patterns in youth networks impacting
many young people. We pray for peace in Northern
Ireland, the Basque region of Spain and Chechnya
in the Russian Federation.

Lord, reach the nearly 400 non-Christian peoples within
Europe's countries that are partially evangelized including
Muslim ethnic groups, Roma minorities, the Jewish
remnant and the many ethnic minorities of the Russian
Federation in the Caucasus, Siberia, the Urals
and the Arctic. Dave Davidson

Evangelists

It was he who gave some to be apostles, some to be prophets, some to be evangelists, and some to be pastors and teachers...
Ephesians 4:11

Lord, we thank You for calling, equipping and sending workers to become evangelists. We pray for the personal ministries of the hundreds of evangelists around the world. Encourage them Lord and give them Your vision that no lost soul would ever perish. Increase the effectiveness of their ministries and protect their lives and reputations from sin and scandal as the devil tries to destroy all who are on the front lines for You.

Prepare now those hearts who will be experiencing the ministries of Graham, Palau and other high-profile evangelistic crusades. Give these servants a solid grounding in Your word and true theology. May these ministries and their supporters be blessed.

Lord may we live by the creed found in Romans 1:16 to not be ashamed of the gospel. Grant all believers evangelism boldness according to their personality and spiritual gifts.
Dave Davidson

Faith, Hope & Love

And now these three remain: faith, hope and love.
But the greatest of these is love.
1 Corinthians 13:13

Lord, we pray that we may be active in sharing our faith, so that we will have a full understanding of every good thing we have in Christ. Philemon 1:6 Lord let us exercise centurion delegating, water walking, ark building, plague escaping, Jericho wall falling,

Goliath headache making,
Mount Moriah, mustard seed faith!

Lord, we know that hope does not disappoint us, because You have poured out Your love into our hearts by the Holy Spirit, whom You have has given us. Romans 5:5 So for me, I will always have hope; I will praise you more and more. Psalm 71:14 In Your name the nations will put their hope. Matthew 12:21 Father, we will use the spirit of power, of love and of self-discipline You gave us. 2 Timothy 1:7 May we above all, love each other deeply, because love covers over a multitude of sins.1 Peter 4:8 Let us love by the definition Your word gives to us. 1 Corinthians 13

Dave Davidson

Family

*He and all his family were devout and God-fearing; he gave
generously to those in need and prayed to God regularly.*
Acts 10:2

We pray for strength and unity in families.

We lift up marriage as the divine component that keeps
families together and ask for diligence to stand against any
forces that oppose marriage. We pray for couples to give
attention to their marriage and make it a priority in their
personal lives. We also lift up single parents and
ask for their support and encouragement.

We pray for understanding

between parents and children. Give parents wisdom for
the balance between freedom and boundaries, which will
instill confidence, security, well-being and love. We ask for
a strengthened commitment from families to spend time
learning biblical ways and understanding God's plan.
We ask for clarity in purpose and a dedication
to following God's will for their lives. Joan Davidson

Fellowship Partnerships

We proclaim to you what we have seen and heard, so that
you also may have fellowship with us. And our fellowship
is with the Father and with his Son, Jesus Christ.
1 John 1:3

Let's just have a word of prayer living God, we thank
and praise you for all that you're doing across the
world today. We realized we're in the midst of the
greatest harvest of people to yourself that has ever
taken place in the world, and we're excited about that.

At the same time, Oh God, we're very aware of
thousands of unreached peoples groups and so many
places in the world where there are a million set still
had not clearly even heard or read the Gospel or
move upon our hearts that we may not only be
excited and challenged and obedient, but that we may
also learn the basic principles on a practical level on
how we can be effective, how we can be committed to
excellence in this task of world missions. As hard as
that is as complex as a challenge. Maybe You guide us
Lord. Help me to really share what's on my heart and
enable people who are listening or reading in many
parts of the world to adopt and contextualize
these thoughts into their own situation.

We thank you for so many local churches and
fellowships that now have this vision and are moving
in mission and world evangelism and we pray for
an increased partnership between missionary
fellowships and local fellowships and powerful
and important structures that you have raised
up that this work may be done guidance now as we
go forward together in the name of Jesus. Amen.

George Verwer

Fiji

*In the Lord's hand the king's heart is a stream of water
that he channels toward all who please him.*
Proverbs 21:1

Oh God in heaven, I come before You in the Name
of Jesus on behalf of the leaders of the nation Fiji Islands.
First of all in accordance with 1 Timothy 2:1-2, I intercede
and give thanks for kings and all in authority and
expect to live a quiet and peaceable life.

I pray for the Word of God to be given free course and
Your people to be delivered from unreasonable and
wicked men (2 Thessalonians 3:1-2).

The heart of the king is in Your hand and You will turn it whichever way You choose (Proverbs 21:1).

I ask You to direct the heart and mind of Fiji's government and church leaders to make decisions that will lead the country in Your ways and according to Your Word.

I thank You, Lord, for bringing change to the politics of the Fiji Islands. Thank You for changing the voices of influence to speak in agreement with Your Word.

I ask You to send labourers filled with the spirit of wisdom and might, to surround the leaders of the Fiji Islands with godly counsel and insight.

Jose Bose

Finances & Resources

Command those who are rich in this present world not to be arrogant nor to put their hope in wealth, which is so uncertain, but to put their hope in God, who richly provides us with everything for our enjoyment.
1 Timothy 6:17

Lord, reveal to us Your priority, balance and grace when it comes to not only giving but giving to world missions. We petition You for an avalanche of financial gifts sending out workers enabling key literature

projects around the world.

Give us discernment to support various ministries. Bless their efforts as good and effective stewards. Lord, flood our faith! May money given to missions be stretched and used wisely. We earnestly ask that churches would take greater ownership in the great commission. Answer our prayers for ministry resources.

George Verwer

Prayer reflects the image of a man's heart.

Dave Davidson

Finland

I will praise you, Lord my God, with all my heart;
I will glorify your name forever.
Psalm 86:12

Now that Finland has had over 100 years of independence
from the Swedes, let them Lord thrive in gospel good news
freedom. May this country of 60,000 lakes be mirror the
reflection of a godly countenance pleasing
and glorifying You Lord.

Dave Davidson

Let us pray for a great harvest of souls in Finland,
that the Lord would move in unprecedented ways.

Let us pray for His people to arise and let the light
of Christ shine. And pray that His purposes
would be fulfilled in Finland!
Europe Shall Be Saved

First World Problems

For the time will come when men will not put up with sound doctrine. Instead, to suit their own desires, they will gather around them a great number of teachers to say what their itching ears want to hear.
2 Timothy 4:3

Our struggle for luxury coffee flavors and our quest for ultimate thrill-seeking consumption falls short of a godly attitude in many new testament themes of living for You. Father God western culture has gone whack. We think a real problem is no Wi-Fi or that we must wait for our food more than a mere moment. Forgive our self-absorbed lifestyles filled with self-sufficiency tendencies and riddled with entertainment dependent busyness addictions. Humble us with the mission burden of our brothers and sisters across the world.
Dave Davidson

Focusing on Christ

"I am the Alpha and the Omega," says the Lord God,
"who is, and who was, and who is to come, the Almighty.".
Revelation 1:8

Let's turn our eyes upon Jesus. You are the Alpha and Omega, the Almighty, the blessed and only potentate the Lord Christ the power of God and the wisdom of God.

Emmanuel, God with us, God of the whole Earth Governor, head of all principality and power, the great I Am, the judge of the quick and the dead, the King of glory, the King of Kings and Lord of Lords, Lord from Heaven, the Lord of hosts, the Lord God Almighty, the Most Holy, the son of God, wonderful counselor, mighty God, the everlasting father, the Prince of peace, the Bishop of souls, desire of nations, the friend of sinners, the faithful witness, the king over all the earth, the Lord of all the Prince of the kings of the earth, ransom for all righteous judge, savior of the world, son of man, stone rejected, author of eternal salvation, gift of God, the Lord of Glory, the Messiah. The offering and sacrifice, the redeemer, the Resurrection, the light source of righteousness. The author and finisher of thing, the altogether lovely. The advocate, the bread from heaven, bread of life, the branch of righteousness.

The bridegroom, the chief cornerstone the chief Shepherd, Christ of God, door of the sheep, eternal life, the high priest, the hope of glory, the King of Kings, a light of the world, the Lord about righteousness, mediator, messenger of the covenant, the Prince of peace, the quickening spirit, the redeemer, the Rose of Sharon, the true light. Let's worship this glorious Christ focusing on him as we pray.

George Verwer

Fruit of the Spirit

I am the vine; you are the branches. If a man remains in me and I in him, he will bear much fruit; apart from me you can do nothing.
John 15:5

Jesus, the gardener of our soul and giver of eternal life, we seek to abide in You and to produce much fruit for your heavenly kingdom. Prune us according to your will and discipline us by Your

unfailing abundant love.

Make us forever realize how connected and grateful we are to You, O Lord. Be our source of strength as we set out to bear fruit and exalt your name with the living worship of our very lives. Father, Thank Your for Your complete forgiveness through the life, death and

resurrection of Jesus.

Help us take a spiritual inventory searching our hearts for those we need to forgive. Remind us to seek Your Spirit and power to

forgive others as You have forgiven us.

Dave Davidson

France

*Abram believed the Lord,
and he credited it to him as righteousness.*
Genesis 15:6

Father in heaven bless the center of western Europe
comprising 30% atheist and only 1% evangelical
believers. Meanwhile as Muslims make up
approximately 7% of France's population, Lord allow
this to be the highest percentage in any European
country no longer. Bolster church attendance beyond
recent years as one of the lowest in Europe (6-8%).
Change these discouraging statistics to find
favor in your will Lord.

We grieve that 80% of French people have never owned
or even seen a Bible. Solve this literate deficit Lord.

We pray for the 50,000 full-time practitioners of occult arts
(tarot, fortune telling, psychic healing, etc) to be influenced
by the 35,000 full-time Christian workers in France.
Dave Davidson

Gabon

Like newborn babies, crave pure spiritual milk,
so that by it you may grow up in your salvation.
1 Peter 2:2

We ask Lord for wiser and more transparent leadership in the spiritual battlefield of Gabon. Spark the evangelical Christians to grow while extending missions to the interior. Work through the spiritual darkness of secret societies, endemic alcoholism, ignorance of the gospel and willingness to mix traditional religious beliefs with Christianity.

Reveal Yourself to the 37 people groups with fewer than 10% evangelicals. Help the Fang group and the Baka (Pygmy) who struggle for civil rights.

Multiply Bible translations, God glorifying broadcasts, and evangelistic literature along with JESUS film distribution. Thanks God that 1,000 people a year come to Christ CMA's Bangolo Hospital.

Dave Davidson

Gambia

It is for freedom that Christ has set us free.
Stand firm, then, and do not let yourselves
be burdened again by a yoke of slavery.
Galatians 5:1

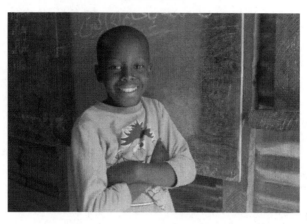

Lord, we pray for continued freedom for the people of Gambia to spread the Gospel. We pray for revival, peace and stability in this nation. Father, as You own everything, we ask of you to release the needed resources in order for Your Kingdom to be built in the Gambia. Will You also make land available for communities to use to the glory of Your name, Lord Jesus. We pray also for unhampered and accurate translation work for many languages with no Bible.

We bring before You, the missionaries who will leave urban Gambia to travel upriver to unreached tribes. Father, we pray also for nominal Christians to deepen in their relationship with You and for them to have a clearer knowledge of who You are. Lord God, we pray for the unreached Muslim majority to discover life in Jesus. prayer.africa/Gambia

Georgia

*When a farmer plows for planting, does he plow continually?
Does he keep on breaking up and working the soil?*
Isaiah 28:24

May the country of Georgia, named from the Greek
word for farmer, be blessed in the rich in fertile soil
and agriculture reap a manifold harvest of saved
souls. Transform the Orthodox Christians whose
religion is merely cultural to meet the Living Christ,
to embrace His grace, and to fulfill Your great
commission. Give unity among all churches as they
present the Gospel. Breakthrough to remote and
largely unreached Svaneti people. As the Persians,
Arabs, Turks, and Mongols all impacted the history
of Georgia, move Christ followers
for Kingdom momentum
Dave Davidson

Germany

Therefore he is able to save completely those who come to God through him, because he always lives to intercede for them.
Hebrews 7:25

Intercessors, sanctify yourselves with sacred oil!
Let the Spirit of Jesus flow into your heart and soul!
May your mouths overflow in sacred ways
With supplication, prayer and praise.
The prayers of the saints, the pleas and requests,
Are poured out on the altar before God's throne,
Where Jesus Christ is our great high priest
Who for all his servants will atone.

If the prayer from one of the faithful souls,
When it touches God's heart, cannot miss its goal;
What now if they all come together before his throne
And present their prayers in unison!
Oh what amazing power is in our prayers indeed.
Without this nothing can be done
In good times and in need.
Step by step it assures the victory of friends,
And to those who oppose it brings an end.

Christoph Karl Ludwig von Pfeil

Ghana

*Therefore everyone who hears these words of mine
and puts them into practice is like a wise man
who built his house on the rock.*
Matthew 7:24

Ghana belongs to God, for Him and Him alone therefore
what shall man plan against the land. The Word of God
has established that forever. Only the counsel of Jehovah
shall stand and he shall forever be our shalom.
Oman Ghana ye do wo,enti ko w'anim. George Sakyi Adade

Heavenly Father as we go on as a country, help us not
to throw away the moral foundations You taught us
through the Word and the inner conscience of Your
Law passed down to us over the generations. As a
country we Pledge Allegiance to the Lamb that as
many countries prosper and forget You, Ghana shall
not but always remember where You picked us from.
All of us for All of YOU. Amen.

Kwame Antwi-boasiako

Glory & Grace

*I have brought you glory on earth by
completing the work you gave me to do.*
John 17:4

Help us to live for You always

and to be hungry for true intimacy with You. Take
away Lord, anything from our lives that doesn't
glorify You. We are truly sorry for the times when
we have failed to honor You and put
You first place in our lives. Jenny Voon

Lord we ask for the discernment in faith to react,
respond and reply by the grace of Jesus in trials and
tribulations. When the very people we are trying to
work with annoy us, Lord, give us a reminder of Your
patience and Your sufficient grace. May we glorify
You, O Lord, as we trust You in our lives. Dave Davidson

God, grant me the serenity

to accept people
that drive me crazy; the courage to get up and get
going; and the wisdom to know you love the
bananas out of me even when I screw things up.
Hugh Myrrh

Governments

And the government will be upon His shoulders...
Isaiah 9:6

Above all God may governments worldwide stand for life,
morality, and righteousness, not death and destruction.
Dave Davidson

Heavenly Father,

we come before You today
to ask Your forgiveness

and to seek Your direction and guidance.

We know Your Word says, "Woe to those who call evil good," but that is exactly what we have done. We have lost our spiritual equilibrium and reversed our values. We confess that: We have ridiculed the absolute truth of Your Word and called it pluralism; We have worshipped other gods and called it multiculturalism; We have endorsed perversion and called it alternative lifestyle; We have exploited the poor and called it the lottery; We have rewarded laziness and called it welfare; We have killed our unborn and called it choice; We have shot abortionists and called it justifiable; We have neglected to discipline our children and called it building self-esteem; We have abused power and called it politics; We have coveted our neighbor's possessions and called it ambition; We have polluted the air with profanity and pornography and called it freedom of expression; We have ridiculed the time-honored values of our forefathers and called it enlightenment. Search us, Oh, God, and know our hearts today; cleanse us from every sin and set us free. Guide and bless these men and women who have been sent to direct us to the center of Your will. We ask it in the name of Your Son, the living Savior, Jesus Christ. Amen

Joe Wright read this at the Kansas senate while some politicians left the room.

Grace Awakening

One who loves a pure heart and who speaks
with grace will have the king for a friend.
Proverbs 22:11

Heavenly Father, I bring before you this increasingly
difficult relationship that I am in and pray that by
Your grace, I may be willing to learn the lesson that
You would teach me through this problematic time.
Lord I know that relationships are not always easy,
but we seem to have slid into a constant cycle of
hostility and accusations. Forgive me for the part I
have played in developing this bitterness and ill-
feeling between us and I pray that You would help
me repent of this wrong attitude - and turn right
away from my own natural, fleshly reactions and
start to walk in spirit and truth. Lord I know that I
cannot do this in my own strength but only in the

power of the Holy Spirit.
And so Lord, I pray that I
may be willing to listen to
Your promptings and to
submit to Your training and
chastening hand on my life.

Help me each day to lay my life before You
and to search my own heart so that I may identify any
seeds of my own bitterness and hostility – and I pray
that I may be honest in my assessment of my own
faults and failings. Teach me Your way and endow
me with wisdom, grace and counsel – so that the
damage to our relationship may be repaired by
Your grace. Help me to live my life as the person
that You would have me be – and in a manner
that is pleasing in Your sight.

Guard my heart and all that proceeds from my lips and may my words be seasoned with salt and pleasing to the Father. Thank You Lord that You are a God Who hears and answers the prayers of Your children and I pray that you would graciously renew a right spirit, within this relationship - in Jesus name I pray, Amen.

Heavenly Father, I come boldly to the throne of grace in the name of Jesus Christ, my Lord and Savior so that in Your loving-kindness and great mercy I may find the specific and sufficient grace that is needed to help in time of need.

Lord the days are getting darker and I need Your abundant grace in so many areas of my life, knowing that it is only as I abide in Jesus by grace through faith, that I will be enabled to be fortified against every evil thought, word and work and live godly in Christ Jesus, to Your praise and glory.

I pray that I may receive grace upon grace as You have promised in Your Word. I am asking to be supplied with God's grace. So that sin will not gain dominion over me, but that I will become a vessel fit to be used in Your service and a channel of Your love and grace to all with whom I come in contact today. May I decrease and Christ increase in every area of my life until it is not I that live, but Christ that lives in me – to Your praise I pray in Jesus name, Amen.

Knowing-Jesus.com

Great Commission

Therefore go and make disciples of all nations, baptizing them in the name of the Father and of the Son and of the Holy Spirit, and teaching them to obey everything I have commanded you. And surely I am with you always, to the very end of the age.
Matthew 29:19,20

Father, we desire to see lost millions come to follow and worship Jesus with their lives, to commit their time and talents, dreams and passion, money and relationships to bringing glory to You in all that they do. Lord, give us Your passion and vision. Todd Morr

Lord, we thank You for allowing us to partner with You as an ambassador of heaven. Produce a ministry of multiplying fruit to further grow Your kingdom and to fulfill the great commission. May we worship You! May we obey like we live as Your chosen people, Lord God. Fulfill Your will and finish!

Yes God Do It!

George Verwer

In some lands

there are hundreds of thousands of congregations and in others maybe only one or two. The wheat and the tares are mixed with obvious divisions and weaknesses, yet the Holy Spirit's working in and through the church in all its diversity of doctrines, denominations, languages and personalities. Through Your Church redemption will be

proclaimed to mankind.

Lord this is why You called Abraham (Genesis 12:3; Galatians 3:8). Christ died for the Church (Ephesians 2:16) and he lives as its Head (Ephesians 1:22). As part of Christ's Body, our longing should be for its up-building and perfection (Colossians 1:24). One day soon the Bride of Christ, the church, will be complete and perfect (Ephesians 5:27; Revelation 7:9-10)!

Your church on earth is only an imperfect manifestation of the one, true and invisible church of the Lord Jesus Christ, yet You promise the gates of hell will not prevail!

Equip us with a clear witness to the uniqueness of Christ in the centrality of the scriptures for local church effectiveness. Help us keep pastors, ministers and elders upheld in prayer. Give Your church spiritual depth against superficial devotion. Evangelize afresh our younger generation. Give us a revival in missionary vision.

adapted from Patrick Johnstone / OperationWorld.com

Greece

*I am obligated both to Greeks and non-Greeks,
both to the wise and the foolish.*
Romans 1:14

Inspired by the Apostle Paul pointing lost Greek souls
from an unknown God to the saving grace of Christ, may
Greece become a beacon of leading people to heaven.

Father God though Greek language and culture paved the
way for the spread of the Gospel in the 1st century, today,
Greece is Europe's neediest mission field with less than
20,000 believers, (around 0.18% of the current population.)

Lord boost the average Sunday church attendance beyond
its average of 15-30 people. Solve the red tape of few
historical churches operating with a valid church permit.
Dave Davidson

Grenada

Rise up; this matter is in your hands.
We will support you, so take courage and do it.
Ezra 10:4

God give Grenada missionaries greater
opportunities to minister in their communities.

Secure them in financial stability with gospel abounding
church-planting momentum as You provide support
for housing, food, and living expenses.

Bless missionary families, who have greatly
missed them in their absence.

Disciple new believers so that they will
understand who they are in Christ.

Dave Davidson

_____

_____

_____

_____

Guatemala

I am he who will sustain you.
I have made you and I will carry you;
I will sustain you and I will rescue you.
Isaiah 46:4

For the people of Guatemala may find safety as they live out their days is hostility. We lift up in prayer the Achi people of Cubulco who practice traditional Spiritism. God protect bible translation teams facing spiritual warfare every day.

Beef up bible study resources for requesting pastors.

Lord, hear our prayer that Guatemalans may find unity, and put aside violence as they confront emergencies, crises, and challenges. Lord, hear our prayer.
Dave Davidson

Guinea & Guinea-Bissau

*Now it is God who makes both us and you stand firm in Christ.
He anointed us.*
2 Corinthians 1:21

Anoint the youth to rise up and lovingly serve you
wholeheartedly in Guinea-Bissau. Lord send the
spiritually mature, trained national workers to move
outside urban areas to minister to the less-reached.
Expand the distribution of oral Christian
materials for the poor and illiterate.

Guide government leaders to stop the movement
of foreign narcotics. God of mercy solve illicit drug
trafficking that has grown almost unchecked, as the
government has no coast guard, police do not have
cars available, and the navy has no boats for
patrolling the North Atlantic shores.
Dave Davidson

Guyana

You wearied yourself by such going about, but you would not say, 'It is hopeless.' You found renewal of your strength, and so you did not faint.
Isaiah 57:10

Father in heaven, please hear our prayer. I have no doubt that it is your will to unite our people. You have afforded us this opportunity Lord, grant us all, the boldness to do your will. Jehovah your word states "...then if my people who are called by my name will humble themselves and pray and seek my face and turn from their wicked ways, I will hear from heaven and will forgive their sins and restore their land." It is time for a new Guyana, we pray for a new Guyana Lord, we pray because we are deeply disappointed with the Guyana we currently have.

We're fed-up with the crime, the corruption, the hopelessness, the suicides.... We commit our land to you, from the east to the west and from the north to the south. We surrender it to you.

Pray For Guyana Facebook Page

Haiti

As the soldiers led him away, they seized Simon from Cyrene, who was on his way in from the country, and put the cross on him and made him carry it behind Jesus.

Luke 23:26

Most Holy Creator God, Lord of heaven and earth,
we bring before you today your people of Haiti.
It is You who set in motion the stars and seas,
You who raised up the mountains of the
Massif de la Hotteand Pic La Selle.

It is You who made her people in your very image:
Their gregarious hearts and generous spirits,
their hunger and thirst for righteousness and liberty.
It is you, O Lord, who planted the rhythms of konpa,
Twoubadou and zouk in the streets of Cite-Soleil;
You who walk the paths outside of Jacmel and Hinche.

Your people, O Lord, cry out to you.

Haiti, O Haiti: The world's oldest black republic,
the second-oldest republic in the Western world.

God, You are the One
who answers the cries of the suffering.
You are a God who sees, frees, and redeems
your people. "I too have heard the moaning
of my people," you spoke to Moses.

Now, Lord, speak again to Chanté, Agwe, Nadege,
and Jean Joseph. Speak now, O Lord, and comfort
Antoine, Jean-Baptiste, Toto, and Djakout. Raise up
your people from the ash heap of destruction and
give them strong hearts and hands, shore up their
minds and spirits. Help them to bear this new burden.

As for us, Lord, we who are far away from the rubble
and the flood, from the sobbing and moans, but who
hold them close in our hearts, imbue us with the
strength of Simon the Cyrene. Help us to carry the
Haitian cross. Show us how to lighten their yoke with
our prayers, our aid, our resources.

Teach us to work harder for justice in our own
country and dignity in Haiti, so that we may stand
with integrity when we hold our Haitian families
in our arms once again. We ask this in the name
of Jezikri, Jesus Christ. Amen.

Rose Marie Berger

Harvest

Swing the sickle, for the harvest is ripe.
Come, trample the grapes, for the winepress is full and the vats
overflow— so great is their wickedness!"
Joel 3:13

Let us pray. Oh God and father, we thank you for
your word and we thank you for these mega
motivating words from your word in Acts 13, and we
would pray in obedience to Matthew 9. Old God, that
you would send for it just as you sent Paul and
Barnabas, that you would send forth laborers,
workers into the harvest locally and across the globe,
and that you would raise up the senders, the
intercessors, the mission mobilizers to make this a
reality that that remaining 25 percent may soon at
least hear or read about Jesus. That after that the
church might be planted among every people's in
every part of the world. In Jesus name, Amen.

George Vewer

Hedge of Protection

*Those who live in the shelter of the Most High
will find rest in the shadow of the Almighty.*
Psalm 91:1

Heavenly Father, I (we) ask You to place a hedge of protection around me (us). It hides me (us) from the enemy, familiar spirits, any and all demon spirits, making it difficult, if not impossible for them to effectively track or trace me in the realm of the spirit. There shall be no perforations or penetrations to these hedges of protection according to your word in Psalm 91. I (we) know that You will answer this prayer because I (we) love You and I(we) trust in Your name only. I pray that Your blood Lord Jesus will cover me(us) and all that You have given me(us). That the enemy will not have access to what has been given to me(us). Thank you for your divine protection in Jesus Name, Amen. MissionariesofPrayer.org

Hell

*Rescue others by snatching them from the flames of judgment.
Show mercy to still others, but do so with great caution,
hating the sins that contaminate their lives.* NLT
Jude 1:23

Lord remind us again and again of the reality,
relevance and resolute resolve of warning others
of unrepentant sin's consequences. Equip
us to snatch souls from hell. Dave Davidson

Lord, You promise that the gates of hell will not overcome
Your church. You have a people and You have a plan that
will not fail. No matter what, Your purposes will prevail.
You are in Your church and indwell Your people. In this
we take great hope. Strengthen Your people, Lord!
Strengthen Your church in this country! Let us rise to the
battle cry and faithfully stand firm! Stir up our passions
and desires for purity, holiness, and intimacy with You.
Let us walk in the unquenchable fire of Your Spirit.
Matthew 16:18 Arabah Joy

Hindus

He is the image of the invisible God, the firstborn
over all creation. For God was pleased to have
all his fullness dwell in him…
Colossians 1:16,19

Lord, turn the Hindu hearts of the world's third largest religious system toward the supremacy of Christ.

Turn their religious beliefs, philosophies, Vedic rituals, idolatry, occultism and animism to a path of Jesus Christ being the only way, truth and the life.

May the Hindu religious absorbing mindset be convinced in faith of the unique "true communion" to Christ and His claims.

May those in movements of the Hare Krishna and New Age also be brought to the gospel without confusing it with yoga, gurus, karma, reincarnation and transcendental meditation.

Have mercy and shed light

on the Hindu caste system, which discriminates, intimidates and represses the poor.
Make governments wise. Dave Davidson

Holy See

But what does it matter? The important thing is that in every way, whether from false motives or true, Christ is preached. And because of this I rejoice.
Philippians 1:18

Lord as the loss of credibility through numerous scandals and aggressive papal doctrinal positions we pray for wisdom for Catholics adapting the Church to 21st Century realities to be biblically relevant. We ask for spiritual renewal and unprecedented doctrinal wisdom especially when the Pope dilutes the gospel trading opportunities for effective impact for environmental gibberish

Leverage Catholic charismatic renewal beyond the 235 countries and 120 million people involved. Use it as a bridge to believers in other denominations and to not be rendered ineffective by the system. Drive nominal Catholics – many millions strong – to experience the radical conversion and cultural transformation that at times their pontiff insists is essential to faith.

Moreover, convict all the leaders at the Holy See
to dump some of the enormous wealth tucked away
in the catacombs of the Vatican to free up for
transforming funds to feed and heal the world.
Until they live out any semblance of such
humble service offering may we otherwise
be discerning to be convinced otherwise
than outrageous hypocrisy.

Dave Davidson

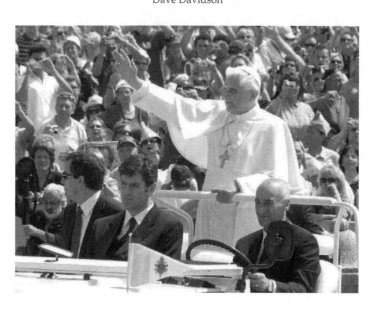

Holy Spirit

But you will receive power when the Holy Spirit comes on you;
and you will be my witnesses in Jerusalem, and in all Judea
and Samaria, and to the ends of the earth
Acts 1:8

Cause us to thirst,
pant and long for more of You and Your Spirit, Lord.
All we want is more and more of You.

Thank You for satisfying us completely. Lead us Lord by your Holy Spirit and equip us to go out and tell precious lost souls about Your love.

Lord, we desire Your Heart for the lost and Your compassion and tears for the unsaved. Jesus, you died openly for us, so empower us to witness boldly to all nations, no matter what the consequences.

Lord, we are willing to be used for Your Kingdom. Send us with Your Holy Spirit's power and anointing, ## to gather precious souls to Your feet.
We desire Lord, to yield to Your Holy Spirit and not to the flesh. Help us to have hunger, thirst and a burning passion for You always - to be like You in every way. Jenny Voon

Homeless

*"Come, you who are blessed by my Father... for I was hungry
and you gave me something to eat, I was thirsty and you gave
me something to drink, I was a stranger and you invited me in,
I needed clothes and you clothed me."*
Matthew 25:34

We pray for friendship and hope, for sustenance and
rehabilitation. May those without a home during storms
have access to practical resources, such as warm and safe
shelter, hygiene services, nutritious food and clothing.
May the homeless be willing and able to connect with
long-term rehabilitation programs, social workers, job
skills programs, mental health care and access to
permanent housing. We pray that the city's leaders
would respond wisely to the challenges operating 24/7
emergency shelters, that God would grant them
energy and compassion to continue their work.
We pray for spiritual renewal.

We must come to
God expecting more.
He loves to provide
our needs when we
ask Him to in faith.

We pray that those experiencing loneliness or hopelessness would find spiritual renewal through a relationship with God the Father; that their hearts would receive comfort from God in a tangible and real way. May they experience God's kindness and care throughout the day to remind them that they are not forgotten and that they are deeply loved by their Father in heaven. May any children experiencing homelessness, Lord would protect and provide for them as they live in challenging conditions.

We pray that He would strengthen their families and show his special favor and love to them in the small, everyday things. We lift up parents in these vulnerable families; that they would make wise decisions and be able to provide both practically and emotionally for their children. May God give them hope for their future and faith that He is with them always. Thank You Lord for organizations serving the homeless. May volunteers and staff to approach people graciously and compassionately, and that those they encounter would connect to the resources they need. We pray also for ourselves - that God would stir up in our hearts a call to compassion, a call to action, and a call to see the homeless as the children of God that they are.
adapted from a prayer list by Hope For New York

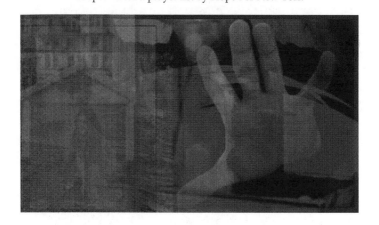

Honduras

I will sing of your love and justice; to you, Lord, I will sing praise.
Psalm 101:1

Praise God for 2.5 years of transformation through the police purge commission! We are celebrating 5,000+ corrupt officers fired, 7,000 new officers hired, and new police laws and training facilities created. As the commission's mandate ends in January, please also pray for wisdom in this period of transition.

Praise God for the expansion of our violence-prevention family and community projects this year! We've seen an amazing response as new organizations and churches implement our methodology in their own communities. We're grateful for this opportunity to see a message of peace and justice spread to hundreds more beneficiaries. Please pray for justice to heal the wounds left behind by Honduras' presidential elections. Next week marks one year since that contentious period. Since then, we have been hard at work on in-depth electoral reforms, calling for more democratic and transparent processes that will benefit Hondurans not only at the next election, but also in their daily lives. Pray for consensus behind important reforms that bring accountability and transparency to public office in Honduras.

Please pray for the public health system in Honduras, which 80% of Hondurans depend on for care and medications. This system faces serious problems, with a backlog of thousands of patients needing surgery and limited surgical materials and medicines. Praise God that AJS has been asked to be involved in reform, and pray with us for transparent and committed authorities!

ajs-us.org/pray

Hong Kong

It is written: "'As surely as I live,' says the Lord, 'every knee will bow before me; every tongue will acknowledge God.'"
Romans 14:11

Father God, You are exalted above the heavens.
Let Your glory be over all the earth! You are exalted over
all nations and people! You are exalted above all things.
Grant not, O Lord, the desires of the wicked.
Let not the evil plots and schemes of the
enemy bring down Hong Kong.

I pray. I declare China belongs to Jesus! Hong Kong, the
pearl of the orient, shall worship You. Let her people bless
the Lord.As this city rages, let her people fear Your Name,
O Lord! For every knee shall bow and every tongue
confess that Jesus Christ is Lord, to the glory
of God, the Father!.

I pray for all protesters to remain calm.
Let them submit their lives to You, O God. For their
destiny and the destiny of Hong Kong rest with You, my
Lord. Let the government of Hong Kong and their Chief
Executive submit to You, O God! By Your grace, mercy
and divine intervention, grant the Chief Executive and
decision makers in the Chinese Government
both wisdom and counsel.

Let Your kingdom come and Your will be done in this city
and nation, I pray. Let Your favor, blessing and glory rain
down on Hong Kong and China, O Lord. By Your grace,
let the Hong Kong government uphold Your righteousness
and justice. Let your people who are called by Your Name
humble themselves and pray and seek Your face and turn
from their wicked ways. Then You will hear from heaven
and will forgive their sins and heal their land. Then Your
eyes will be open and Your ears attentive to their prayers
that is made in the city of Hong Kong (2 Chronicles 7:14-15).

Lord, remember that You would have spared Sodom
if Abraham could find just 10 righteous souls (Genesis 18).
Remember O Lord that You told Jeremiah that if he can
find one man of integrity in Jerusalem, the man's presence
would gain pardon for the whole city (Jeremiah 5:1).

Let Hong Kong remember Your promise, that You are
looking for a man who would stand in the gap for the land
before You, O God, so that You will not destroy it
(Ezekiel 22:30).

Let the church of Hong Kong remember when they enter
the place of prayer, that mercy triumphs over judgment.

Have mercy, Lord! Hear the cries and prayer of Your people in Hong Kong. Deliver them from all evil and heal their land, I pray. What the enemy intended for evil, Lord, You will turn it for good, for Your purposes and glory in Hong Kong. No weapon formed against Your people and Hong Kong shall prosper and every tongue that arises against them, I condemn. By Your grace, Lord, let peace that surpasses all understanding guard the hearts and minds of Your people in Hong Kong.

Let Hong Kong and China see their salvation and the goodness of the Lord in the land of the living, I pray. Be glorified, Lord! In Jesus' Name I pray, Amen.

Jill MacKillop

Human Trafficking

Captives also enjoy their ease;
they no longer hear the slave driver's shout.
Job 3:18

Oh God, we didn't see them, but you did...The hundreds
and thousands of human beings Trafficked each year to
join the millions who are trapped in modern-day slavery.
Under terrible conditions, they work in factories, plow
fields, harvest crops, work quarries, fill brothels, clean
homes, and haul water. Many are children with tiny
fingers for weaving rugs and small shoulders for bearing
rifles. Their labor is forced, their bodies beaten, their faces
hidden from those who don't really want to see them. But
you see them all, God of the poor. You hear their cry and
you answer by opening our eyes, and breaking our hearts
and loosening our tongues to insist: No more. Amen.

Catholic Relief Services

Jesus, when we pray for a horrible

injustice like human trafficking it's easy to forget our
own sins that play into this atrocity. We all have root sin
causing us to desire to rule over others, even God himself.

God, we also acknowledge that we struggle with selfishness, lust, and greed, three factors that greatly feed the evil of human trafficking. Please forgive us for our sins. Help us to repent and change. Enable us to serve and love others. Make us different, shining like the stars in the heavens.

Father, we beg for the liberation of victims. Please bring freedom to the 30 million slaves in the world. Remove the chains of their oppressors and help them escape. Just as you helped Paul and Silas escape the jail, free these people supernaturally. Free them through the repentance of oppressors. Free them through the work of your people to administer justice. However you do it, please grant freedom.

Jesus, you know the roots of this atrocity. They are poverty, greed, and lust. God, first we want to pray for those in poverty. Would you help bring people out of positions that lead to desperation, making them vulnerable to traffickers. Please bring work into these areas - animals, crops, and industry. Father, grant a way for people to care for their families and themselves so that they are not easily stolen away. We are so broken over the other roots as well, lust and greed. Would you open hearts and eyes to the sickness of lust and greed. Would you make them see that feeding off the flesh and backs of others is wrong and leads to nothing but emptiness.

Rachel Baxter

Hungary

*Who among the gods is like you, Lord? Who is like you—
majestic in holiness, awesome in glory, working wonders?*
Exodus 15:11

Lord it's time to love on the central Europe landlocked
country of Hungary. Speak your Word in the Magyar
(Hungarian) language unique to nearby neighbors.

Pun intended Lord, may Hungarians eat up the truth
of the gospel even amidst postmodern culture distractions.
Recommit the church to evangelism, holiness, and spiritual
maturity. Give government grace to ease restrictions on
witnessing. Praise God the Hungarian Bible Society was
revitalized in 1989, in time for the 400th anniversary
of the original Hungarian new testament version.

May Bible distributing ministries abound while Christian
literature is in demand with new Christian publishing
companies. Carry Christian media in more broadcast
hours across the country and back again. Dave Davidson

Hungry & Thirsty

I am the bread of life. He who comes to me will never go hungry, and he who believes in me will never be thirsty.
John 6:35

We pray for the millions of men, women and children who suffer from hunger. Lord, Your sustaining Spirit nourish bodies and souls of those longing, searching for food to eat and those who go to bed every night with an empty stomach. Bless ministry and relief agencies that help to feed those suffering from starvation and malnutrition. Lord, improve third world countries in areas of sanitation, irrigation and farming methods.

Help those who hunger

physically that they would also hunger for Your righteousness. As the true Bread of Life, Lord provide Your manna from heaven today for Your hungry people. Dan Davidson

Lord, thank you for Your word in Isaiah 55:1,

"Come, all you who are thirsty,
come to the waters;"

Thank You Jesus

for revealing in Your word, "If anyone is thirsty, let him come to me and drink." (John 7:37) and for being the finisher who said, "It is done. I am the Alpha and the Omega, the Beginning and the End. To him who is thirsty I will give to drink without cost from the spring of the water of life." Revelation 21:6

Lord, let us hear you say someday at the throne of heaven, "For I was hungry and you gave me something to eat, I was thirsty and you gave me something to drink, I was a stranger and you invited me in... Matthew 25:35

Lord, give those who are thirsty throughout the world a pure drink to sustain their life so that they may know you. Answer the prayers of those needing clean water. Have your servants drill wells, O Lord, to spring forth life in desolate barren areas.

We lift up water scarcity causing conflict in the Amu arya/Oxus of Central Asia, the Tigris-Euphrates (Turkey, Syria, Iraq, Iran) the Jordan (Israel, Syria, Jordan) the Nile (Egypt, Sudan, Ethiopia) the nations to the north and south of the Sahara Desert the Amur (Russia, China).

Lord, meet the needs of thirsty.

Dave Davidson

A population growth of about 80 million annually
is straining food, water and fuel resources globally.
Lord we know you're in control!

Iceland

*So we fasted and petitioned our God about this,
and he answered our prayer.*
Ezra 8:23

Our petition is Father God that more Icelanders
would hear the gospel, respond in repentant faith, and
become coworkers in God's harvest in their own country.

Lord our hearts break that Gunnar Ingi Gunnarsson
convincingly calls Iceland "Europe's Most Godless
Country." We pray for him and the few pastors like him in
the handful of healthy churches there. Jehovah Rapha heal
Iceland as they top the list for antidepressant
consumption per capita.

Its' baffling how 85% of Icelanders are supposedly
Christians. It's also the world's sixth-most atheistic nation.
Lord address the cultural worldwiews that cause Iceland
to lead the world in out-of-wedlock births with 29.5%.
Lord reveal Your presence in this overlooked
Scandinavian mission field "hidden in plain sight."
Dave Davidson

Identity in Christ

Therefore, if anyone is in Christ, the new creation has come:
The old has gone, the new is here!.
2 Corinthians 5:17

No weapon formed against me shall prosper,
and every tongue that rises against me in judgement,
I condemn, (Isaiah 54:17).

I am established in righteousness, and oppression is far from me,

(Isaiah 54:14).

The weapons of my warfare are not carnal but mighty
through God to the pulling down of strongholds,

(2 Corinthians 10:4).

I take the shield of faith,

and I quench every fiery dart of the enemy,

(Ephesians 6:16).

I take the sword of the Spirit, which is the Word of
God, and use it against the enemy, (Ephesians 6:17).
I am redeemed from the curse of the law. I am
redeemed from poverty. I am redeemed from
sickness. I am redeemed from spiritual death,

(Galatians 3:13).

I overcome all because greater is He that is in me
than he that is in the world, (2 John 4:4).

I stand in the evil day having my loins girded
about with truth, and I have the breastplate of
righteousness. My feet are shod with the gospel of
peace. I take the shield of faith. I am covered with the
helmet of salvation, and I use the sword of the Spirit,
which is the Word of God, (Ephesians 6:14–17).

I am delivered from the power of darkness and translated into the kingdom of God's dear Son, (Colossians 1:13).
I tread upon serpents and scorpions and over all the power of the enemy, and nothing shall hurt me, (Luke 10:19).

I do not have the spirit of fear

but power, love, and a sound mind, (2 Timothy 1:7).
I am blessed with all spiritual blessings in heavenly places in Christ Jesus, (Ephesians 1:3).
I am healed by the stripes of Jesus, (Isaiah 53:5).
My hand is upon the neck of my enemies, (Genesis 49:8).
You anoint my head with oil; my cup runs over.
Goodness and mercy shall follow me all the days of my life, (Psalm 23:5-6).

I am anointed to preach,

to teach, to heal, and to cast out devils.
I receive abundance of grace and the gift of righteousness, and I reign in life through Christ Jesus, (Romans 5:17).
I have life and that more abundantly, (John 10:10).

I walk in the light as He is in the light, and the blood of Jesus cleanses me from all sin, (1 John 1:7). I am the righteousness of God in Christ, (2 Corinthians 5:21).

I am the head and not the tail, (Deuteronomy 28:13). I shall decree a thing, and it shall be established in my life, (Job 22:28). I have favor with God and with man, (Luke 2:52). Wealth and riches are in my house, and my righteousness endures forever, (Psalm 112:3).

I will be satisfied with long life,

and God will show me His salvation, (Psalm 91:16). I dwell in the secret place of the Most High, and I abide under the shadow of the Almighty, (Psalm 91:1).

No evil will befall me,

and no plague shall come near my dwelling, (Psalm 91:10).

My children are taught of the Lord, and great is their peace, (Isaiah 54:13). I am strengthened with might by His Spirit in the inner man, (Ephesians 3:16).

I am rooted and grounded in love,

(Ephesians 3:17).

I bless my natural enemies, and I overcome evil with good, (Matthew 5:44). from Prayers That Rout Demons by John Eckhardt

Idols

"Dear children, keep yourselves from idols.
1 John 5:21

Unfortunately, Lord many speak of prayer today without any mention of a person to whom it is offered as if it were the very activity of prayer that is important. Prayer is of no use when offered to any other person but to You the true and the living God. Throughout Your word there are examples of men praying to idols of gold and silver and wood and stone. Men pray to manmade statues, to fallen angels, to deceiving spirits, to false gods and to meaningless idols. We know these prayers are unacceptable to You God. Thanks to the Lord Jesus Christ who took upon Himself our sins and died on the cross. May we not bow to, succumb to, or be tricked by idols. Rather may our devotion be to the One who tore the temple curtain from top to bottom, thereby making access to God through the blood of atonement. May our prayers only be to the Savior, the Lord Jesus Christ.

Dave Davidson

If 7:14

If my people, who are called by my name, will humble themselves and pray and seek my face and turn from their wicked ways, then will I hear from heaven and will forgive their sin and will heal their land.
2 Chronicles 7:14

Lord continue to mobilize "If 7:14" as an agent of an urgent and compelling call to revival based upon 2 Chronicles 7:14.

Give us a greater glimpse of Your heart God and a template for revival as we seek it answering the urgent "if" call.

Ignite of a global rhythm of prayer with those committing to pray for revival twice a day...

Once at 7:14 AM and once at 7:14 PM.

Expand this worldwide prayer movement.

adapted from Bob Vander Plaats if714.org

India

The Lord is not slow in keeping his promise, as some understand slowness. He is patient with you, not wanting anyone to perish, but everyone to come to repentance.
2 Peter 3:9

We praise You God for the growing number of Christians in India with over 300,000 churches. Thanks for the continued freedom for Indian Christians to proclaim the gospel despite efforts to limit the Holy Spirit through intimidation and persecution. May the many Indian Christian leaders, apologists, theologians, preachers, writers and mission leaders impact India's numerous and large people groups with no Christians, churches or workers.

May the church rise to complete this task.

May Christians be united and be courageous in the face of widespread and localized persecution with the increase of attacks. We pray for unity in India churches to mature and develop a godly testimony. May there be a greater cooperation and accountability between local churches and sending agencies. Lord, train and equip Christian workers for the health and growth of the Church and transform complacent hearts of nominalism, syncretism and Hinduism.

Thank You for the pastors, seminaries,
Bible schools, training centers, and cell groups.

Lord God, reach the North India Ganges plains, the
great cities, the highly populated slums, the Brahmin
people group, other forward castes, Dalit groups,
tribal peoples and the Sindhi. Minister to the affluent
250 million of the middle classes, the 10 million
students, the young people including 100 million
school drop-outs, the severely malnourished, children
in crisis, the 70 million child laborers, the 1.5 million
leprosy sufferers, the 10 million blind, the 10 million
with AIDS and those suffering we can't account for.

Lord we can't miss praying for

the minority religious communities of 140 million
Muslims, the 24 million Sikhs, the Buddhist Tibetans,
the Jains, the Parsees and the 22 million Indians
in other lands. Continue Your significant work
in mighty and miraculous ways!

Dave Davidson

Take 8 minutes to Pray Along for India. Download 10/40 Window Prayer Bucket List titles about India at PrayAlong.com and share.

Andrew Murray once said, "The man who mobilizes the Christian church to pray will make the greatest contribution to world evangelization in history."

Get in on the action with a click by sharing FREE Pray Along ebook links with world mission prayer theme social media memes.

Indonesia

Devote yourselves to prayer, being watchful and thankful.
Colossians 4:2

Thank the Lord for those workers who tirelessly serve among unreached groups of people, who day after day seek to engage new families and new communities with the good news of Jesus Christ.

One worker expressed his burden and his commitment...
"I'm thankful for God for He is always with my ministry. With joy and hope in Christ, the team and I share with anyone who hasn't received salvation yet. True salvation isn't just a dream. It is sad that many people do their religious rituals but never experience the guarantee of salvation. I'm thankful for the fact that I can go through my life, day by day, with the help of the Lord."

We pray for those who have committed their lives to reaching Indonesia's unreached with good news of eternal salvation in Jesus Christ. We pray for courage, boldness, clarity and love as they speak the truth of the gospel. We pray for the Holy Spirit to produce fruit for their labor.

Praying For Indonesia Facebook

Integrity

… I will not deny my integrity.
Job 27:5

Loving Father thank You for Christ Jesus our Lord
Who was the perfect example of a man with a godly
character and integrity of spirit. Lord I long to be
more like Jesus in all my actions and attitudes and
pray that You would guard my heart; strengthen my
character; teach me Your ways; uphold me with Your
righteous right hand and develop in me the grace and
integrity that only comes from being in Christ.

Help me to be true to Your word and righteous in all
my doings and enable me to conquer the temptations,
tests and trial that will inevitably come my way, in a
manner that is pleasing to You. Help me to be diligent
in my work; faithful in my witness; helpful to those
with whom I come in contact and be ready to wait
on You for Your right timing and for

Your best direction.

Give me I pray more of Your grace so that I may
speak the truth in love. Enable me to grow in sincerity
and wisdom and in the light of Your perfect love,
search out any dark area in my heart that needs to be
cut away or pruned back, so that I may be fruitful in
Your service, grow in grace and be increasingly
conformed into the image of the Lord Jesus Christ –
in Whose name I pray, Amen. Knowing-Jesus.com

International Students & Influential People

Whatever you have learned or received or heard from me, or seen in me—put it into practice.
Philippians 4:9

Father as international students encounter different cultures, may they also encounter caring Christians who reflect the love of your Son, Jesus. Help us to be gracious and bold in our witness that they might understand your gospel and come to a saving faith.

May they be a godly influence

in their leadership role to bring many others to Christ. May those who return to their countries as new Christians be equipped to meet possible hardship and persecution. Prepare them to be a witness that glorifies You, Lord.

Mary Ann Smith

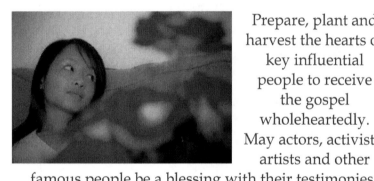

Prepare, plant and harvest the hearts of key influential people to receive the gospel wholeheartedly. May actors, activists, artists and other famous people be a blessing with their testimonies. Nurture and train them in Your word. Dave Davidson

_____
_____
_____
_____
_____
_____

Internet

The path of the righteous is like the first gleam of dawn, shining ever brighter till the full light of day. **Proverbs 4:18**

Lord, we claim the Internet for You. May key domain names and search engines lead people to Your truth. Make us grasp a vision for the potential of cutting-edge outreach. We ask for more effective evangelistic sites. Use email communication to bless and encourage mission workers and to witness to the lost.

We ask for more specialist web ministries to Muslims. Give vision to groups and individuals to use the Internet for Your glory. Increase the ministry sites in Chinese, Japanese and Arabic languages. We pray for Muslims in the Middle East to consider the claims of Christ in a loving and non-threatening way.

Protect Christians from online pornography. Stir our hearts to support evangelistic web ministries with online giving. May there be an insightful and compassionate witness by Christians in chat rooms. May those being discipled tap into the godly resources in cyberspace. We pray for new evangelistic strategies to take advantage of mobile 'wireless' Internet access and other advancing technologies to come.

Dave Davidson

Iran

Their outcry echoes along the border of Moab; their wailing reaches as far as Eglaim, their lamentation as far as Beer Elim.
Isaiah 15:8

Lord we echo the 40 prayer focus points from PrayforIran.org
Prayer for the Church, Open Hearts, The Word of God, The Internet, The Nuclear Crisis, Children, Iran's Students, Workers for Iran, Iran's Economy, Iran and Pentecost, Drug Addiction, Christian literature, Depression, That they may be one, Iranian Schools, Family Life, Iran and Soccer, Iranians in Diaspora, Church in Diaspora, Tehran, Law Enforcement, Ayatollah Khamanei, Disasters, Discipleship, The Iranian Military, The Media, Miracles and Healings, Women, The Vulnerable in Iran, Leaders, Cities, Satellite TV, Government, Repentance Mullahs in Iran, Villages, Ethnic Groups of Iran, Love Iran, and Revival. PrayforIran.org

Iraq

*Deliver me, O my God, from the hand of the wicked,
from the grasp of evil and cruel men.*
Psalm 71:4

Lord, you are God and there is no other.
Your Name is unfailing. Righteousness and justice are
the foundation of Your throne: love and faithfulness
go before You. There is none like You, a great
Savior and One who delivers the helpless.

We thank You that Your ears are open to the cry of the
righteous. We come before Your throne of grace with
confidence through the authority of Your sacrifice.

Together, we ask that You would protect and preserve
the leaders in Baghdad whose lives are under threat.

Lord, release escapes from death, we ask for Your angels
to intercept and intervene on behalf of the men and
women who are in positions of influence. Protect these
people who will guide Baghdad and the nation forward in
constructive and life-giving paths in the days ahead.

Father, we bind the one who comes to "kill, steal, and destroy" in Jesus name. We ask that You would deliver these leaders from loss and destruction; that You would preserve them and prepare them to be the ones to rebuild this city and nation. We also lift up the Prime Minister in this time of transition, and we ask that You would protect him and give him grace, wisdom, and vision to lead his nation forward. Let Your will be done, and let your kingdom come, we ask this in Jesus name. Amen!

pray4eurasia.org/iraq

We pray for all Iraqis to hear the gospel at least one time before their time on earth is over! Many believe, in Iraq, and all over the world that there is more then one way to heaven. It's simply not true.

_____
_____
_____
_____

Ireland

For the law was given through Moses;
grace and truth came through Jesus Christ.
John 1:17

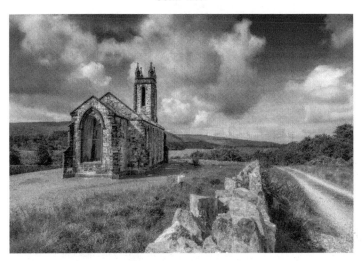

Christ be with me. Christ before me.
Christ behind me. Christ in me. Christ beneath me.
Christ above me. Christ on my right. Christ on my left.
Christ where I lie. Christ where I sit. Christ where I arise.
Christ in the heart of every man who thinks of me.
Christ in the mouth of every man who speaks of me.
Christ in every eye that sees me.
Christ in every ear that hears me.
Salvation is of the Lord.
From Saint Patrick's Breastplate

Israel

Pray for the peace of Jerusalem.
Psalm 122:6

Father God, We come to you in Jesus' Name to pray
for Israel. In Psalm 122:6, Your Word says we should
pray for the peace of Jerusalem, so we know it's Your
will to bless Israel and all the people who live there.
We ask You, Father, to keep them safe in this time of
unrest. And, we thank You, Lord, that no weapon
that is formed against Israel shall prosper (Isaiah 54:17),
for You are protecting them according to Your Word.

In addition, we pray for the people of Israel and the
country itself to be healed and prosperous, because in
Psalm 23:6 we are told that goodness and mercy
follow those who have called you their Shepherd. Let
this supernatural protection and deliverance cause
many people who hear of it to give glory to You, Sir

(Jeremiah 33:9). Kcm.org

Dear Heavenly Father,
You are the Rock and Redeemer of Israel.
We pray for the peace of Jerusalem. We are sad to see
the violence and suffering as men, women, and
children are injured and killed on both sides of the
conflict. We don't understand why it has to be this
way, nor do we truly know if war is right or wrong.
But we pray for justice, your sovereignty and
righteousness, Lord. And at the same time, we pray
for mercy. For everyone involved we pray, for
governments and peoples, militants and terrorists, we
ask for your kingdom to come and rule over the land.

Shield the nation of Israel, Lord. Protect the soldiers
and civilians from bloodshed. May your truth and
light shine in the darkness. Where there is only
hatred, may your love prevail. Help me as a Christian
to support those who you support, Lord, and to bless
those who you bless, my God. Bring your salvation to
Israel, dear God. Draw every heart to you. And bring
your salvation to the whole earth. Amen.
Mary Fairchild

Italy

*Ask the former generation and find
out what their ancestors learned.*
Job 8:8

Lord remind us Italy for missions since only 1%
of the Italian population is evangelical Christian.
Help mission agencies reprioritize since Italy
is less reached than China and other
nations of focus missions' efforts.

Lord reveal Your Spirit and reach out in a revolutionary revelation to the 80% of Italians are cultural Catholics in name, yet only a very small percentage of them attend church more than 3 times a year including weddings, funerals, and holidays. Guide mature believers to be effective disciple makers just as gondola drivers steer canals for tourists. Unfortunately, a large portion of the population has never heard the name of Jesus. May that hell-bent reality not be! Unravel truths in Your word.

Redirect generations with supernatural discernment to turn from empty secularism, atheism, and agnosticism. It's no wonder there's disillusionment with the cultural Catholicism that offers them no relationship with Jesus.

The people of Italy desperately need the great Gospel of grace, so enable the church in Italy to overcome obstacles more miraculous than miracle lovers ever dreamed. Lord redefine and reestablish the small Evangelical community in Italy that has faced much persecution being viewed as a misunderstood cult.

Dave Davidson

Jamaica

When someone tells you to consult mediums and spiritists, who whisper and mutter, should not a people inquire of their God? Why consult the dead on behalf of the living?
Isaiah 8:19

Our Father in heaven, hear my voice as I call unto You, O God Most High. Unto You, I present the people of Jamaica. Lord, I place their future in Your hand, I ask that You will give them divine direction; and an ever renewed sense of Your purpose. Help them to never be resistant to change, instead. to always be open to new things that You want to do in their lives

I take authority in the name of Jesus Christ against every yoke of bondage upon this nation the economic crisis, mismanagement, disunity, robbery, murder, drug-trafficking, corruption, idolatry, violent crime, limitation and any unspoken challenges be broken in the mighty name of Jesus Christ
I release the various communities that are known trouble spots from the circle of limitation in progress, their career that have been dormant will begin to walk, their business will begin to flourish, you will begin to live out your destiny in the name of Jesus Christ.

I break sin power over this nation, and I reverse
every curse. I cancel all plans of assign agent of the
devil in the mighty name of Jesus.

I release families from the cages of destruction, and yoke
of generational curse be dismantle, satanic power that are
influencing people's mind to do evil things be confounded
in the mighty name of Jesus, I reverse wrong thinking in
the name of Jesus. Thank You Lord for healing and
restoring this nation from the many challenges.

Lord, I ask that You will give them the desire to draw close
to You today, grateful that You will draw close to them as
You promised in Your Word. Help them to become
separated from the world without becoming isolated from
it. Lord help them to set aside time each day to meet with
You alone as You teach them to pray

I pray that You will have mercy upon the people of
Jamaica. O God according to the multitude of Your tender
mercies, blot out all their transgression, create in them a
clean heart, and renew a steadfast spirit within.

Do not cast them away from Your presence,
but lead them in the way everlasting O Lord, I pray for a
financial breakthrough in the lives of the many people
who are experiencing hardship, may You abundantly bless
their provision, so that the poor among them will be satisfy
with food, and jobs, enabling them to pay their bills.
Lord, let there be no more lack.

The scripture declare: Behold, the eyes of servant look unto
the hand of their master and as the eyes of a maiden unto
the hand of her mistress; so our eyes wait upon the Lord
our God, until that He have mercy upon us. Dear Lord, let
these word manifest now; in the lives of the people in the
name of Jesus. Thanks be to God, who gives us victory
through our Lord Jesus Christ...Amen. Sonia Cranston

Japan

*"I have posted watchmen on your walls,
O Jerusalem; they will never be silent day or night.
You who call on the Lord, give yourselves no rest,
and give him no rest till he establishes Jerusalem
and makes her the praise of the earth."*
Isaiah 62:6-7

Japan is indeed a nation in search of its soul.
Lord we pray for signs, wonders and miracles to
awaken the Japanese people and spiritually jolt them
from their stiff intelligent approach and logic-oriented
perspective. We need to present the Gospel to them in
such a way that it will open their minds, but also they
are in dire need of seeing a demonstration of the
power of God. Thank You Lord the Japanese are
indeed responding to the gospel one by one.
Enable church members to live out the Christ's
identity reaching lost souls. Provide proper finance
for churches in Japan to pay bills and expand
all church plant vision and mission action.

Grow the church with a mix of honoring cultural tradition while communicating the cross in relevant methods. May the men of Japan step up, humble themselves, and melt in repentance to thus live and lead by example. May men get saved, get anointed, and get on Ephesians 6 armor with discipline of a samurai warrior. As leaders in Japan see themselves as "a super power without a moral compass," shatter the well-meaning moral and religious ethic inspired Shintoism and Confucianism past.

Japan needs miracles. There is no social reason for a Japanese to come to the Lord. (In their mind there is no economic, educational, or social benefit in changing from nominal Buddhism to Christianity. But when they see the power of God and the supernatural revelation of the reality of Jesus Christ comes to them, they become some of the most disciplined and motivated believers on Earth.) We pray that God would grant more supernatural signs and wonders to the church here, so that the eyes of their family, friends, and co-workers would be now wide-eyed.

Show the Japanese preoccupied with materialism and those glaring at the god of money a biblical life solution. Lord address in Your sovereign way: Growth of Buddhist offshoots, the rise of new cults, uniqueness of Jesus, pressure to conform, aging pastors, spiritual vacuum, and authentic friendships. Answer the plea of a young man on Asian video saying, "I don't know what is Truth, so please tell me!" Dave Davidson

Jesus Film

For God, who said, "Let light shine out of darkness," made his light shine in our hearts to give us the light of the knowledge of the glory of God in the face of Christ.
2 Corinthians 4:6

Lord, we thank you for this powerful tool of evangelism that has been translated and reproduced all over the world! We pray for the millions of people who have seen this film. Continue to use this tool to introduce the salvation of Your Son, Jesus to many nations around the world. Lord, we pray for support teams and volunteers working together to coordinate this complex, enormous and effective ministry. We pray for the multiplication of evangelistic films. Thank You for Christian film success throughout the world in many languages. Thank You for JesusFilm.org, various visual bible

websites and other media ministries.

Dave Davidson

Lord bless the over 200 million people have indicated a decision to place their faith in Jesus Christ from the 4 billion people who have seen the Jesus Film.

Jonah's Salvation

Jonah 2:2-9

"In my distress I called to the Lord, and he answered me. From deep in the realm of the dead I called for help, and you listened to my cry.

You hurled me into the depths, into the very heart of the seas, and the currents swirled about me; all your waves and breakers swept over me.

I said, 'I have been banished from your sight; yet I will look again toward your holy temple.'

The engulfing waters threatened me, the deep surrounded me; seaweed was wrapped around my head. To the roots of the mountains I sank down; the earth beneath barred me in forever.

But you, Lord my God, brought my life up from the pit.

"When my life was ebbing away, I remembered you, Lord, and my prayer rose to you, to your holy temple.

"Those who cling
to worthless idols
turn away from God's love for them.
But I, with shouts of grateful praise,
will sacrifice to you.
What I have vowed I will make good.
I will say, 'Salvation comes from the Lord.'"

Jordan

They left the mountains of Abarim and camped on the plains of Moab by the Jordan across from Jericho.
Numbers 33:48

Praise God for the protection Christian Camp Gilead has received from any fanatic attacks. Also praise God for the many converts from Islam that security continues.

Lord Finish and sustain the building and ministry of Jordan Evangelical Theological Seminary, now that the government has approved it. Father God move in the peace process between Israel & Jordan to continue and for religious freedom to peak in the reign of King Abdallah.

adapted from arabicbible.com

Kazakhstan

God sets the lonely in families, he leads out the prisoners with singing; but the rebellious live in a sun-scorched land.
Psalm 68:6

Lord we pray for healing and courage for those in Kazakhstan and Central Asia who are beaten and imprisoned for leaving Islam and turning to Christ.

Expedite salvation of government authorities who seek to suppress or eradicate Christianity.

May Christian leaders under surveillance experience the peace and rest only found in and through the love of Jesus.
adapted from opendoorua.org

Kenya

For every battle of the warrior is with confused noise,
and garments rolled in blood; but this shall
be with burning and fuel of fire.
Isaiah 9:5

If you are going to join the spiritual battle for the soul of Kenya at this
time, your prayers have to go beyond the kindergarten, Sunday school
level of prayer.   This is advanced warfare ... reserved for battle-
hardened Christian warriors, the type moving mountains for
JESUS in the spiritual trenches day and night...

1. I cover myself and my family with the blood of Jesus.

2. O LORD ignite our mouths with fire to destroy all contrary powers rising up against Kenya in Jesus name.

3. Let all forces of darkness hindering the move of God in this nation be paralyzed in the name of Jesus.

4. Every power that does not want Kenya to enjoy peace and prosperity, we bury you today in the name of Jesus.

5. Let the global champions and promoters of Sodom be disgraced in the name of Jesus.

6. O God of Abraham, Isaac and Jacob release your sword of judgment on the sons of Sodom, their agents and sponsors in the name of Jesus.

7. Let the joy of the enemy concerning Kenya be turned into sorrow in the name of Jesus.

8. Let the heavenlies reject every satanic instruction against this nation of Kenya in Jesus name.

9. We speak destruction unto every evil prophecy against Kenya and her people in the name of Jesus Christ.

10. O LORD release confusion into the camp of all the enemies of our nation in Jesus name.

11. We de-program every evil in the heavenlies against the destiny of Kenya and her people in Jesus name.

12. Every ancient altar activated against the destiny of this nation, become desolate by fire in mighty name of Jesus.

13. Every enemy of Kenya, fall down and die in the name of Jesus.

14. Every incantation, occult and witchcraft activity against this nation, be consumed by the fire of God's judgment in Jesus name.

15. Blood of Jesus, wipe out all evil ordinances against our country Kenya in the name of Jesus.

16. Let the fire and the thunder of God clear the heavenlies over Kenya in the name of Jesus.

17. O heavens, disgrace all the enemies of Kenya by fire in the name of Jesus.

18. We paralyze all satanic advice contrary to the divine destiny of Kenya in the name of Jesus.

19. Every arrow of fired against Kenya, gather yourself together, go back to your senders in the name of Jesus: Poverty, untimely death, international occultists, economic stagnation, spiritual failure, and leadership failure.

20. Let the spiritual strongman in charge of this nation be bound and be disgraced in the mighty name of Jesus.

21. All the multitude of nations that fight against Kenya, O LORD of hosts, visit them with thunder, and with earthquake, and great noise, with storm and tempest, and the flame of devouring fire in the name of Jesus Christ.

22. Every international gang-up and evil unity against Kenya, be scattered unto desolation in the name of Jesus.

23. O God arise and visit Kenya with your fire of deliverance in Jesus name.

24. We release confusion of tongues into the nations gathered against Kenya in Jesus name.

25. O LORD, the God of Abraham, Isaac and Israel, in this time of crisis let it be known that You are the One who rules affairs of men.

26. O LORD, forgive our sins and let the precious blood of Jesus avail for our nation in Jesus name.

27. O LORD, turn the heart of our people back
to You in this time and season in Jesus name.

28. Father forgive the transgressions of your people and
deal with us according to your great mercy and
compassion in Jesus name.

29. Ancient altars of darkness energized against Kenya, both within and without, catch fire and burn to ashes in Jesus name.

30. Let the shield of the Rock of Ages protect Kenya from terrorists and their sponsors in Jesus name.

31. Let the weapons and missiles of the enemy backfire against them in the name of Jesus.

32. O LORD arise to the defense of Kenya in the name of Jesus.

33. Every nation strengthening the enemies of Kenya, receive the wrath of God in Jesus name.

34. Every evil agreement against the destiny of Kenya be cancelled, be nullified by the blood of Jesus.

35. Every evil verdict against Kenya and her people, be reversed by the power of the blood of Jesus.

36. All the satanically-inspired voices raised against Kenya in the global media be silenced by the thunder fire of God in Jesus name.

37. Every wicked campaign and propaganda against Kenya in the media, receive failure and defeat in the name of Jesus.

38. Every power engineering evil propaganda against Kenya be silenced by fire in the name of Jesus.

39. O LORD re-assign all the enemies of Kenya to useless and fruitless purposes in the wilderness in Jesus name.

40. Let every evil unity, evil agreement and evil gathering against Kenya be scattered unto desolation in Jesus name.

41. Every worldwide movement to discredit Kenya be scattered unto desolation in Jesus name.

42. By the spirit of prophecy, every power assigned to divert the destiny of Kenya shall be disgraced by the Mighty One of Jacob in Jesus name.

43. All those manipulating the spirit realm against Kenya, fall down and die in the name of Jesus.

44. Every ancient power invoked to fight against Kenya, be consumed by the fire of the God of Elijah in Jesus name.

45. Let all the attackers of Kenya become like small dust, and the multitude of the terrible ones be as chaff that passes away in Jesus name.

46. Every strongman behind the economic onslaught against Kenya, be arrested by the warrior angels of the Almighty in Jesus name.

47. Every weapon of the wicked targeted against Kenya, begin to malfunction and backfire now in the name of Jesus.

48. What the enemy meant for evil, O LORD turn it to good for Kenya in Jesus name.

49. O LORD raise up a million true intercessors for the nation of Kenya in Jesus name.

50. Every anti-Kenya decision on the world stage, be cancelled, be reversed in the name of Jesus.

51. Thou spirit of the wasters working in the lives of our youths, we break your backbone today in the name of Jesus Christ.

52. Every demon mobilized in the global campaign against Kenya, be bound with hot chains and fetters of God in Jesus name.

53. Every mouth raining curses on Kenya, receive your curses back by fire; for no one can curse whom the LORD has blessed.

54. Economic war machine set in motion against Kenya, catch fire and burn to ashes in Jesus name.

55. O LORD anoint the leaders of Kenya with divine wisdom, strength and courage in Jesus name.

56. Every demonic brain trust assembled against our nation, be roasted by fire in Jesus name.

57. Divine protection of the Living God, come upon Kenya and all those who love and support her in Jesus name.

58. Powers manipulating the dust of Kenya against her people, fall down and die in the name of Jesus.

59. Every evil gathering against Kenya, O LORD stretch out your hand and render them desolate in the name of Jesus.

60. Let satanic altars within the nation become desolate in Jesus name.

61. O LORD fill our nation with brightness of your glory.

62. O LORD restore health unto this nation and heal Kenya of her wounds in Jesus name.

63. Every triangle of darkness operating against Kenya, we curse you to die in the name of Jesus.

64. Every power assigned to waste lives and drink blood in this nation, we command you to eat your own flesh and drink your own blood in the name of Jesus.

65. O LORD begin to cleanse and purge your Church in this nation in the name of Jesus.

66. Those that seek the destruction of Kenya shall go down into the lowest parts of the earth in the name of Jesus.

67. Let the glory of this nation that has departed be restored.

68. O Lord, let this be a golden opportunity for all the un-evangelized areas of this nation to be reached by the Gospel of our Lord Jesus Christ.

69. We dismantle the stronghold of poverty in this nation.

70. Let righteousness begin to reign in every part of this nation in Jesus' name. firesprings.com/70bulletskenya.htm

_____
_____
_____
_____
_____
_____
_____
_____
_____
_____
_____
_____
_____

Kingdom Come

"Repent, for the kingdom of heaven has come near."
Matthew 3:2

YAHWEH, I hear you when you say, you are the
One True God. I accept the great commandment to
Love you with all my heart, soul and strength. Abba,
we will work together to see your Kingdom come as
we proclaim your word and love others with food,

water, shelter and friendship.

Abba, you have given us everything we need to work
with you in your Kingdom. I receive your affirmation
in the gift of salvation and baptism. Thank you
for making me a new creation in Christ:
the old has gone and the new has come.

Fritz Trost

Kiribati

Pray this way for kings and all who are in authority so that we can live peaceful and quiet lives marked by godliness and dignity.
1 Timothy 2:2

On behalf of the people of Kiribati, we humbly ask you to join us in praying for Kiribati. We are standing in faith believing God will save the lost and bless our nation, if we pray and seek His face!

Lord we pray for our officials, courts, police, military and all public servants. Lord we pray for the Churches in Kiribati to glorify Jesus Christ and declare that Jesus is Lord.

We pray for every man, woman, boy and girl to hear the Gospel and turn to the Lord. We ask for peace to come to our people and land. Now is the time to humble ourselves, pray, seek His face and turn from our wicked ways.

Adapted from United States National Prayer Council

Kosovo

*I wash my hands in innocence,
and go about your altar, Lord.*
Psalm 26:6

God ever and forever save Kosovo.
Prayers to the Father, the Son, and the Holy Spirit
ever rise from Kosovo, from her heavy hearts, from
her spiked rivers, from her blood-saturated soil,
where, of her faithful, many receive
the crown of martyrdom.

God ever and forever protect His holy remnant in
Kosovo, standing watch over the relics of His holy
martyrs. Prayers to the Father, the Son, and the Holy
Spirit ever and forever rise from Kosovo, from her
altars and cells, her huts and coops, her wells and
sheds, where her faithful stand for charity and
fellowship, as hoards of enemies slander them.

God ever and forever bless His heavenly kingdom in
Kosovo. Prayers to the Father, the Son, and the Holy
Spirit ever and forever rise from Kosovo, from her
hymns and saints, her monastics and hierarchs, her
children of Simeon, Sava, and all Nemanje, where all
the hosts of heaven and the Most Holy Mother
of God embrace her in righteous renewal.

Amen. Prayer from Kosovo The Saint Gregory Palamas Outreach

Kuwait

*My prayer is not for them alone. I pray also for those
who will believe in me through their message.*
John 17:20

Praise God that there are Kuwaiti believers and that
they have a history of meeting together in small
groups. We pray for more! We pray for the Lord of
the Harvest to bring in more of his sheep into the
sheepfold so that there will be one flock, hearing
the voice of the Good Shepherd (John 10:16).

As with any church, roots of bitterness have
separated some of the national believers in Kuwait.
We pray for conviction of sin, brokenness, and
reconciliation. We pray for a fresh understanding
of forgiveness since God has forgiven
us first of much more (Ephesians 4:32).

We pray for long-time workers in Kuwait who have seen a history of new, national believers coming together and then dispersing. We pray for renewed faith, Spirit-led strategies, and the time and determination to carry them out.

We pray that the message of the gospel will reach many Kuwaitis through various avenues such as social media and other forms of technology. We pray to the Lord to send workers to Kuwait who have a variety of skills that can be used to reach out to the Kuwaiti people.

One Kuwaiti man is an elderly national believer who has been a believer in Christ for some years. Two of his grown sons have also professed faith in Christ, but their decisions remain hidden from the public. We pray that God will help them be bold witnesses in His timing and plan. We pray for more families to come to faith! We pray for second, third, and fourth generation believers.

One Kuwaiti man is an elderly national believer, who has been a believer in Christ for some years. Two of his grown sons have also professed faith in Christ, but their decisions remain hidden from the public. We pray that God will help them be bold witnesses in His timing and plan.

Responses to Arabic Christian media have led many to faith in Christ. We pray for effective contact with on the ground believers who can disciple them. We pray that those who are new in their faith will grow and become established in local bodies.

adapted from pray-ap.info/kuwait

Kyrgyzstan

Do not hold against us the sins of past generations; may your mercy come quickly to meet us, for we are in desperate need.
Psalm 79:8

Lord do Your mustard seed faith thing in Kyrgyzstan, a nation of mountains and 6 million people, 75% Sunni Muslims. Heavenly Father address the depressed economic situation to improve so that families don't have to choose between living together and providing financially.

Inspire righteousness in mothers of sons who play a very large role in Kyrgyz family structure, controlling everything. Build loving marriages and intervene in relationships of daughters-in-law to not be treated like slaves. End the bride kidnapping mentality and practice common in rural areas as women face threat of being kidnapped and forced to marry a stranger. May it no longer be.

Lord have mercy, that Kyrgyz wives in desperate situation believe that suicide is their only way out. Yikes! If they don't become pregnant during the first two years of marriage, the husband is often forced by his mother to dismiss his wife and marry another woman. Lord recue, reach, and revive many children growing up with the feeling of being abandoned and unloved separated from their families, cared for by extended family or sent to orphanages. Touch special needs children with grace.

Strengthen and protect Kyrgyz church house groups teaching Christian discipleship principles for family life, where it's difficult for believers to profess their faith in Christ within traditionally close family structures due to being ostracized by their family or friends. Dave Davidson

Laborers

*How beautiful on the mountains are the feet
of those who bring good news…*
Isaiah 52:7

An image flashed across my TV screen;
Another broken heart comes in to view.
I saw the pain and I turned my back.
Why can't I do the things I want to?
I'm willing yet I'm so afraid. You give me strength…

I want to be Your hands.
I want to be your feet.

I'll go where you send me. I'll go where You send me,
and I try, yeah I try to touch the world like You touched my life
and I find my way to be your hands. I've abandoned every
selfish thought. I've surrendered everything I've got. You can
have everything I am and perfect everything I'm not. **I'm
willing, I'm not afraid…** This is the lifetime I turned my back on
You. From now on, I'll go so send me where You want me to.
I finally have a mission I promise I'll complete.
I don't need excuses when I am Your hands and feet.

Mark Stuart, Bob Herdman, Will McGinniss, Tyler Burkum & Charlie Peacock
from the song "Hands and Feet"

Laos

Loving God, as we reflect on the year past and the
new one ahead, we are reminded of your presence
and abundant blessings in our lives. Thank you God,
for peace and strength in times of stress, uncertainty,
and sadness. Thank you for rejoicing gladness and
laughter in the moments we share with those we love.

Gracious God, be with the beautiful land and Lao people, specifically the Lao Evangelical Church. Guide the children as they carry out Lao traditions bringing light into the future of this developing community. Build in them a tolerance and acceptance for differences. Remind them -through you - we are one. Bring wisdom, wholeness, and clarity to members of the Lao Evangelical Church as they plan, educational Bible workshops, youth camps, worship services, church leadership meetings. Be with them as they join in youth fellowship and fun, celebrate new beginnings in births and weddings and during times of illness and death.

Holy provider, we ask for clean water in the rural villages of Laos. Remind the Lao people they are not alone in their challenges and times of need. Through Christ, we accomplish far more in the community than alone. In all these things, we pray, Amen.

globalministries.org/prayer

Latin America

You came out to deliver your people, to save your anointed one.
You crushed the leader of the land of wickedness,
you stripped him from head to foot.
Habakkuk 3:13

We thank You for the growing number of evangelicals in Latin America. We pray for more breakthroughs, Lord, through the power of Your Spirit in the Roman Catholic Church in the Charismatic movement and the challenge to face the doctrines of false cults throughout this region. Lord, we thank You for the huge impact of media ministries that significantly reach and influence millions of people. We thank you for increased Bible translations and we pray for the mega-cities, for the university students and for

various governments.

We pray for CRU throughout the Latin world and for immigrant communities with a minority presence like the Chinese, Japanese and Muslims. We pray for major financial breakthroughs for ministry resources and the maturity in churches to train future pastors, workers and missionaries for Your work, despite socioeconomic boundaries. Dave Davidson

Latvia

*We have sinned, even as our ancestors did;
we have done wrong and acted wickedly.*
Psalm 106:6

Send harvest workers to embrace the younger
generation before following in the footsteps of their
atheistic ancestors. Living God heal cynical despair
and hopelessness of suicide. Spark renewal and
revival among lethargic churches filled with
nominal believers. adapted from prayercast.com/latvia

Leadership

For the Lamb at the center of the throne will be their shepherd;
'he will lead them to springs of living water. "And God will
wipe away every tear from their eyes.'".
Revelation 7:17

Lord, I pray for discernment in exposing any
schemes of the enemy against my leaders. Show our
congregation how to pray against all powers of this
dark world and the spiritual forces of darkness in
heavenly realms. And, Lord, protect us as we wage
warfare on behalf of our leaders (Eph. 6:11-12).
Lord, let my leaders have a discerning mind to
prioritize the precious minutes in the day. Let my
pastors discern what is most important and be
guarded against the tyranny of the urgent.
(2 Cor. 11:14, 1 Jn. 4:1).

Father, I thank You that no weapons formed against
my leaders will prosper. Every tongue raised against
them will be cast down. Rumors and gossip will be
turned aside. My leaders will dwell in the shadow of
the Most High God and will be delivered from terror,
darts of doubt, and diseases (Ps. 91:5-6). Set Your angels
about my leaders (Ps. 91:11) and no power of the
enemy shall harm them (Lk. 10:19).

I thank You, Father, that Your eyes are on the
spiritual fathers and mothers of our house and Your
ears are attentive to their prayers and Your face is
against those who plot evil against them (1 Pet. 3:12). For
I know that in all things You work for the good of my
leaders who loves You (Ro. 8:28). Who can accuse my
leaders who are daily interceded for by Christ Jesus?
(Ro. 8:33-34). Therefore, in all things my leaders
are more than conquerors (Ro. 8:37).

Father, allow my leaders to glory only in the cross (Gal. 6:14). Keep my pastor from pride and pity. Let the cross be their reason for ministry. Jesus keep my pastors holy in every way (1 Pet. 1:16). Protect my shepherd from seducing spirits especially when he/she is tired and hard-pressed. Give mission leaders comrades to help protect them and to share with in personal holiness As my pastor draws near to You, draw near to my pastors (Jas. 4:7,8).

I pray that the eyes of my leaders may be enlightened to know the hope to which we are called and know the riches of our glorious inheritance in the saints. Let them know the incomparable great power which is in us who believe (Eph. 1:18-19). Let my leaders see the full revelation of Jesus Christ (Gal. 1:12). Place in them a desire to know Christ and the power of His resurrection (Phil. 3:10).

Lord, I lift up the hands of my leaders and their family. Place them in your shelter, oh Most High to rest in your shadow, Almighty. I will say of the Lord, You are their refuge and fortress. You will preserve their family time. You will cover their home.

Your faithfulness will meet their financial needs in Christ Jesus (Phil. 4:19). You will command Your angels to guard them as they travel and win the lost. You have said, "I will be with [them] in trouble, I will deliver [them] and honor [them]. With a long life, I will satisfy [them] and show [them] my salvation" (Ps. 91:15-16). In Jesus' name

I cancel all assignments of the enemy against them.

In Jesus' name I speak to church hurts, abuse, and ungrateful forces to move. I speak to mountains of criticism and inordinate expectations to be cast into the sea. I speak to stress, excessive phone counseling, and fatigue to be cast into the sea, and I believe every need, vision, and dream of my leaders will be completed (Mk. 11:22-24, Phil. 4:19).

Adapted from Legacy Church

Lebanon

*Let me go over and see the good land beyond the Jordan
—that fine hill country and Lebanon.*
Deuteronomy 1:7

To God be the glory after a long, bloody history filled
with wars and turmoil at the very center of the entire
Muslim world. With over 1 million refugees, tens of
thousands homeless, most suffer emotional and
economic devastation. All the while Lebanon balances
between stability and risk of being drawn back into
violence near its northern border. We pray that this
open door in the Middle East would not be slammed
shut since Lebanon is the only Muslim-majority
country in the Middle East where evangelism is legal.
Dave Davidson

Lesotho

*A bruised reed he will not break, and a smoldering wick
he will not snuff out. In faithfulness he will bring forth justice;
he will not falter or be discouraged till he establishes justice on
earth. In his teaching the islands will put their hope.*
Isaiah 42:3,4

Lord let Lesotho be a land locked 'Lighthouse of
the Region'. Praise God prophetically, the LORD is
mightily at work in Lesotho and a spirit of prayer is
gaining momentum. Father, may churches in Lesotho
bear fruit, united in their efforts to further God's
Kingdom not peripheral agendas.

Banish animistic traditions in the church of Lesotho
bringing the blood of Jesus Christ forefront.
Transform testimonies in the lives of the youth with
unity under guidance of the Holy Spirit, while nation
and church leaders surrender their hearts
to heaven yielding to Christ. Dave Davidson

Libya

Shake off your dust; rise up, sit enthroned. Free yourself from the chains on your neck, oh captive daughter.
Isaiah 52:2

We pray for the placement of many more workers from the west and global south. We pray that the existing prayer network will continue to mobilize many individuals, churches, and agencies to pray for the nation. We pray for righteous leadership that will assist instead of hinder the gospel. We pray for Libyan people to rise up and stand before the Lord to repent for their people. The land is so stained with blood from the past centuries and some progress must happen in the area of repentance, forgiveness and healing. We pray for reconciliation following the recent war and for a generation to grow up that is no longer "in the dark" but enters new thinking. We pray for an explosion of the Spirit's power to cover the nation and lead many into the Kingdom.

anonymous from prayna.org

Liechtenstein, Luxemburg, & Monaco

They promise them freedom, while they themselves
are slaves of depravity—for "people are slaves to
whatever has mastered them."
2 Peter 2:19

Lord may the spiritual vision of Liechtenstein, the
tiny 62-mile nation of tucked between Switzerland
and Austria realize the futility of Islam and atheism.
Also, may the financially secure be illuminated to
their eternal depravity. Confront the disinterested
and irreligious with a hell escaping rescue
embracing the need for a personal savior.

Bordered by Belgium, France, and Germany,
over 500,00 people need You Lord in Luxembourg.
Let the power of the living Christ to triumph over
materialistic ritual as the word of God disseminates
available in Lëtzebuergesch. End the stigma of
suspicious attitudes toward evangelicals
and grant the gospel favor in this the last
remaining Grand duchy in the world.

May many see the emptiness of materialistic hedonism compared to the fullness of freedom in Christ in the magnificently scenic, royally renowned, and prestigious nation of Monaco. Manifest culturally appropriate witness from the expatriate Christian community. All the while revive nominal believers with vibrant expressions of Christian faith in the second smallest nation in the world bordered by France on three sides. Dave Davidson

Literature

Here I am—it is written about me in the scroll—
I have come to do your will, O God.
Hebrews 10:7

Lord, use literature and godly resources to help build your kingdom. Increase the production and distribution of top quality Christian teaching books and magazines to nations where resources are scarce or non-existent.

Raise up authors, translators, publishers and distributors in nations where there are few or none. Urge western Christians to serve with training, advice and financial support.

May books offered be culturally relevant and spiritually challenging. Bless the work of literature ministries seeking to 'feed your sheep'. Lord, use the printed word for spiritual breakthroughs!

Jan Mungeam, Director of Sovereign World Trust

Supply of Christian literature is hindered in the places of greatest need because of poverty, difficulty of distribution, cost of printing, using expensive materials from the West and rampant inflation. We pray for adequate funding... Patrick Johnstone

Lord may we feel naked and not ready
to leave the house without being locked
and loaded with a gospel tract.
Dave Davidson

Lithuania

*In those days and at that time, when I restore the fortunes
of Judah and Jerusalem, I will gather all nations and bring
them down to the valley of Jehoshaphat.*
Joel 3:1-2

Dear Lord, the mighty God, the one who keeps his
covenant and shows mercy to those who love him
and obediently fulfill his word. Oh almighty God the
Father, the Son and the Holy Spirit, on the behalf of
Lithuanian nation we humble ourselves before you in
repentance, fasting and prayer, and beg you to
forgive our nation for its active involvement in the
holocaust, bloodshed of innocent Israelites and all
injustice done to them. Oh Lord, you are great,
gracious and merciful, but you judge fairly, hate
sin that brings death, and curse to those who
disobey and rebel against your will.

You expelled your chosen nation from their land and spread them widely across pagan lands for their unbelief, rebellion and idolatry. However, you commanded the gentiles to do no harm to the children of Israel in Joel 3:1-2.

...There I will put them on trial for what they did to my inheritance, my people Israel, because they scattered my people among the nations and divided my land. We know that God will submit serious charges against Lithuanian nation and his trial will be fair since many Israelites have lived in our lands...

Lithuania scores the highest (or high) in the Europe ranks of suicide, alcoholism and car crashes; almost a third of our population has emigrated. Child abuse and murders are often; the respect to parents and teachers is decreasing... Therefore, we, the church of God, government and a society as a whole have to confess and repent for the massacre of Israelites during the holocaust. We must turn away from all forms of anti-Semitism, intolerance and disrespect towards Israelites and other nations.

However, it is impossible without the help of God, therefore, we humble ourselves and pray: Oh almighty God, hear our prayer and begging. Listen to us; look at us and all the troubles we experience in Lithuania. We pray for your favor and forgiveness not because we deserve it, but because you are merciful. Lord Jesus, hear us, forgive us and act so that everyone knows that you are almighty God, and that there is nothing that you cannot do. Amen.

Gyvenimas Ir Ramybė

Long Term Missions

...so that you can help me on my journey, wherever I go.
1 Corinthians 16:6

Lord God, we thank You for the dedicated Christians who have taken up the call to be a missionary committed for the long haul to an area, a ministry project or to a lost people. Bless their lives and ministries with a fruitful abundance of disciples who worship You, with their life. Lord, with such a calling and vision comes a different realm of spiritual warfare in their Christian walk. Guide, direct and protect these servants in the face of the schemes of the devil. Recruit, retain and renew teams of enthusiastic and supported long-term workers devoted to a significant world mission need. Deliver dedicated groups of people and churches to support their ministries now and in the future. Dave Davidson

Macau

*"Again, the kingdom of heaven is like a merchant
looking for fine pearls."*
Matthew 13:45

Father we lift up in prayer Macau, a Special
Administrative region (SAR) of China on the south
coast of China on the Pearl River estuary.
Show Yourself a Savior! Dave Davidson

Macedonia

Come over to Macedonia and help us.
Acts 16:9

One of the poorest regions of the former Yugoslavia north of Greece, is modern day Macedonia bound both religion and language influenced by Roman, Byzantine, Turkish, and Bulgarian culture. Unleash an unprecedented movement of the Holy Spirit in the Macedonian Orthodox church.

Annihilate racial and ethnic tensions in the vibrant growing Church. Oh God prod the success among indigenous Christian groups getting out word.

Dave Davidson

Madagascar

*'And these signs will accompany those who believe…
they will pick up snakes in their hands, and if they drink
any deadly thing, it will not hurt them'.*
Mark 16:17-18

Holy God, Thank you that Your loving care is over
all your Creation. We ask your blessing on the
peoples of Madagascar, overrun by plague and
sickness. Strengthen those who work to eradicate
plagues. Give compassion to those who care for
the sick, and healing to all who are affected.

May your own image shine through all Creation,
that all people may know fullness of life through you.
Amen. Adapted from Rev Canon Richard Bartlett

Malawi

"A new command I give you: Love one another.
As I have loved you, so you must love one another.
By this everyone will know that you are my disciples,
if you love one another."
John 13:34-35

We are all affected by HIV/AIDS; we are the body of Christ. We have lost close relatives; heal our bodies. We have lost close friends and neighbours; heal our hearts. We have lost church and work mates; heal our spirits.

We have lost our hope; heal our minds. We put our trust in you. You are Emmanuel, you are God With Us. You will never leave us or forsake us. You will be with us to the end of the ages.

Fulata L. Moyo, Malawi, & Musa W. Dube, Botswana

Malaysia

The Lord is compassionate and gracious,
slow to anger, abounding in love.
Psalm 103:8

O God of Life, you have placed us on this earth
to usher in Your Kingdom of love and compassion.
Forgive us when our social witness has failed
to build bridges of peace and understanding
among all peoples.

Let there be growing spaces of understanding,
tolerance and harmony among the different ethnic
and religious communities. Grant that Your church in
Malaysia will deepen its influence to work for peace,
to be prophetic in calling for justice and caring in
sustaining a sharing fellowship with all people.

So rule our hearts and prosper our endeavors of
good, to the honor of Your Holy name, Jesus Christ
our Lord, we pray. AMEN Council of Churches in Malaysia

Maldives, Malta, & Marshall Islands

*They must keep hold of the deep truths
of the faith with a clear conscience.*
1 Timothy 3:9

Lord there is none of us who cannot be some type
of philanthropist in prayer. Push us to dive in.
Dave Davidson

Mali

*After this I looked, and there before me was a great multitude
that no one could count, from every nation, tribe, people and
language, standing before the throne and before the Lamb.
They were wearing white robes and were holding
palm branches in their hands.*
Revelation 7:9

God of the Bible maximize ministries which help
people engage with God's word in Mali. Triple
trauma healing counseling, literacy, relief efforts and
youth work. God open ways for the use of minority
languages in the school system in Mali unfortunately
unrecognized by the government.

May Malians be receptive of Christ-centered
evangelism, disregarding Islamic faith. Lord, deliver
unprecedented wisdom handling extreme poverty
hindering development. We also pray for the
evangelization of the Bambara people, which would
also impact other tribes coming to Christ.

Allow African and Malian ministries working in Mali
to collaborate. Galvanize national churches. Establish
righteous leaders in government, business,
and the church in Mali.
Dave Davidson

Marriage

*He and all his family were devout and God-fearing; he gave
generously to those in need and prayed to God regularly.*
Acts 10:2

We pray for strength and unity in families.
We lift up marriage as the divine component that
keeps families together and ask for diligence to stand
against any forces that oppose marriage. We pray for
couples to give attention to their marriage and make
it a priority in their personal lives. We also lift up
single parents and ask for their support and
encouragement. We pray for understanding between
parents and children. Give parents wisdom for the
balance between freedom and boundaries, which will
instill confidence, security, well-being and love.

We ask for a strengthened commitment from families
to spend time learning biblical ways and
understanding God's plan. We ask for clarity in
purpose and a dedication to following God's will for
their lives. Joan Davidson

Lord may husbands grasp the privilege of marriage
in striving to love their wives like Christ
loves the church. Dave Davidson

Martyrdom

*from the blood of innocent Abel
unto the blood of Zacharias son of Barachias.*
Matthew 23:35

Lord God, Father of our blessed Savior,
I thank Thee that I have been deemed worthy
to receive the crown of martyrdom and that
I may die for Thee and Thy cause.

Polycarp

Lord help us wrap our minds around and understand
that an estimated 150 000 Christians are martyred
every year and more than 200 million Christians are
restricted from being Christ followers. Lord intervene
for the Jesus believers in more than 65 countries who
suffer interrogation, arrest and even death for their
faith in Jesus Christ with millions more facing
discrimination and alienation. Ease the incessant
beatings, physical torture, confinement, isolation,
rape, severe punishment, imprisonment, slavery,
discrimination in education and employment,
and death around the world.

Dave Davidson

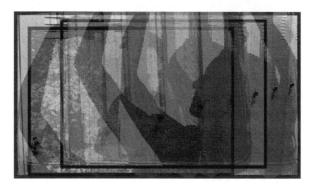

Martyrs

*And they sang a new song: "You are worthy to take
the scroll and to open its seals, because you were slain,
and with your blood you purchased men for God from every
tribe and language and people and nation."*
Revelation 5:9

Lord may we have the attitude of...
"I am not going to apologize
for speaking the name of Jesus.
I am not going to hide the light that God has put
in me. If I have to sacrifice everything I will take it.
If my friends have to become my enemies for me to
be with my best friend Jesus, that is fine with me."
from the journal of Columbine martyr Rachel Scott

If we go to jail or die for our faith, we
want the whole Christian world to
know what is happening to their
brothers and sisters.
Bishop Haik Hovsepian-Mehr

Mauritania

"He the reached down from heaven, all the way from the sky to the sea. He reached down into my darkness to rescue me! He took me out of my calamity and chaos and drew me to himself, Taking me from the depths of my despair!"
Psalm 18:16 TPT

Thank You Lord for your hand over Mauritania.
You are the God who reaches down. We pray that
your mighty arm will meet yielding hands
when you reach down to Mauritania.

We thank you that in your steadfast love and perfect
timing, you draw Mauritanians to yourself. We lift
you up as the only one who can rescue and save.
Show us what you desire to do among Mauritanians,
and we will declare in prayers.

prayna.org/pray-for/mauritania

Mauritius & Micronesia

Praise be to the LORD, for he has heard my cry for mercy.
The LORD is my strength and my shield; my heart trusts in him,
and he helps me. My heart leaps for joy,
and with my song I praise him.
Psalms 28:6–7

Lord it's been said "no man is an island."
You Lord desire no island to lose a man's soul
to this strangely dim world. Be a welcoming
light showing heaven's hospitality.
Dave Davidson

Media

Let love and faithfulness never leave you;
bind them around your neck, write them
on the tablet of your heart.
Proverbs 3:3

Lord, we thank You that Your gospel message can freely be sent forth over radio waves around the globe. We thank You for the broadcast of Christian stations and programs, even in remote countries like Belarus and Ukraine. Lord, we pray for the agencies WRMF, TWR, FEBC in the Philippines and Micronesia. We pray for FEBA and Seychelles and Sim in Liberia and Ibra in Sweden and Lebanon and for ministries like ICRE. We pray for the effective use of television and video, Lord, and for the people who are listening that may never have heard Your word before. **We pray for their hearts to open up to receive the message of Your gospel and** the teachings **of the Holy Spirit.**

We also pray for tape, record and cassette ministries as well as the global recordings mission, the UBS and the WBT, Lord. We pray for these relevant sound media tools all over the world that mission agencies use, including tape players with a hand powered motor. We give You all the praise for these innovative ways to take the gospel to the ends of the earth.

Dave Davidson

Medical Needs

Is anyone sick? ... And the prayer offered in faith
will make the sick person well; the Lord will raise him up.
James 5:14,15

Lord, Jesus, thank You for the gift of the Holy Spirit
that enables us to go to all the world to preach Your
gospel. Thank You for the power of Your Spirit that
heals the sick. Sharon L. Smith, Medical Missionary

Lord Jesus, I come before you
today praying for a heart of
brokenness- a heart that
begins to understand Your
full measure of love and
grace for Your children.

In Your word you have said
that whatever we do to the
least of our brothers we do
also to you. Lord fill my heart
with compassion for the sick,
those who are in prison and
those without clothes. I pray for the lonely who feel
like strangers in this world. I ask you to bless those
who are hungry and thirsty - fill them will Your
bread of life and living water.
Dan Davidson

Give us your heart of compassion as we meet people
with various medical, emotional and spiritual needs.
Joan Davidson

Mega-Cities

"The Lord did not choose you because you were more numerous, for you were the fewest of all peoples. But it was because the Lord loved you."
Deuteronomy 7:7,8

Lord God, all cities are in need of your presence, but the megacities in the 10/40 window are strategically in need of a flourishing

Christian witness.

Lord, we pray for the millions of people in Kabul Afghanistan, Tirana Albania, Algiers Algeria, Baku Azerbaijan, Manama Bahrain, Dhaka Bangladesh, Cotonou Benin, Thimphu Bhutan, Bandar Seri Begawan Brunei, Ouagadougou Burkina Faso, Phnom Penh Cambodia and N'Djamena Chad.

Lord, we pray for all those in urban areas, as half of the world's population lives in or near a city. We pray for the inner cities of the western world with their poverty, drug abuse, crime, displaced families and addictions.

Lord Jesus, we pray for these mega-cities in China. Break the strongholds in Beijing, Changchun, Chengdu, Chongqing, Guangzhou, Hohhot, Jinan, Lanzhou, Lhasa, Nanjing, Shanghai, Shenyang, Taiyuan, Tianjin, Urumqi, Wuhan and Xian.

Lord, reveal Your loving grace in Djibouti Djibouti, Cairo Egypt, Asmara Eritrea, Addis Ababa Ethiopia, Banjul Gambia, Gaza Gaza Strip, Conakry Guinea and Bissau Guinea-Bissau.

Lord, show these cities in India who is the true God by Your Holy Spirit… Ahmedabad, Amritsar, Calcutta, Delhi, Hyderabad, Jaipur, Kanpur, Lucknow, Patna, Pune and Varanasi.

Bring a gospel breakthrough
to Jakarta Indonesia, Mashhad Iran, Tehran Iran, Baghdad Iraq, Jerusalem Israel, Tel Aviv Israel, Fukuoko-Kita-Kyushu Japan, Osaka-Kobe-Kyoto Japan, Sapporo Japan, Tokyo-Yokohama Japan, Amman Jordan, Almaty Kazakhstan, Pyongyang North Korea, Kuwait City Kuwait, Bishkek Kyrgyzstan, Vientiane Laos, Beirut Lebanon, Tripoli Libya, Kuala Lumpur Malaysia, Male Maldives, Bamako Mali, Nouakchott Mauritania, Ulaanbaatar Mongolia, Casablanca Morocco and Yangon Myanmar. (Burma)

Lord, may You be glorified as the King of new Christian hearts in Mogadishu Somalia, Colombo Sri Lanka, Khartoum Sudan, Damascus Syria, Taipei Taiwan and Dushanbe Tajikistan. Lord, reveal Your eternal redemption in the hearts of those living n Kathmandu Nepal, Niamey Niger, Kano Nigeria, Muscat Oman, Karachi Pakistan, Lahore Pakistan, Doha Qatar, Mecca Saudi Arabia, Riyadh Saudi Arabia, and Dakar Senegal.

We earnestly pray that amongst the great numbers of these populations, Your gospel would grow every day. Bring unique socio-economic melting pots into Your kingdom.

Bring Your compassion and love to Bangkok

Thailand, Tunis Tunisia, Ankara Turkey, Istanbul Turkey, Izmir Turkey, Ashkhabad Turkmenistan, Abu Dhabi United Arab Emirates, Tashkent Uzbekistan, Hanoi Vietnam, El Aaiun Western Sahara, and Sana'a Yemen.

We pray that Your word would spread

quickly throughout mega-cities. We are believing for a holyrevival to begin a divine harvest of souls for Your kingdom. Dave Davidson

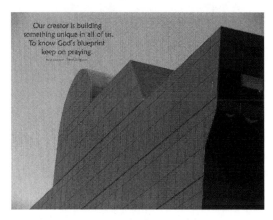

Our creator is building something unique in all of us. To know God's blueprint keep on praying.

Lord may we reap an unprecedented harvest being won in Africa, Asia and Latin America in contrast to stagnation in North America, the Pacific and a decline in Europe.

Mexico

*I tell you the truth, you can say to this mountain,
'May you be lifted up and thrown into the sea,' and it will happen.
But you must really believe it will happen
and have no doubt in your heart.*
Matthew 11:23

Mexico! A beautiful country filled with culture and
romance! Pray for Mexico. May her culture and love
be her strength and the hope of her people
reign over all tribulation!

The drug cartels in Mexico have no mercy and no regard/reverence for anyone. From kidnapping innocent children, students and now priests. It is obvious that there is only one solution: Prayer! With the corruption and drug war of Mexico it is obvious that Divine intervention needs to occur. Only God can help the innocent people of Mexico and only His glory will manifest when the people call out to Him! Unite us in prayer for Salvation in Mexico!

10,000 victims of human trafficking in Mexico City forced into modern day slavery... The issue is a lot closer to home than some think... Let's raise this awareness and pray!

Mexico is filled with culture, traditions, color and love. Despite the tragedies and corruption there are a lot of things to still be grateful for in this beautiful country!
Pray For Mexico Facebook

_____
_____
_____
_____
_____
_____
_____
_____
_____

Middle East

Jerusalem, Jerusalem...How often have I desired to gather your children together as a hen gathers her brood under her wings, and you were not willing.
Matthew 23:37

Gracious God, we pray for everyone in Israel and Palestine as they continue to struggle for peace in their land. In the midst of great tensions, conflict, deaths and turmoil, we ask that the Spirit of your peace be upon all people in the region. Give them wisdom and understanding to realize the preciousness of human life. Breathe love into our prayers with a desire for nothing other than peace: peace in our hearts, peace for all creation, and especially
peace in the land that is called holy.

God of hope, we lift up

the city of Jerusalem, distracted and divided, yet still filled with promise as all the cities of the world. Jesus, ride again into our cities, temples, Upper Rooms and Gethsemanes, that we may be given sight to recognize you.
adapted -Mideast Prayer Vigil Lutheran Office

Lord God, we pray for Islam's power to be broken. We ask that people would commit their lives and missionary efforts as trainers, Prayer warriors and financial supporters.

May Christian women rise

to the challenge of targeting the Middle East countries

because Islamic cultural tradition dictates that only
women can reach women, which is more
than half of the population.

Father God, may Muslim people open their hearts
to the gospel, in spite of dangers that may follow
their conversion. Give courageous transforming faith!
Lord, we ask that the government remains non-Islamic.
Powerful God, break the iron fist of the Syrian dictator.

God of Power we ask You to give
persevering strength for Christians in prison in Saudi Arabia.

Listening God, who answers prayer,
we beseech You to intervene so that the government will lift
restrictions on Christian nationals in the United Arab Emirates.
Give strength to Turkey Christians facing persecution.

Lord God, we humbly trust You
to change the hearts of the Iraq leaders to bend their knees
to You, causing many to surrender their lives to Christ.

Father God Almighty, we ask You
that believers will experience empowerment of the Holy
Spirit to share the gospel, breaking barriers in Cyprus.

Just and sovereign God, we ask that
You raise a standard of justice and
righteousness on behalf of Christians
in Kuwait. May Yemen believers be
strengthened and encouraged daily, and
that nationals will be won for Christ.
We ask that You give Christians creative
ways to share the gospel inside Iran.
O Lord, rise up an army of believers in
Qatar. Jesus, we pray that Christian foreigners will have
opportunities to share Christ with the citizens of Oman.
Dave Davidson - inspired from Persecution.com

Military

Have I not commanded you? Be strong and courageous.
Do not be afraid; do not be discouraged, for the Lord
Your God will be with you wherever you go.
Joshua 1:9

Almighty God, Lord of Hosts, we call out to you as the One
who is sovereign over all. Watch over and protect our
nation's military members and their families. Sustain them
with your everlasting arms. Take into your most gracious
protection our service members currently deployed. May you
be their comfort and their guide as they live and walk in a
foreign land. Give them reassurance that you are a shield
around them, an ever-present help in time of need. Grant our
service members courage so that in all things they may serve
without reproach. Encourage them while they
also encourage one another.

As they serve around the world, we ask that you guard their
families and loved ones back home. Provide them with peace
and surround them with love as they mourn the absence of
their loved one and long for their return. May they find hope
and strength in you for the trials of each new day. Be with
military children who endure the difficult burden of knowing
their father or mother is in harm's way for months on end.
Guard these children's hearts and minds despite the
loneliness and uncertainty of having a parent deployed.

Lord God, be with marriages in the military.
Preserve the bonds of husband and wife despite the stress
that military life brings, stress only compounded by the
decade of war our nation is in. Help military chaplains in
their efforts to equip military marriages with ways to stay
connected and communicate effectively despite the challenge
of frequent deployments. Give husbands and wives strength
and resilience to endure separations, frequent moves,
and all the uncertainty military life brings.

For some, Lord, service takes their toll permanently in physical and emotional damage. For those wounded in battle, we pray you would come beside them. Sustain and strengthen them amidst treatment, pain, and adjustments to life with an injury. Help them to find competent care and support, and to not be afraid to reach out for a helping hand or a listening ear. Be with their caregivers in the demanding role they have. Give caregivers renewed energy to offer support and love as they tend to the needs of the injured. Strengthen them as they both monitor and advocate for their loved one.

We know that war is very costly. Some have made the ultimate sacrifice, laying down their precious lives in service to our nation. Each one of them was a son or daughter, perhaps a husband or wife, father or mother. For all those who feel the pain and the toll of this war in the loss of their loved one, comfort them. Be a father to the fatherless and defender of widows. As they cast their cares on you, may they know the consolation of your love. We thank you for the freedoms these service members fought for which we enjoy today. For each and every veteran who has served our country through the years, we thank you for their sacrifice. Comfort those who struggle in life after war. Help us to honor and care for those who have given so much for us. Be with our nation's leaders as well, and all those who make decisions for our military. Give them wisdom and discernment in everything they do. Father God, we long for the day when swords will be beaten into plowshares and spears into pruning hooks. We long for your peace, for your shalom. In Christ's name we pray, Amen.

Kristi Hofman

Miscarriage & Infant Loss

Blessed be the God and Father of our Lord Jesus Christ,
the Father of mercies and God of all comfort.
2 Corinthians 1:3

Heavenly Father, as our friend's and family's losses weigh on our hearts and perplex us in ways we can't understand, remind us that each season of life is there for a reason. Lord, help us to have an eternal perspective and to remember that we aren't made to be happy and whole in this life. Help us to be willing to walk beside our friends and family in whatever season we are given, whether rejoicing or grieving. Lord, we ask you to break our hearts for the things that break yours. God, we may not understand the depth of grief from a parent who has lost a child. We may not know the loss of a child ourselves. Maybe we know a different kind of loss. Give us the clarity to remind ourselves that each and every life comes from you. Each child, no matter the time here, is perfectly made and loved for eternity. Let us reflect that truth back to those who mourn for the life of a child.

Rachel Baxter

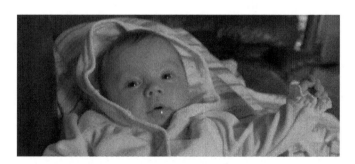

Mission Agencies

We are therefore Christ's ambassadors, as though God were making his appeal through us. We implore you on Christ's behalf: Be reconciled to God.
2 Corinthians 5:20

Lord, we pray for the many faithful mission agencies and ministries throughout Your world. We ask that You use these outreaches to bring Your love to Your children created in Your image that do not yet know You as the one True Savior and Lord. We pray that mission agencies will continue to make a major impact in their steadfast missionary efforts. Create and strengthen new partnerships and affiliations among agencies that will multiply Your worldwide gospel outreach.

Dan Davidson

Lord let us pray that no church is too small, too large, too rich or too poor to be involved.

George Verwer

Mission Mobilization

...The harvest is plentiful, but the workers are few. Ask the Lord of the harvest, therefore, to send out workers into his harvest field. **Luke 10:2**

Lord, we thank You for the many agencies and missionaries that work together from all over the world, many even from

different denominations.

Thank You Jesus, for new countries sending out missionaries today and for the efforts of strategic ministries that mobilize resources and people in specific global evangelization plans.

We pray for the leadership and coordination of those who are in positions to lead mission movements, mission events and mission outreaches. We pray for the continued coordination of large global ministries.

Dave Davidson

Lord we are your chosen people, not your frozen people. We pray for a defrost. Mobilize mobilizers around the world to take ownership of the great commission. George Verwer

Mission Supporters

The share of the man who stayed with the supplies is to be the same as that of him who went down to the battle. All will share alike.
1Samuel 30:24

Everyone who calls on the name of the Lord will be saved. How, then, can they call on the one they have not believed in? And how can they believe in the one of whom they have not heard? And how can they hear without someone preaching to them? And how can they preach unless they are sent? Romans 10:13-15 How then Lord can we sit by and not take part in the sending to those who have not heard?
Dave Davidson

Use us Lord, to send the teachers, the preachers, the funds, the supplies, the equipping ones, the helpful ones, and to minister the love of Jesus. Make us more like You. Burn away the chaff Lord, anything that separates us from You. Jorge Parrot

 Lord, I want them to be and experience all you have for them. Don't let fears hold them back. Give them wisdom. Open their eyes to temptation and sin and make them strong in You to resist the evil one. Lord, I pray that they will always be confident of my love and support that I am cheering them on.
Diane Buchelt

Missionaries

*However, I consider my life worth nothing to me;
my only aim is to finish the race and complete the task
the Lord Jesus has given me—the task of testifying
to the good news of God's grace.*
Acts 20:24

Give them protection from illness while providing strength and stamina. 1 Peter 3:13 Make them effective and productive witnesses, while strengthening and protecting new believers. 2 Peter 1:5-8 Keep them from discouragement and homesickness as they follow you. Joshua 1:9 Keep them alert - shrewd as snakes and innocent as doves. Mathew 10:16-17 Send more workers to the fields. Matthew 9:37,38, Galatians 6:9 Use them as intercessors for those they serve. Ezekiel 22:30,31 May they do everything you ask them to do. Acts 13:22b Create a bond between them and those they serve. Romans 12:10 Give them opportunity to demonstrate your love. Romans 12:21 Convert their willingness to serve into a spiritual fervor. Romans 12:11 Use threats against them to create holy boldness. Acts 4:29 Use hospitality. Create desire to associate with the lowly. Romans 12:16 Live in peace and don't seek revenge. Romans 12:17-19

 Give them the spirit of wisdom and revelation. Ephesians 1:17 Meet all their needs as they serve. Philippians 4:19 Help them persevere to the completion of their mission. 2 Thessalonians 3:3-5, 2 Timothy 4:7 Teach them the truth of your Word and how to use it for your purpose. 2 Timothy 2:15 Keep international missionaries in His comfort as they are away from their families.
Prayer Tower

Missionary Kids

*All your children will be taught by the LORD,
and great will be their peace.*
Isaiah 54:13

Lord may missionary kids have...

Healthy, scriptural view of wealth and poverty.
Contentment and gratefulness for God's provision.
Eternal rather than temporal thinking. Daily trust in the
Lord's ability to provide all they need. Fun and lasting
friendships despite changes. Trust in and reliance on God
during transition flexibility and social skills. Adequate
and appropriate educational opportunities.

Ability to adjust to home culture after high school.
Grace to handle being observed. Protection from
enticement of host culture. Discernment and strength
when facing temptation. Love for the people in host
and home culture. Upright behavior. Recognition
of their own need for spiritual growth. Thirst
for a deeper relationship with Christ.

Hunger for His truth found in Scripture.
Pursuit of excellence and holiness.
Honest and joyful relationships with parents.
Balance between ministry and family.
Appreciation for their parents' ministry.
Other adults to encourage and guide them.
Connection with extended family despite distance.
Emotional dependence on God's protection.
Rest in God's sovereignty. Protection,
health and safety. Absence of fear.
Awareness of potential dangers.
Send.org

Missionary Needs

*For this is what the Lord has commanded us:
'I have made you a light for the Gentiles, that you
may bring salvation to the ends of the earth'.*
Acts 13:47

Please help them to put on the whole armor of God,
that the fiery darts of the devil are extinguished, and
after doing everything to stand, please strengthen
them to "stand on." Philippians 3

I ask Lord, that the joy of the Lord would be
their strength…may their hearts trust in you."
Psalm 28:7

Thank you that the one who watches over Israel,
neither slumbers nor sleeps. Please guard our
missionary's going out and coming in, and may they
remember that their help comes from the Lord.
Psalm 121

Thank you Lord, that you are faithful. I pray that you
will strengthen and protect the missionary from the
evil one.
II Thessalonians 3:3

May our missionary experience and recognize the faithfulness of the Lord, and may the new mercies He sends each and every morning. Lamentations 3:22-23

Dear Father, please provide for their needs according to your riches in Christ Jesus. Philippians 4:19

Give them the grace and discipline to study hard to show themselves approved of God, that they will be able to rightly divide your Word of Truth to others. II Timothy 2:15

Father, please direct our missionaries by your eye, instructing them and teaching them in your ways. Please uphold them with your righteous right arm. May the lamp of your word guide them today and may your words be found in their mouths as they speak to others about Jesus. Psalm 32:8:8, Isaiah 41:10, Psalm 119:105.

Please give ears to hear to those to whom the missionary speaks. Please prepare the listener and let your words fall on good soil. Give the missionary success for your glory. Matthew 13:8 - Annie Armstrong

Lord we pray for solid family relationships. The tasks of full-time ministry, often in a foreign culture, can cause a strain on the relationships within a family -- husbands and wives, parents and children. We ask that You Lord would strengthen family bonds and draw them close together. We pray for the health, safety, and encouragement of these family members. Strength in the "inner man" (Ephesians 3:16).

Loneliness, discouragement, despair -- these struggles occur in the lives of missionaries, and sometimes frequently.

Lord, may the hearts of missionaries be encouraged and strengthened into deep commitment and obedience to Your will. Provide for their physical needs. (Philippians 4:19).

We pray for a strong personal walk with God. May missionaries be faithful daily to spend time in God's Word in the midst of ministry busyness. Lord protect and strengthen them spiritually and cause them to grow with God. Give them good physical health in foreign lands. Nurture strong relationships with co-workers. Reconcile personality conflicts and relationship struggles among missionaries as they seek to work together to bring people to Christ. Foster unselfishness, kindness, and humility in these cooperative efforts (Philippians 2:3-5).

Grant them the ability to speak accurately, discern decisively, and act accordingly. Lord cause them to speak with clarity and precision as they declare God's Word Offer opportunities to relax time and time again. Grant a balance of servanthood, rest and restoration. Give wisdom in all they do.
(Colossians 4:3-4 James 1:5). Dave Davidson

Moldova

*So also, when we were underage, we were in slavery
under the elemental spiritual forces of the world.*
Galatians 4:3

Father God provide food to live a healthy life. Psalm
132:15 Create chances for employment in Moldova.
Deuteronomy 28:12 Let the young people have the
education. Exodus 36:1 Protected the young from human
traffickers. Help them to make decisions that are wise
and not out of desperation. Help the vulnerable
to know who to trust. Psalm 5:11 Intervene on the
part of people that might be trafficked.
Save them before they are sold. Psalm 55:11, Psalm 45:4
Present people to know the love, grace, forgiveness
and salvation of Jesus Christ in Moldova. Hebrews 9:28
Trap traffickers to be caught and brought to justice.
Have law enforcement pursue organized crime
exposing and dismantling corruption. Judges 5:26, Judges
2:16 God bring supernatural freedom now to all the
victims trafficked anywhere in Moldova. 1 Chronicles 16:34-
36, Hebrews 9:28 Remind me Lord to stand in prayer for
Moldova and the women, men and children
trapped into a cycle of slavery. adapted from
prayerforfreedom.com/moldova-and-prayers-for-freedom

Mongolia

Therefore, since we have such a hope, we are very bold.
2 Corinthians 3:12

We pray:
For Christians everywhere to be concerned for the
unreached millions in Mongolia who have never
heard the name of Jesus, especially those who live
nomadic lives in the remote countryside.

For the Lord to send Christians to Mongolia to see for
themselves the spiritually needy people and to return
to their home churches with a new zeal to pray,
to support the ongoing work in Mongolia,
and for some to consider serving in Mongolia.

For Mongolian believers to boldly share the Gospel
with their families and friends. For the Bible school
students to become godly leaders and to model
authentic biblical spirituality in contrast to the certain
aspects of the culture such as the acceptance of
premarital intimacy, abortion, and alcoholism. For the
local churches to grow in quality and quantity, and
for churches to become financially indigenous.

For the local pastors and church leaders to persevere and become mature in God's service in the midst of difficulties, such as lack of resources for the church.

For the missionaries and Christian workers serving here to have effective ministries: meeting the practical and spiritual needs of the people, discipling and mentoring believers, and influencing churches to be mission-minded — reaching out within Mongolia and beyond.

asianaccess.org

Mourning & Grieving

*Grieve, mourn and wail. Change your laughter
to mourning and your joy to gloom.*
James 4:9

Lord, soften our hearts with compassion for those
suffering loss in their lives. Help us to rejoice with
those who rejoice and to weep with those who weep.
Send Your Holy Spirit to care for the grieving.
Encourage, strengthen and counsel Your people in times
of grief and sorrow. Help them to fully experience Your
comfort, so that they may be able to help comfort others
in the future. Give us godly sympathy as we pray for
discernment for supportive ways to minister to those
carrying heavy burdens in life. Equip us with
a listening heart and a spirit of understanding.

Through the resurrection power
of Your Son, Jesus, turn their mourning into
joy in Your perfect timing. Dan Davidson

Dear God 74 nations persecute religious believers mostly Christians where 400
million live. Make Your sovereign way through these barriers of darkness.

Mozambique

For where your treasure is, there your heart will be also.
Matthew 6:21

Rejoice over the "Land of Smiles" of Mozambique located off the southeastern coast of Africa. Just as 40% of the world's unmined rubies are waiting to be found, may valuable souls be mined in Christ.

Despite rich natural resources of stunning beaches, turquoise water, and coral coastline, Mozambique remains one of Africa's poorest countries. May citizens identify the treasure to store up in heaven.

We pray for lasting peace to overcome all threats to the nation's fragile stability and for true freedom for those in bondage to poverty, disease, witchcraft, and animism. Father, grant church leaders to grow in spiritual maturity and Biblical understanding.

We also ask that Your blessing and provision over 17 Bible translation projects. Lord, our prayer is that the love of Christ will extend the Church of Mozambique.

Dave Davidson

Muslims

You will seek me and find me when you
seek me with all your heart.
Jeremiah 29:13

For those who have never heard the gospel among the
Muslim peoples due to religious restrictions in their
country, we pray they will hear your gospel in such a
way that they will understand the message and have
the grace to respond to your love even under difficult
circumstances. Thank You Lord for Arabic media that
is reaching thousands with the message of your
gospel. Thank You for those following you under
great pressure. We pray You will build communities
of believers in the nations of North Africa and the
Middle East. Protect them as they follow You. We
pray for those who are earnestly seeking the truth,
that as they read of the person of Jesus in the Koran it
would fuel a desire to find Jesus of the bible. Reveal
yourself in dreams and visions to those who seek
after You according to Your word. Ruth Boctor

Myanmar

*As long as it is day, we must do the works of him who sent me.
Night is coming, when no one can work.*
John 9:4

In this very moment we share Myanmar's "greediness" for peace with "too long lists" requiring a multitude of prayers. In this very moment when the people of Myanmar deeply desire peace, we pray with them for the lasting peace they seek. In this very moment may they find genuine forgiveness among diverse religious and ethnic groups, leading to reconciliation between ethnic armed groups and the state military. In this very moment may there be peace and healing for those who have suffered 50 years of civil war, in addition to the devastation of annual floods, fires, landslides and droughts. In this very moment we echo Myanmar's prayers for their government, and the determined efforts of those working for a nationwide ceasefire agreement. In this very moment we pray for strength and wisdom for the continuing work of the Peace Studies Centre within Myanmar, and for all efforts for peace in the world. In this very moment we pray for peace. Amen.

Monica Scheifele

Namibia

"For the mountains may leave and the hills be removed, but my grace will never leave you, and my covenant of peace will not be removed."
Isaiah 54:10

Father, we pray for life-sustaining jobs for the 27% of Namibians who are unemployed.

Lord, we also pray for continued religious freedom in Namibia. We pray for reformation among Christians who cling to un-biblical beliefs. We pray that purity in worship and in the Church will be restored in the lives of Namibian Christians. Lord, we ask that all may hear the Gospel once again and for many to turn back to Christ. Father will you please establish unity and cooperation among all groups seeking to uplift Christ in this nation.

Father we praise you for many in government and leadership positions who follow you. We trust that you will encourage them and make them lie down in green pastures, lead them beside quiet waters, and restore their souls. Lord, we pray for wisdom and discernment to develop specific approaches to reach the unreached people groups. We ask this in the mighty name of Jesus Christ. Amen.

movingintoaction.co.za/country/namibia

Nations

Blessed is the nation whose God is the LORD,
the people he chose for his inheritance.
Psalm 33:12

We would follow the example of the Father
(Abraham) of the faithful and pray for all great cities,
and indeed for all the nations. Lord let Your kingdom
come. **Send forth Your light**
and Your truth. Chase the old dragon from his throne
with all his hellish crew. Oh! that the day might come
when even on earth the Son of the woman, the Man-
child, should rule the nations, not with a broken staff
of wood, but with an enduring scepter of iron, full of
mercy, but full of power, full of grace, but yet
irresistible. Oh! that that might soon come, the
personal advent of our Lord! We long for the
millennial triumph of His Word. Amen!
Charles Haddon Spurgeon

Lord, Your blessing has been upon this nation and I thank
You for your kind mercies! But Your word says the blessed
nation is the one whose God is the Lord and our nation has
turned from You. God, on behalf of myself and my
people, I confess our disregard of You. Bring Your people
to repentance and let this nation once again be
one who calls You "Lord." Arabah Joy

Nauru

*Surely the nations are like a drop in a bucket;
they are regarded as dust on the scales; he weighs
the islands as though they were fine dust.*
Isaiah 40:15

Thousands of miles from any other land, the tiny
island of Nauru sits isolated in the Pacific awaiting
our prayers. Home to just over 10,000 people, this
small island of only 21 square miles is the
world's smallest republic.

We pray for God's provision for the 90% who are
unemployed in this predominantly Christian nation.
We pray for the despair of people's economic
condition to turn their softened hearts to Christ.
We pray for great spiritual growth in the midst of
increased poverty. Although its location is exotic, its
people are quite westernized. The island has seen
both independence and brutal occupation, immense
wealth and dire economic meltdown.

adapted from Prayercast.com

Nepal

We are witnesses of these things, and so is the Holy Spirit,
whom God has given to those who obey him.
Acts 5:32

Lord God, I give you thanks and praise
for my sisters and brothers in Nepal.
For their dedication to walk miles upon miles to share
your love with others… For their witness to their
surrounding neighbors who do not know the depth of
your grace…For their hospitality to accept strangers
into their homes and into their hearts… For their
commitment to enact justice and to heal wounds of
brokenness among them… For their confidence in
your faithfulness to reach out to you in prayer.

Through the witness of my Nepali sisters and
brothers, O God, I humble myself before you.
I humble myself recognizing you are holy and you are
love and you are power. And through your grace,
I come to you, seeking to be made obedient to your
will, seeking to be strengthened in my commitment
to serving you with the same obedience and passion
as my sisters and brothers.

Lord God, as my heart cries out with tears of joy for
their loving witness and tears of sadness for the
distance between us, I pray that you may continue to
fill me with your compassion that I may serve you
where I am. And as my tears fall upon the road I
walk, I pray for others to encounter my tears and for
my tears to serve as a witness to the deep, profound
ways you have broken my heart for the beautiful
people of Nepal, as fellow bearers of your love and
grace. Please protect them and watch over them,
renew their hearts day by day, give them good
health and courage to continue to share
your Word with others.

Lord God, I thank you for my sisters and brothers
and for the continued ways in which you let me
experience your love and grace, through the many
witnesses around the world, and ultimately, through
the death and resurrection of your beloved, Son,
in whose name I offer this prayer.

Jane Larson

Netherlands

*In the same way, those of you who do not give up
everything you have cannot be my disciples.*
Luke 14:33

Thanks God for historically deep Dutch Christian
roots. Thanks for disciples who make disciples.
Nudge the Netherlands to national spiritual maturity
and personal repentance. Ramp up revival and
regeneration for believers to stand strong in the face
of spiritual apathy masked as Dutch tolerance. Raise
up mission workers, righteous servants, and wise
leaders filled with grace. Transform young lives
who consider Christianity as irrelevant.
Dave Davidson

New Age

For the time will come when men will not put up with sound doctrine. Instead, to suit their own desires, they will gather around them a great number of teachers to say what their itching ears want to hear.
2 Timothy 4:3

Bring the conviction of the Holy Spirit and pierce hearts to respond in repentance over New Age deception. Lord cut through horrific satanic bondage and wash the consciences tricked and deceived from scarlet sins as white as snow.

Shake down the mysterious mystical New Age experience to completely pale in comparison to Your redemptive truth. May the shiny crystal schemes of Satan's glowing counterfeit fineries appear cheap as filthy rags like the "Emperor's New Clothes" story compared to God's gospel Truth.

Dave Davidson

God could have made us all manequins, but He wanted us to talk to Him on our own initiative.

Dave Davidson PrayAlong.com

New Years

To proclaim the year of the LORD's favor and the day of vengeance of our God, to comfort all who mourn.
Isaiah 61:2

Lord, we look back to last year.
Thank you for every sign of your grace.
For every life transformed.
For every broken life healed.
Every lost person found.
Everyone far off brought near.
Every sinner saved.

Lord it is all about you our grace,
Your love, Your mercy, Your glory.
Only you can make a difference to every life.

Lord, this year we pray for:
greater love for the lost,
deeper compassion for the broken,
stronger faith in your saving power,
bolder witness to your presence,
believing that the kingdom is advancing.

Help your Church rise up to seize the day
believing that there are no "no-go" areas for you Lord.

No people that cannot be reached.
No chains that cannot be broken.

So Lord, send us into this year longing for your presence and for your glory to fall anew. Igniting us with an unquenchable flame. Bringing light, hope and love wherever you send us. In Jesus' name Amen.

Fred Drumond

New Zealand

*"Then all the nations will call you blessed, for yours
will be a delightful land," says the Lord Almighty.*
Malachi 3:12

We pray for Godly leadership and wisdom for those
who lead and govern our nation, including: the
Queen, Governor General, Prime Minister, Cabinet,
Members of Parliament, Mayors and Councillors.
We pray for all who lead in the areas of education,
business, media, church, family, government,
arts, entertainment and sport.

We pray that our nation will be strong morally,
encouraging what is good and right, and rejecting
what is evil and immoral. We pray that our laws will
uphold Godly living and do all they can to discourage
what is evil and detrimental to our nation.
We pray against various evils by name,
and for those things which are good.

We pray for law and order, justice and peace in the
land. We pray strong family relationships, for loyalty,
love, mutual support. We pray against abortion,
sexual immorality and those things which are
destructive to good family life. We pray that parents
will love, support and discipline their children, and
that children will respect, honour and love their
parents. We pray for older single people, and
those who are lonely, poor and needy.
We pray about the issues of abortion, divorce,
de facto relationships and single-parent families.

We pray the young people of our nation: that they
will be set good examples by older people; that they
will not be led astray into crime, violence, immorality,
the occult or false religions, suicide, drugs, etc. We
pray for all Christian youth groups and organisations,
that they will lead many to Christ and help
them to grow and mature as Christians.

We pray a nationwide return to God's laws and God's
ways. We pray for unity within churches and
between churches; and for unity within the nation,
between various racial groups. We pray for a strong
Church and a strong nation because of Godly unity.
We pray against things which cause hatred and
division: pride, prejudice, selfishness, greed, etc.

We pray all evangelistic efforts being made by individual Christians, by churches and Christian organisations. We pray that many people will be saved. We pray that New Zealand will be a strong missionary-sending nation. We pray that those who are unsaved, in other religions, in the cults, nominal Christians and unbelievers, will be drawn by the Holy Spirit to receive Jesus Christ as their Lord and Saviour. We pray especially for unsaved loved ones.

We pray Church leaders and members; for an out-pouring of the Holy Spirit, bringing revival to the Church and nation. We pray for the tearing down of satanic strongholds and for victories in Jesus' Name! We pray that the Lord will be worshipped in Spirit and in Truth; for Bible-centered preaching and teaching; and for Spirit-filled Christians who will glorify the Lord in everything they do.

adapted from pray-for-the-nation.org

Nicaragua

Do not let the oppressed retreat in disgrace;
may the poor and needy praise your name.
Psalm 74:21

Hear, O God, the cries of your oppressed people.
It is a fight between good and evil,
between justice and injustice.
Lord, make your light shine upon us,
and guide us by your Spirit,
for we are cast down, but not defeated,
afflicted, but not in despair.
This is not a fight against flesh and blood,
but against principalities,
against powers,
against the hosts of evil in heavenly places.
Come, Lord, free us from the yoke of oppression
that has been laid upon us!
It is as if we were in a dark tunnel,
but we know that in your light we shall see light.
Do not leave us in the hands of our enemies,
who have joined against us,
all those who selfishly seek their own good
and act violently, trampling over their neighbours,
so as to reach their goals.

They thus hate justice,
they wish to devour us, destroy us,
day and night they are plotting evil.
Why do you tarry, Lord, in making your power felt?
They put their trust in money,
in influence, in bribery...
But we, Lord, put our trust in you,
our salvation comes from you.
May those who desire evil for us
be confounded and put to shame.
Amen.

Mendelson Dávila Amaya, Nicaragua

Niger

*"For so the Lord has commanded us, saying,
'I have made you a light for the Gentiles, that you
may bring salvation to the ends of the earth.'"*
Acts 13:47

We pray that as Nigeriens accept Christ, they would be filled with an insatiable passion to see their nation won to Christ. Pray that the persecution and hardships would not quench their fiery passion for the Lord, but would compel them to be the Light of the World in a dark place.

We pray that Nigerien believers would be a light to their Muslim brothers and sisters so that they may bring salvation throughout the country of Niger. Many widows are neglected and scorned by their community in Niger. Many Nigerien widows are forced to leave their houses, have their children taken from them, and endure great difficulty finding work.

We pray that Nigerien believers would care for the widows and that many would come to know Christ. Storytelling is a big part of the Sokoto Fulani culture. Typically, in the evenings, the older men tell stories and legends to the younger men and women in their communities.

We pray that they will share
the stories of Christ for generations to come.

We pray that the Gospel of Jesus Christ would
become known among the Sokoto Fulani people.

As the Pray for Niger global prayer movement grows,
our desire is to partner with other Christian
organizations serving in Niger. Pray for partnership
opportunities to grow as the Pray for Niger
ministry moves forward.

We pray that the Lord will speak to the people of
Niger through dreams and visions. We pray that
Nigerien believers would boldly proclaim the Gospel.

prayforniger.org

_____

_____

_____

_____

_____

Nigeria

*"'And in the last days it shall be, God declares,
that I will pour out my Spirit on all flesh, and your sons and your
daughters shall prophesy, and your young men shall see visions,
and your old men shall dream dreams;"*
Acts 2:17

Father I thank You for this great country of Nigeria.
I thank You for all the things that You have done,
all You are doing and about to do over there.

Lord, I ask that You awaken this land and cause the
people to hear Your voice, oh God! Father, send forth
Your Spirit of Truth in every part of Nigeria and
provide laborers for Your harvest, Lord that the
Gospel will be preached in every dwelling home.
Convict them, oh God, of sin, unrighteousness
and judgement. christianstt.com

_____
_____
_____
_____

North Africa

Walk by faith, not by sight.
2 Corinthians 5:7

Father, we lift up North Africa before you. We pray that you might be exalted in these countries that at one time had a strong church, but now lie in spiritual darkness. We pray that You and You alone are the Great God over this whole earth. Our Heavenly Father, we ask that You would rise up the laborers especially for your church in Latin America where the believers have such an affinity with North Africa. Move by your Spirit among the young people and speak to leaders in the Latin church to call them forth as ambassadors of your Kingdom. We thank you that a crack is beginning to form in the Islamic curtain in North Africa and soon it will be torn. Thank You for speaking to individual Muslims through dreams and visions. Father, move upon your church worldwide so that when North Africa opens, the church will be ready to move as well. Thank You that North Africa will come to know You. Frank Dietz

Lord our hearts break for 160 million North African and 157 million sub-Saharan Muslims.

North Korea

All the nations you have made will come and worship before you,
O Lord; they will bring glory to your name. For you are great
and do marvelous deeds; you alone are God.
Psalm 86:9,10

Blessed are the peacemakers, for they shall be called
the children of God. In this region of hostility, send
your Spirit to establish peace between nations. We
bring before you the disunity of Northeast Asia, its
history of injustice and oppression, the fear of the
unknown, and, now, threats of nuclear war. May your
church be a voice of reason, reaching across divides to
speak peace to a region that has endured 70 years of
hostility and division. Lord, as your people, we pray
for the power to be gentle; the strength to be
forgiving; the patience to be understanding; the grace
to be compassionate toward our enemies; the
endurance to accept the consequences of holding to
what we believe to be right. Lord, strengthen the will
of all those who work for reconciliation and peace,
renew your church, and give us the peace
which the world cannot give. Amen.

Donna Rice

Norway

*Multitudes who sleep in the dust of the earth
will awake: some to everlasting life, others
to shame and everlasting contempt.*
Daniel 12:2

Praise God freedom of religion is granted,
with the Church of Norway being Lutheran.
Christianity was introduced when King Olaf I
was converted and made it the state religion in 995.

Thanks be to God that the Church emphasizes
missions, and Norway is one of the top missionary
sending nations in the world. Though the majority of
the population are church members, a large number
of them are no longer committed. So light a spiritual
fire of fervor to reignite fundamental discipleship
basics. Lord address the challenge that Islam is now
the second largest religion in Norway, with many
Muslims immigrating from places such as Pakistan
and Iran. Reach out to those who are not fully
committed to the Islamic faith and
are open to the Gospel.

We pray for a movement of the Holy Spirit among
the 86% of the population who are church members
but do not attend worship. We pray for vibrant
churches to be planted in Oslo among Muslim and
Asian immigrants. We pray for spiritual awakening
among increasingly secular high school
and college students.

adapted from Prayercast.com

Obedience

Jonah obeyed the word of the Lord and went to Nineveh.
Jonah 3:3

Take my hands, take my feet. Take my heart, soul,
mind and strength. So the captives can be free. Speak
through me. Use Your words, use Your truth. Make
this vessel pure for You. So the thirsty can believe,
pour through me. Lord run Your kingdom through
my heart. Crucify self, set me apart, so that the
nations hear Your truth. Send this ambassador for
You. Move through me. Take the scales from my
sight. Pierce my darkness with your light so blinded
eyes can finally see. Shine through me. Let me wipe
away their tears. Show compassion, calm their fear,
so wounded hearts will surely heal. Love through me.

Bill Drake from "Move Through Me" BillDrake.com

Prayer is like a day at the beach,
to have the best experience...
Get your feet wet!

Oman

*Thus you nullify the word of God by your tradition that
you have handed down. And you do many things like that.*
Mark 7:13

Lord we echo prayer Christians in Oman ask
us to pray for: Many Omanis are influenced by
globalization. We pray that their experience outside
of traditional Omani life will bring them to the Cross
of Christ as they look for answers beyond the borders
of their land. Social media is of great influence
in Oman. We pray that this media will be a means
for Omanis to be exposed to the truth of Christ.

The fear of evil spirits is a reality to many Omanis.
They often carry out practices to appease the spirits.
We pray that God would release them from fear and
reveal Himself to them in dreams or visions. Bahla,
Oman is the center of black magic in the country. Pray
for the Holy Spirit to reign in Bahla! Hundreds of
Omanis study abroad. Many also go outside the
country for medical care. We pray that Christians
in these countries will reach out to them with
hospitality, care, and love in Jesus' Name.

Omani international students have already come to Christ in these countries. And a few Omani university students in Oman have given their lives to Christ through the witness of young adult believers.

Important decisions are made collectively as families, clans, and tribes. We pray that whole families will believe the Gospel. We pray that God's church will be firmly established in Oman and that nothing will prevail against it. Many areas of Oman are almost completely untouched with the Gospel message. We pray that God would call believers to these unreached areas. The good news is that some of these unreached areas are slowly being populated with believers, but many more are needed!

We pray for Sultan Qaboos. He is dearly loved by his people and has great influence over them. We pray for his salvation and that he would lead his country to salvation! We pray that he would continue to rule with justice, righteousness, and wisdom.

We pray for the people of Oman, that God would take out the hearts of stone and give them new hearts of flesh (Ezekiel 11:19). We pray that the Spirit would cause them to walk in His statutes (Ezekiel 36:27). We pray that God would show Himself through signs and wonders and various miracles and gifts of the Holy Spirit according to his will (Hebrews 2:4). Pray that He would open their hearts so that they will believe the Gospel (Acts 16:14). Adapted from pray-ap.info/oman

_____
_____
_____
_____

Orphans

*Religion that God our Father accepts as pure and faultless is
this: to look after orphans and widows in their distress and to
keep oneself from being polluted by the world.*
James 1:27

God of all
comfort,
(2 Corinthians 1) fulfill
your promises to
those who have
lost their parents
as a child. Bring
godly people
into their lives to
love, care,
support, nurture,
befriend and
disciple these
precious children
throughout the
world. We pray
for the orphans
of Malawi
wondering
around the fields
with no orphanage, mentor or direction. Lord, bring
Christian workers to these children and others like
them in the world. Father of the fatherless, be the
Abba father to these children. As they grow up and
struggle to survive, show them firsthand how to trust
You with their very soul. Lord, break our hearts with
compassion for the children of the world. Protect and
keep them safe in Your hands. Dave Davidson

Pakistan

It is he who will build the temple of the Lord, and he will be clothed with majesty and will sit and rule on his throne. And he will be a priest on his throne. And there will be harmony between the two.'

Zechariah 6:13

May the church in Pakistan know and experience your loving hand and comfort.

Please bring peace, harmony and understanding to this nation.

Loving and merciful God, we thank you for the church in Pakistan and thank you that it has stood firm in the midst of all the troubles it has experienced.

releaseinternational.org

Lord we prayer for Pakistan that You would address these key categories with Your almighty power according to Your soverign will:

- The President, prime Minister and all in positions of political authority.

- National stability and peace with Pakistan's neighbours. - The role of the Army and the politics of the USA, India and Afghanistan. - Population explosion. - The state of the nation. - The state of the economy. - The breakdown of basic amenities: electricity and power. - Wisdom is dealing with terrorism and Islamic extremism in all its forms. - The state of education. - The education emergency: 50% school-age children in school. - The disastrous state of Government education. - The tragedy of expensive Private Schools and Church schools. - The bias towards Islam in text books and the curriculum. - Christian teachers – leaders of tomorrow's Church. - The state of the Christian community.

- Living in the shadow of Islam and the Blasphemy law. - The curse of prejudice, discrimination and persecution. - The tragedy of marginalisation and the minority complex. - The urgency of equipping the children before it is too late. - The Christian heroes who are making a difference. - The need for massive infrastructure support. - The loss of leaders and the educated overseas. - The urgency of Christian education. - The prospect of a lost generation.

StarfishAsia.org

Palau

We and our kings, our princes and our ancestors are covered
with shame, Lord, because we have sinned against you.
Daniel 9:8

Lord since there's a strong sense of Palauan identity,
they're slow to the gospel letting go of their ancestral
roots. Imagine if Christians clung to their identity in
Christ. Lord may followers of the local religion of
Modekngei personally meet the all-powerful and
compassionate God. Father show the full moon
esteeming people of Palau who equate it with peace,
love, and tranquility, that You are their Creator. May
local believers be raised up as evangelists to the
smaller unreached island communities. Just as the
islands of Palau are surrounded by a 70 mile (113 km)
barrier reef located east of the Philippines and north
of Indonesia, may there be a circle of protection from
barracuda type demons looking to penetrate godly
legacies on Palau. Hand out hope and freedom to
those imprisoned by addictions to alcohol and drugs.

Dave Davidson

Palestinian Territories

*Listen to the fugitives and refugees from Babylon
declaring in Zion how the Lord our God has taken
vengeance, vengeance for his temple.*
Jeremiah 50:28

In the name of Elohim, the most merciful.
May the Palestinian people receive the healing
powers of our prayers. May they be granted safety,
success, love, security, and hope. May they enjoy the
fruits of freedom and equality that they — and all
human beings — deserve. We remember that the Holy
Land is a shared space and pray to see the day when
Jews, Muslims, Christians, Druze, and all religions
will live there together in peace.

We hope for the day when Palestinian refugees may
return. We pray that together with their Jewish
neighbors they can rehabilitate their history and
rebuild what could be the best place on Earth...
A place of many cultures and true equality.

We pray that Palestinians will be able to live lives free
from violence and oppression. We ask God to help us
build bridges of peace with them. May we be the light
that brings peace and hope to our Palestinian friends
and to all the world. Amen. Ritualwell.org

Panama

I am the servant of the Lord.
May it be done to me according to your word.
Luke 1:38

Merciful Father, You call us to live our lives as a way of salvation. Help us to recall the past with gratitude, to embrace the present with courage and to build the future with hope. Lord Jesus, our friend and brother, thank you for looking upon us with love. Let us listen to your voice as it resonates in the hearts of each one with the strength and light of the Holy Spirit.

Grant us the grace of being a Church that goes forth with vibrant faith and a youthful face to communicate the joy of the Gospel. May we help to build up the kind of society we long for, one where there is fairness and fellowship...

Official Prayer for WYD Panamá 2019

Papua New Guinea

...I know that you acted in ignorance, as did your leaders.
Acts 3:17

We pray for 'Ring of Fire' in the Pacific Ocean, where
culturally diverse New Guinea is the second largest
island in the world. We pray for an end to tribal
fighting, revenge killing, and sorcery-related violence.
We pray for audio discipleship materials in all 300+
languages still needing translation work. We pray
for unity of the Spirit across isolated and
diverse church communities.
adapted from Prayercast.com

We pray for the government of Papua New Guinea
that they may seek God's wisdom and love to serve
their people with fairness and honesty. We pray
especially for our leaders and decision makers that
they may seek God's wisdom and knowledge in order
to make wise and honest decisions for the good
of the people of Papua New Guinea.
Julie Felix

Paraguay

This is the way he governs the nations
and provides food in abundance.
Job 36:31

We give glory and praise to the God of open
doors and abundant life for the Paraguayan people.
Thank you, God, because we have witnessed your
intervention with the indigenous communities, where
you have been refuge, safety, and salvation. Thank
you for the believing people who hold this Ministry
where we can reach a town that needs medical care,
support, and food security. Give us your
understanding so that the daily journey is one that
blesses and cares for this land and this people. Protect
them from thieves and evil-doers who harm, hurt,
and corrupt in pursuit of their own interests. Provide
this beloved people their daily bread and may they
experience your peace. Amen. Amelia Casillas

Pastors

*And when the Chief Shepherd appears, you will receive
the crown of glory that will never fade away.*
1 Peter 5:4

Lord, we pray for our pastors.

We pray for the results of open doors, (2 Corinthians 2:12)
fruit that will last (John 15:16) and laborers for the harvest
(Matthew 9:37). Lord, we pray for their teaching and
preaching… for the message to spread and be
honored, (2 Thessalonians 3:1) for clear teaching and
presentations (Colossians 4:4) and for divine wisdom and
knowledge (Colossians 2:3). Lord, we pray for their
ministries… that they will be well-received, (Romans
15:31) for boldness, (Ephesians 6:20) for deliverance from
frustrating circumstances (2 Corinthians 1:10-11) and for
fruitfulness (John 15:16). Lord, we pray for the personal
lives of pastors… for moral purity, (1 Timothy 4:12) to be a
person after God's heart (Acts 13:22) and a person of the
Word, (Psalm 119:11) deepening prayer life, (Psalm 63:1)
and filled with the Holy Spirit (Ephesians 3:16-19).
Lord, we pray for family relationships… marriages
that honor and reflect Christ, (Ephesians 5:22-33) a
harmonious family life (1 Peter 3:8-9) and children as a
source of joy and blessing (Psalm 127:3,5). Lord, we pray
for their spiritual lives to be devoted to prayer and
ministry of the Word, (Acts 6:4) to intercede for people, (1
Samuel 12:23) to equip the saints (Ephesians 4:11-12) and for
protection from the evil one (2 Thessalonians 3:3). Lord, we
pray for their physical needs in health, (3 John 2)
in material needs, (Philippians 4:19) in protection (Psalm 91:11-
12) and in the binding of Satan (Matthew 18:18). Linda Corbin

...Enable your servants to speak Your word with great boldness.

Stretch out your hand to heal and perform miraculous signs and wonders through the name of your holy servant Jesus. After they prayed, the place where they were meeting was shaken. And they were all filled with the Holy Spirit and spoke the word of God boldly. Acts 29,30,31

People Groups

*…what he opens no one can shut,
and what he shuts no one can open.*
Isaiah 22:22

Father, You know each of the 13,000 people groups in the
world by name, as well as those missed by human
calculations. You intimately understand each culture and
have created them to love and know You. How You must
grieve over those who have no opportunity to hear of You!
Open the eyes of these unreached peoples groups.
Grant repentant hearts to follow You,

whatever the cost.

Lord, rise up international laborers for those without
any witness. In Your sovereignty, link them with
teammates who have a similar vision, and help them
to persevere when people tell them it cannot be done.
Humble them and above all, keep them close to Your
heart and faithful in prayer. We want to reflect
You more by loving, serving, and interceding.

Caryn M. Pederson – Pioneers

Persecuted & Tortured

Others were tortured and refused to be released,
so that they might gain a better resurrection.
Hebrews 11:35

Lord God, we pray that the persecuted
will not seek to retaliate, but entrust themselves to Him
who judges justly. (1 Peter 2:23) May believers stand firm in
their faith. (1 Peter 5:8-10) May they not be fearful but trust in
God. (Rev 2:10) May they will not repay evil for evil but will
seek to live at peace with everyone. (Romans 12:17-18) May
they not take revenge, but leave that completely with God.
(Romans 12:17-21)

Enable them to rejoice,

even in suffering. (1 Peter 4:12-13) May they forgive those who
persecute them. (Luke 23:34; Colossians 3:13) Have them love their
enemies. (Matthew 5:43-44) May they bless those who have
persecuted them. (Romans 12:14, 21; 1 Peter 3:9) Have them
persevere under tribulation. (Hebrews 10:32-39) Enable them to
proclaim the Gospel even while suffering. (2 Timothy 4:16-18)
Keep their eyes on Jesus to persevere, and not grow weary
or lose heart. (Hebrews 12:1- 3) May they rely on the
Lord's strength and not on their own.
(2 Corinthians 1:8-9) adapted from Sim.org

Thank You Lord for the persecuted believers who
have remained faithful witnesses for Christ. We pray
for their spouses, children, and families. Lord, make
the provision of Bibles and other Christian literature
and rise up new leaders among the **persecuted**
church. May the churches in communist lands be
strong in the face of government oppression. May
the churches in Latin America act with wisdom
amid all the social, religious, and political changes.

May converts boldly share
their faith without fear of repercussions. May Islamic
world laws forbidding evangelism, apostasy and
"blasphemy" be eradicated. Lord, we pray for
churches n the former Soviet Union, that new political
and legal freedoms will persevere and believers
will remain steadfast encountering
discrimination and harassment.

Dave Davidson

Heavenly Father, I lift up before You all of our
persecuted brothers and sisters around the world.
Watch over them and protect them. Let Your favor
surround them as a shield. Help them to stand strong
in their faith, unwavering in the face of danger. May
You be their source of encouragement and strength.
I thank You for their strong example in the
front lines of spiritual warfare.
You will make a way for them where it looks like
there is no way. Use them mightily to reach many lost
souls in areas unreached with the Gospel. Send your
Holy Spirit before them, to draw the hearts of men
and women to You for salvation. Lift the darkness of
deception from the eyes of their persecutors, and help
them to truly see the love of the Lord Jesus Christ
through the very ones they're persecuting.

Help them to see You, Lord Jesus, as the only way to
salvation. Lord, bless those who are persecuted and
do not ask for deliverance from their situations, but
deliverance for their persecutors. I pray that You
would continually flood their hearts and minds with
Your love, courage, faith and boldness as they
walk by faith and **not by sight.**

Lynn Hitchcock - Gospel Revival Ministries

Personal Evangelism

*Let your conversation be always full of grace, seasoned with salt,
so that you may know how to answer everyone.*
Colossians 4:6

Lord, You have given everyone one of us the gifts,
strength, power and faith to be a shining witness for
Your kingdom. Make us realize our role in the body
of Christ with our unique experience, zeal,
personality and opportunity. Let us not be influenced
by devilish lies of lacking boldness, wisdom,
compassion, discernment and

spiritual confidence.

Instead, may we
confidently share your
gospel message through
social media, websites,
smart phone apps,
prayers, testimonies,
tracts, songs, sermons,
gifts, visits, calls, emails
and letters.
Convince us to participate
in the crusade of investing
our time and talents
towards reflecting Your
eternal love. Encourage us
Lord, and ignite our faith to depend on Your
strength in Your battle.

Dave Davidson

Please never allow me to fall into the trap of calling

myself a Christ-follower if Your passion doesn't reside in me. Give me a passion for those who are seeking You. Let the flame of evangelism burn red-hot within me. Jesus, I ask You to give me as many opportunities as possible to share the hope I have in

You. Help me continually realize that each person I come in contact with has an eternal soul and that they will spend all of eternity with or without You. You said that you came to "seek and save that which was lost". Jesus, never allow me to get so caught up in my own life that I don't remember the lost.

May my love for You be evident, so unchurched, seeking people will sense Your love, service and grace. Keep my heart soft and always sensitive to Your leadings. Allow me to see those who are hurting and seeking You. Give me constant opportunities to share my faith and trust in You with those who are feeling hopeless and empty. Thank You for Your love and grace and reaching out to me. Thank You for the privilege I have to share my love for You. Jeff Mullen

Peru

The Lord brings death and makes alive;
he brings down to the grave and raises up.
1 Samuel 2:6

Lord we agree in pray with these Peru prayer points:
1. Leadership Culture Matthew 9:35-38, Ephesians 1:17-18
"Father, your heart is broken for the people of Earth
because many are harassed and helpless like sheep
without a shepherd. Today we petition you again as
the Lord of the Harvest to raise up workers that are
filled with a spirit of wisdom and revelation in the
knowledge of your Son. Spirit of God blow on the
eyes of the global workers that will be raised up
through MULTIPLi that the eyes of their hearts may
be enlightened towards the hope which we
have been called.

Raise up an inheritance that is filled with the same power that conquered the grave and walks as if they were from another age for another age. Thank you Father of Glory that we can trust you for a culture of Leadership that will be raised up in Peru and beyond. In Jesus name..."

2. Assistance Culture Isaiah 58, James 1:19, Luke 18:1-8 "Father, your word says that pure and undefiled religion is caring for orphans and widows and keeping ourselves unpolluted from the world's culture. It is at the core of your heart and mission to raise up cultures of assistance through your emboldened bride. Thank you that you are the God who blesses the hungry and gives them the kingdom. Thank you that you are the God who prepares places for the homeless refugee. Thank you that you clothe the naked sinner with your own flesh and blood through the cross of Christ.

Thank you, sweet Spirit, that you bring justice speedily to your elect who cry out for you day and night. Father, we ask that You would raise up a culture of assistance in keeping with your character through MULTIPLi. This is who you are, and this is what you did and do. Jesus, re-create a church planting movement empowered by your example that acts as your hands and feet among the hurting and hopeless. Great Helper of mankind, raise up a culture of helpers who bear your image.

3. Marketplace Culture Genesis 1:28, Matthew 25 "Father, much of your Son's work was done in the public domains. Many of your parables used economic terms to teach us about the Kingdom of Heaven. From talents to treasure in a field, you know that places of monetary exchange were kingdomwbattlegrounds.

Your word teaches where our treasure is
there our heart will be found also. Therefore
we ask for a marketplace culture to emerge.
We are praying their treasures and their talents
would be submitted under the allegiance of the living
God. We ask you for great influence in the public
spheres of society, so that your kingdom can fulfill its
mission of transforming cities and nations from the
inside out. Father, the original mandate you gave
mankind was to take the seed currency you gave us
and to become fruitful, multiply and fill the earth.
Cause those involved with the marketplace to grasp
Your heart for the seed of influence you have placed
in their lives. Cause them to come to the knowledge
of who they are and what they carry in the Kingdom
of Heaven. Thank you Father, raise up men (and
women) and money through the marketplaces of Peru
and beyond that will cry our for the coming of
a Kingdom and a King who is worthy.

4. Prayer Culture Isaiah 56:7, 1 Timothy 2:1-2, 2 Chronicles 7:14, Hebrews 11:6 "Father, you called what you are building through Jesus a "house of prayer" for all nations. We ask you boldly to raise up a culture of prayer in Peru and beyond. Raise up houses of prayer that are both attractional and missional for your name's sake. Father, cause each and every church that is planted through MULTIPLi to be a host of your presence that the nations may know that you exist and that you are a rewarder of those who diligently seek you. Father, make it a matter of first importance that a culture of prayer is raised around kings and all who are in high positions of leadership.

Draw people to a place of humility and seeking your face as a response to the great commandment to love you with all our hearts. Father, cause all involved in the MULTIPLi story to believe deeply that if we will humble ourselves, pray, seek your face and turn from our wicked ways that you will hear from heaven, forgive our sin and heal our land. Make this a reality. Thank you Father. In Jesus Name we ask you for these dreams, Amen.

Josh Foliart

Philippines

Blessed is the nation whose God is the Lord; and the people whom He has chosen for His own inheritance.
Psalm 33:12

Dearest Lord, We praise and thank You for calling us to be Your people. We thank You for the times of triumph despite the ongoing challenges we face as a nation, knowing You have been with us always. Have mercy for our failures Lord and make us into a people who will not forget You. Give us the grace to grow in love, service and obedience to Your laws. We pray for our nation - strengthen and defend us in our daily battles. Help us to fight for our country by being good citizens and being part of the solution. Keep safe our families and the Godly values we hold dear.

We pray for our people - that we may grow united in love and appreciation for who we are as Filipinos. May we extend a hand to each other in selfless giving even when we feel we are the ones in need. Teach us to choose our leaders well. We pray for our leaders - give them Your heart and wisdom to govern humbly and justly. Make them worthy examples of righteousness for the youth to emulate. We claim Your victory in Our land Lord!
Papemelroti

Pioneer Ministries

In bringing many sons to glory, it was fitting that God, for whom and through whom everything exists, should make the author of their salvation perfect through suffering.
Hebrews 2:10

Lord, You were a pioneer! Thank you for creating other pioneers in Your image. May those who are not using this gift for Your kingdom, be restless until they obey, and may those who have stepped out to follow you, be strengthened in task.

Anoint every farmer,

teacher, computer specialist, and entrepreneur with a consistent heart for their true calling. Give them wisdom and courage to wait for your implementation timing. Keep their ministries biblical, honoring You before any other culture or value. Guard them from personal temptations that crouch close by in places with little fellowship. Instead, keep them hungry for Your word, faithful in prayer, and consistent in their accountability with their sending churches. In the name of Jesus, our pioneer, Amen.

Caryn M. Pederson – Pioneers

Poland

Very truly I tell you, you will weep and mourn while the world rejoices. You will grieve, but your grief will turn to joy.
John 16:20

Dear God, The souls of Poland's leaders have now returned to you. We offer our deepest prayers for their safekeeping and our heartfelt gratitude to them for the noble ways in which they served their country and humanity.

We all know that life includes death and that tragedies may be serving purposes beyond our knowing. And yet we still ask for your grace to pour onto the hearts of Polish people everywhere to ease them in this time of loss, confusion, and devastation. It is a bitter thing to lose so many cherished leaders in a single moment. We are with the Polish people in this grief over their fallen comrades and we ask you to bless them with healing.

May Poles be able to grieve the loss so completely that their tears cleanse even more ancient wounds born of centuries of warfare. And may the rest of us honor the memory of these leaders by ourselves striving to open our hearts and more fully embrace the Polish people, to understand both their history and their unique gifts.

I cannot help but feel that this was a heroic choice of these souls at a higher level, that they chose the time and place of their deaths in order to mend an ancient wound between two nations. And still deeper, to dissolve a pattern that has kept humanity at odds with itself for far too long.

They sacrificed themselves, I sense, to help heal the wounds of war, which fester in humanity after millennia of invasions, militarism and fear. These leaders went to Russia to memorialize a long-past massacre and in offering their deaths, their souls are giving us all a chance to heal the lingering rifts between nations and between hearts.

Poland has taken more than its share of blows in the long story of humankind's brutality. And as I pray for her to heal from this current tragedy, I also sense that there is a spiritual gift in it, that in some mysterious way it is helping to propel Poland to a destiny as a teacher and leader among nations, showing us all how to cleanse the traumas of the past and create something of beauty from them.

Holy Father, let us honor this sad moment by redoubling our commitment to be people of peace, to be healers of ancient rifts, and to be menders of broken relationships. Let us come together in this moment as one world, offering solidarity of heart and soul with the Polish people.

I pray that we each have the courage to reach out with solace and support to our Polish friends. And in that reaching out, that we help turn the tears into a triumph of the human spirit, transcending the past to forge a more peaceful future. Stephen Dinan

Poor & Oppressed

...the good news is preached to the poor.
Luke 7:23

Lord, the needs of the poor are to be provided through our generosity as the Bible says we will always have poor among us. Lord, some are poor people as innocent victims; others from wrong choices, yet we are not to harden our hearts (Deut. 15:7,11; I John 3:17), make excuses, or send them away empty-handed (James 2:26). Lord You did not tell us to give only to the deserving poor, but to give as an act of mercy undeserved. adapted from Loren Cunningham

And now that we have Your ear we would pray for this poor world in which we live. We are often horrified by it. O, Lord, we could wish that we did

not know anything about it for our own comfort. We have said, "Oh, for a house in some vast wilderness!"

We hear of oppression and robbery and murder, and men seem let loose against each other. Lord, have mercy on this great and wicked city. What is to be done with these millions? What can we do? At least help every child of Yours to do his utmost. May none of us contribute to the evil directly or indirectly, but may we contribute to the Good that is in it.

Charles Haddon Spurgeon

Portugal

*So the churches were strengthened in the faith
and grew daily in numbers.*
Acts 16:5

So what is Your next move here Holy Spirit?
Bound by a single language, Lord the Portuguese
people have retained their national unity and ethnic
identity for thousands of years. As a predominantly
Catholic country, Portugal is even further unified by
the culturally embedded traditions and practices of
the church. So we pray for traditional religion to be
replaced with genuine faith for those in the Roman
Catholic Church. We pray for believers to catch a
missions vision and seize evangelistic opportunities
in the greater Portuguese-speaking world.

We pray for the Portuguese Evangelical Alliance's
initiative to plant a church in every one of Portugal's
316 counties be successful, fruitful and effective for
the kingdom. adapted from Prayercast.com

Praise

I will praise you, O Lord, with all my heart;
I will tell of all your wonders.
Psalm 9:2

Lord, may our worship of You be reflected every bit
as much in our lifestyles as it is in our words and
songs. May our obedience to You be reflected in how
we seek first Your glorious Kingdom. I pray for that
this kingdom obedience would find it's fullest
expression in being involved in Your mission -
Genesis to Revelation that is seeking to reconcile this
world to Yourself through Your Son Jesus Christ.
Lord, spare us from the hypocrisy of saying that we
worship you, if that worship of You does not find it's
fullest expression in a gratitude motivated obedience
that speaks, sings, and acts in a manner that pursues
Your Great Commission and expands Your Kingdom.
We worship You because You are worthy. May the
fruit of our lips and the message of our lives clearly
and unashamedly "tell of" Who You Are, and what
You have done. Lord, You say that You inhabit the
praises of Your people; and we know that
you inhabit our hearts through Your Holy Spirit.

Teach us to revel in Your presence. **Enable** us to celebrate Your goodness. **Empower** us to tell of Your purposes. **Envision** us to long for that blessed day when people from every nation, tribe and tongue will be found praising and lifting You up forever and ever.

Bill Drake

Have a heart of celebration when giving thanks to God.

Dave Davidson PrayAlong.com

Pray Along

*They went to a place called Gethsemane,
and Jesus said to his disciples, "Sit here while I pray."*
Mark 14:32

Lord we take a moment to ask You to improve and upgrade the prayer habits in our personal lives. Bolster our prayer motivation more than mundane obligation and inspire us in intercession beyond entertainment's grip of wasting time. Use the dynamic of agreeing in the prayers of others have thought through to supplement supplications, empower petitions, and draw nearer in devotion with you.

Faithful God bless any ministry that equips people with prayers to "Pray Along" to. Bless the Pray Along book series to help ramp up world mission ministries around the world. Leverage podcasts, publishing, periodicals and social media posts with ready to go Pray Along prayers.

Dave Davidson

PrayAlong.com

Prayer Bucket List

The LORD responded: "Write down this message!
Record it legibly on tablets, so the one who announces
it may read it easily. **Habakkuk 2:2** NET Bible

_____

_____

_____

_____

_____

_____

_____

_____

_____

_____

_____

_____

_____

_____

_____

_____

_____

_____

_____

_____

_____

_____

_____

_____

_____

_____

_____

_____

_____

_____

_____

_____

_____

_____

Write out a prayer list of worthy topics not found in this book.

Prayer in Church

*...for my house will be called a **House Of Prayer For All Nations**.*
Isaiah 56:7

Father, forgive us who go to a church that does not make time to

pray for the nations

of this world during church service times. When we do pray Lord, it is usually about our own needs, which You also call us to do. Lord, make our churches

Houses Of Prayer For All Nations.

May pastors, leaders, elders, members and even visitors carry the torch in initiating a simple system of remembering to pray for world mission prayer concerns while the church meets together. Lord, we fear that if we don't pray for nations in our churches, how then will we be discipled and led to a personal prayer

ministry for the nations of the world.

Make us an army aware of the power of prayer, especially how it can affect the world and God's great commission in our very own local churches. Dave Davidson

Prayer Ministries

*What is the conclusion then? I will pray with the spirit,
and I will also pray with understanding...*
1 Corinthians 14:15a

Jesus set the perfect example of obedience in prayer.
Although His day was filled from morning to night with
many pressures and responsibilities - addressing crowds,
healing the sick, granting private interviews, traveling, and
training His disciples - He made prayer a top priority.
If Jesus was so dependent upon this fellowship in prayer
alone with His Father, how much more you and
I should spend time alone with God.

The lives of the disciples and other Christians who have
been mightily used of God through the centuries to reach
their world for Christ all testify to the necessity of prayer...
As Samuel Chadwick said, "Satan laughs at our toiling,
mocks at our wisdom, but trembles when he sees the
weakest saint on his knees." Prayer is God's appointed
way of doing God's work. Bill Bright In the matter of
effective praying, never have so many left so much
to so few. Brethren, let us pray. Leonard Ravenhill

Pray with all your heart: "Father, grant me the
Spirit of wisdom, that I may experience this
power in my life." Pray for God's Spirit to
enlighten your eyes. Believe in the divine
power working within you. Pray that the
Holy Spirit may reveal it to you, and
appropriate the promise that God will
manifest His power in your heart,
supplying all your needs. Andrew Murray

Prayerless people cut themselves off

from God's prevailing power, and the frequent result is the familiar feeling of being overwhelmed, overrun, beaten down, pushed around, defeated. Surprising numbers of people are willing to settle for lives like that. Don't be one of them. Nobody has to live like that. Prayer is the key to unlocking God's prevailing power in your life. Bill Hybels

Let us stop complaining that we don't have enough people, enough money, enough tools. That simply is not true. There is no shortage of anything we need – except of vision and prayer and will. Prayer is the one resource immediately available to us all. If more Christians were on their knees praying, more Christians would be on their feet evangelizing.
W. Stanley Mooneyham

And when I see professed believers in the clutches of this age. Claiming truth and inspiration, when so little has really changed.

Where are the true disciples,

who have denied themselves? Taken up the cross and followed to live for nothing else? And they read and they pray, but they go their own way. Can't they see, they're in such hypocrisy? But

when I take a look inside me,

I begin to understand for I share the same condition, for I too am a fallen man. I want to stand up for the gospel, yet I've bowed my head in shame. How can I claim to want the heart of God, and yet not share His pain? Lord I've tried, and I've cried, watched my holiness run dry. Can you use me to bring glory to your name? There's an answer, on my knees.
Bill Drake from the song "There's An Answer" Bill Drake.com

Prisoners & Injustice

*Remember those in prison, as if you were their
fellow prisoners, and those who are mistreated us
if you yourselves were suffering.*
Hebrews 13:3

Lord, we refer to Acts 12:4 "So Peter was kept in prison, but the
church was earnestly praying to God for him." Like the church
inActs we intercede now for prisoners. Be near them. Encourage
those falsely accused. Give strength, grace, mercy, forgiveness
and perseverance to those in who suffer in bondage.

Lord God, You and only You are the Just Judge and Kind King!

Father, in situations of injustice grant those involved a touch
from Your Holy Spirit to bring a healing grace and peace to hurt
hearts. Lord, we thank You that You will be near to prisoners
and take care of injustice. Impart Your comfort and serenity.
Dave Davidson

Prison Ministry

Therefore I, the prisoner of the Lord, implore you to walk in a manner worthy of the calling with which you have been called.
Ephesians 4:1

Loving heavenly Father, we pray for the many Christians who are being held in prisons, both at home and abroad, simply because they trust in the Lord Jesus as Savior - many of whom have been falsely accused of crimes or deliberately set up to fall foul of the law- simply because they are believers in Your name.

Lord we pray that You would be with each one in their imprisonment. Break any bonds of fear and bitterness - and may the love of Jesus be shown forth in their actions and attitudes, so that those with whom they have to do, recognize that there is something very special about them, and the God Whom they serve. Set each one free we pray not only from their physical incarceration but also from their spiritual prison - Help them to rest in the Lord Jesus, knowing that in a small part they are participating in the fellowship of His suffering. Use each one as a witness of Jesus Christ and may many be drawn into the kingdom of God, simply because of their gracious love they display in their time of great difficulty.

Heavenly Father, we lift up the many people that have devoted their lives to ministering to men and women in our prisons and pray that you would use their life and witness to draw many into a saving relationship and faith in Jesus Christ. Lord we know only too well the path that has led each prisoner to be convicted of their crime and confined to a prison cell – but we pray that in Your grace and mercy You would reach out to all such men and women and send laborers into this harvest field to share the good news of the gospel of Christ.

Prepare each heart to receive the message of Salvation with joy and hope and may many prisoners be brought into a saving faith in Jesus Christ our Lord. Thank You Father that there is no crime so great that You cannot forgive and no sin too big that it is beyond the power of the blood of Christ to cleanse completely.

Where there is a feeling of hopelessness in the heart of any prisoner or a doubt that God could ever forgive their particular crime – we pray that You would convict them of their need to turn to Christ for forgiveness - and to believe on His redemptive work on the cross - knowing that He is willing and able not only to forgive all their sins, but to clothe each one in His own garment of righteousness – simply by believing in Jesus Christ as Savior. in Jesus name we pray. Knowing Jesus

Redeeming Lord may prison ministries experience revival to rival when Paul and Silas were freed from prison. Dave Davidson

Purity

*Flee the evil desires of youth and pursue righteousness,
faith, love and peace, along with those who call
on the Lord out of a pure heart.*
2 Timothy 2:22

Father, we thank you that your word is very clear on this
issue and we want to be in obedience to what Paul said.
We want to flee youthful lust which war against the soul,
whether it comes through a magazine or a picture or
whether it comes alive or whether it's fantasy. Whether
we are just lying on bed and manufacturer thoughts over
movies, we want to be men and women of purity. We
want crucified minds. We want disciplined and dedicated
bodies. We thank you more than anything else that when
we fail in this area that you love us and you accept us and
cleanse us and you renew us. Deliver us Lord from any
kind of false perfectionism on one hand or lasciviousness.
On the other hand, that we may find a balance of
discipline, holiness in our lives. Lord that we would know
what it is to worship you in spirit and in truth and live in
purity and honesty, reality and integrity all the days
of our life. In Jesus' name, Amen. George Verwer

Qatar

*"I see him, but not now; I behold him, but not near.
A star will come out of Jacob; a scepter will rise out of Israel."*
Numbers 24:17

We pray for the people of Qatar to see you Lord,
Jesus, King of Kings and Lord of Lords.

PrayForQatar.com

Race of Faith

I have fought the good fight,
I have finished the race, I have kept the faith.
2 Timothy 4:7

Oh God, we want to continue in prayer.
We believe that you are creating an atmosphere of reality
in which we can pray in a realistic way and exercise great
faith. Whether it's to release finance or to release spiritual
energy. Whether it's the penetrate Turkey or whether it's to
reach into the back streets of Birmingham. Whether it's the
resolve in somebody's personal difficult crisis that
they're facing in their own life right now.

So we come to you running the race of Hebrews 12,
exercising the faith that Hebrews 11, yet with balance.
Acknowledging our human factor, our own limitations
and our fears, our unbelief. Knowing that great faith is not
created in the absence of doubt or unbelief, but it's created
as we battle faith daily on your promises, praying,
persevering, refusing discouragement, refusing to feed.

So we asked you to meet us now as we worship,
pray together in Jesus' name, Amen.
George Verwer

Race Reconciliation

I have seen the burden God has laid on the human race.
Ecclesiastes 3:10

Lord Jesus, perform the same healing that you did between Jews and Gentiles in the first century with all races and peoples today. We look forward to the time in heaven when every nation, tribe, people and language will worship and glorify You together before Your throne in heaven! Lord, reconcile denominations, ministers, prophets, evangelists, teachers, genders and generations separated by age differences. Lord, show compassion and forgiveness to Ireland and throughout Eastern Europe. Humble the hearts of those suffering in Sudan. Transform prejudices and heal America's discriminations. Bring Your hope to those fighting in the former Soviet Union, Iraq, Afghanistan and in racial and religious clashes the world over. Dave Davidson

Ramadan

*And this is eternal life, that they know you, the only true God,
and Jesus Christ whom you have sent.*
John 17:3

Father, we pray that as they set their hearts to
worship their god Allah, that You might make them
to "know You, the only true God, and Jesus Christ
whom You have sent" (John 17:3). Help them see that
Jesus is Your eternal Son through whom
they can have eternal life.

Father, we pray that as their bodies hunger and their
tongues thirst, that You would show them Jesus who
promised "I am the bread of life; he who comes to Me
will not hunger, and he who believes in Me will never
thirst" (John 6:35). Help them see the insufficiency of
their works and lead them to hunger and thirst
for the righteousness that only Jesus can give.

Father, we pray that as they practice self-restraint that
You would show them Jesus who, before He was
crucified for sinners, denied Himself and "prayed,
'My Father, if it is possible, may this cup be taken
from Me. Yet not as I will, but as You will'" (Matthew
26:39). Help them believe that He truly died on the
cross and drank fully from the cup of Your wrath.

Father, we pray that as they give alms to the poor that
You would show them Jesus who "though He was
rich, yet for your sake He became poor, so that you
through His poverty might become rich" (2 Corinthians
8:9). Help them see and treasure the eternal
glory of Your Son Jesus.

Father, we pray that as they gather together to feast in the evening, that You would show them Jesus who invites sinners of all sorts to abandon their false gods and by faith join "those who are invited to the marriage supper of the Lamb" (Revelation 16:9). Show them the resurrected and ascended King of Glory who desires them to draw near to Him.

Father, we pray that you would give Your church love for Muslims across the world. Make us like Jesus who "felt compassion for them because they were like sheep without a shepherd" (Mark 6:34). Guard us from self-righteousness that would lead us to having hard hearts toward those who do not know You.

Father, we pray that you would give Your church opportunity and courage to proclaim the Gospel to Muslims throughout the world. Lift our eyes to Jesus who promised to empower us when He said "I am with you always even to the end of the age" (Matthew 28:20). Let us not fear any consequence of faithfully taking the Gospel to those who desperately need Your grace. Garett Kell

Refugees

...do not betray the refugees.
Isaiah 16:3

Gracious God and Father to the fatherless, helper to the helpless, hope to the hopeless, source of refuge to those who have lost their homes, escaped homelands and suffered oppression,

We confess our failure

to show compassion to those who have fled their countries and lack food, water, shelter, medical care, jobs and education for their children. Forgive us for not even inviting those living nearby into our homes for a meal and to share truth from Your Word.

Thank you, Lord Jesus, that you understand the trauma of refugees since you had to flee your homeland as a child. Thank you for being a sure refuge to all who call out to you in times of trouble. Meet both the physical and spiritual needs of the millions of refugees. Lead to repentance those who have caused their suffering, and have mercy on their innocent victims.

Gordon Magney - serving Afghan refugees with OM for 4 decades

O Lord help half of world's 21.5 million refugees who are children.

Revival & Repentance

My ears had heard of you but now my eyes have seen you.
Therefore I despise myself and repent in dust and ashes.
Job 42:5-6

Dear Jesus, I pray that You would place within
all Christians, a hunger and thirst for you. I pray
that you would indeed place a burning passion
in their heart for You. Set their hearts on FIRE with
the desire to reach the lost. Give them such a sight for
the value of precious souls that they would say: "Woe
to me if I do not preach the gospel". Do not let our
love and passion for You to die. We are crying out
Lord for you to light the FIRE again. I pray that you
would make us so desperate for You that we are
constantly crying out to You to come near to us.
Give us a vision Lord and never let it die. Jenny Voon

Romania

This, then, is how you should pray:
Matthew 6:9

Tatăl nostru Care eşti în ceruri,
Our Father who art in heaven,

Sfinţească-se numele Tău.
Hallowed be Thy name.

Vie împărăţia Ta,
Thy kingdom come,

Fie voia Ta, precum în cer aşa şi pe Pământ.
Thy will be done, on earth as in heaven.

Pâinea noastră cea de toate zilele,
Give us this day our daily bread,

Dă-ne-o nouă astăzi – şi ne iartă nouă greşalele
noastre
And forgive our trespasses

Precum şi noi iertăm greşiţilor noştri.
As we forgive those who trespass against us.

și nu ne duce pe noi în ispită,
and lead us not into temptation,

Ci ne izbăveşte de cel rău.
But deliver us from evil.

[Că a Ta este împărăţia şi puterea şi mărirea, acum şi pururea şi în vecii vecilor.]
[For Thine is the kingdom and the power and the glory forever.]

Amin Amen
The Lord's Prayer in Romanian

Russia

Be merciful to those who doubt;
Jude 1:22

Our Father All-Merciful!
Don't abandon your own long-suffering Russia
In her present daze,
In her woundedness,
Impoverishment,
And confusion of spirit.
Lord Omnipotent!
Don't let, don't let her be cut short,
To no longer be.
So many forthright hearts
And so many talents
You have lodged among Russians.
Do not let them perish or sink into darkness
Without having served in Your name.
Out of the depths of Calamity
Save your disordered people.

Alexandr Solzhenitsyn (translated by Ignat Solzhenitsyn)

_____
_____
_____
_____
_____
_____
_____
_____
_____

Rwanda

They slay the widow and the foreigner;
they murder the fatherless.
Psalm 94:6

Father we sometimes don't understand how an 80%
Christian nation can allow atrocities to take place like
they did in the civil war in the 1990's. Therefore we
pray, Lord, that you will cement in the people's hearts
an authentic Christian foundation which
they will start to live out.

Father we pray that You will raise up spiritual leaders
in Rwanda and that You will help those who have
fled the country during the violence, to return.

Since less than 10% of pastors have received formal
training, Lord, we pray that leaders will be trained
and established to be witnesses of Your love and
redemptive plan. We pray for the mission agencies
that are working with the people of Rwanda, that
You will bless the work which they are doing.
Lord we also pray for forgiveness in the country
between the Hutus and Tutsis.

We pray for those who are still suffering trauma and sorrow, Lord, that You will meet them in their desperation and bring them the comfort they need. We pray for the process of healing and reconciliation to continue, especially in the young generation.

And we ask you to establish unity in the Rwandan Church and effectiveness of her effort in the healing and reconciliation process. In the name of Jesus Christ we pray. Amen. prayer.africa/rwanda

_____
_____
_____
_____
_____
_____
_____
_____
_____
_____
_____

Saint Kitts & Nevis, Saint Lucia, Saint Vincent and the Grenadines

Religion that God our Father accepts as pure and faultless is this: to look after orphans and widows in their distress and to keep oneself from being polluted by the world.
James 1:27

With breathtaking Caribbean beaches, lush rainforests, and majestic mountains, these island host magnificent landscape as idyllic destinations. So, we pray for those exhibiting a semblance of religion to gain true faith in Christ.

We pray for great missionary fervor in ministering to the throngs of tourists who visit the island. We pray for the Church to model Christ-like morality and compassion to the massive group of single mothers.

adapted from Prayercast.com

Sanctity of Life

*For you created my inmost being;
you knit me together in my mother's womb.*
Psalm 139:13

Heavenly Father, You created mankind in Your own
image and You desire that not even the least among
us should perish. Now, in Your love, protect against
the wickedness of evil, those little ones to whom
You have given the gift of life. Mother Teresa

Lord, we thank you for Your miracle of life.
From the moment of conception You know each of
Your children. Protect the unborn created in Your
perfect image. Bless pregnant mothers and their
babies-to-be with good health. Lord, preserve the
sanctity of life in the world today. Help leaders make
godly decisions involving controversial medical
research in areas of cloning and embryonic stem cell
studies. Help us understand Your value of life
in the elderly and terminally ill.
Dave Davidson

Lord, You are our source of life and health. We will rejoice in Your compassion and minister the same with others.

Dr. Ronald D. Williams

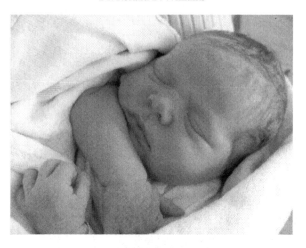

O, God, help us to not forget what we have been charged to do.

Paul O. Lonbard, Jr.

Lord God, I thank you today for the gift of my life, And for the lives of all my brothers and sisters. I know there is nothing that destroys more life than abortion, Yet I rejoice that you have conquered death by the resurrection of Your Son. I am ready to do my part in ending abortion. Today I commit myself never to be silent, never to be passive, never to be forgetful of the unborn. I commit myself to be active in the pro-life movement, and never to stop defending life until all my brothers and sisters are protected, and our nation once again becomes a nation with liberty and justice. Not just for some, but for all. Through Christ our Lord. Amen! Priests For Life

São Tomé and Príncipe

"It is not the healthy who need a doctor, but the sick."
Luke 5:31

Lord help us envision the smallest African country
by 386 square miles area of two major islands 87 miles
apart named São Tomé and Príncipe, with 194,000
people. Lord we pray for São Tomé and Príncipe's
evangelical churches and for the growth of the
nation's economy so that healthcare and
education may be improved.

We are thankful Operation World ranks this country
13th among nations with the fastest evangelical
growth rate of 6.5% annually. Thanks God over
87% of the population is nominally Christian, though
4.3% is evangelical. Meanwhile we ask You to
supernaturally address how 54% of the population
is below the poverty line. Of course, Lord the way
You designed family must flourish since Christian
marriage is primarily regarded reserved for the elite.
Unfortunately, adults usually have multiple partners.
Men typically support children in multiple
households. Dave Davidson

Satanic Conspiracies

*Hide me from the conspiracy of the wicked,
from the plots of evildoers.*
Psalm 64:2

I loose confusion against every satanic and
demonic conspiracy against my life. Let the
secret counsel of the wicked be turned into
foolishness. Let those gathered against me be
scattered. Send out Your lightning, O Lord, and
scatter the enemy. Destroy, O Lord, and divide their
tongues (Psalm 55:9). No weapon formed against me shall
prosper. The gates and plans of hell shall not prevail
against me. I overcome every strategy of hell against
my life. Every strategy of hell is exposed and brought
to light. I receive the plans of God for my life,
thoughts of peace and not evil to bring me to
an expected end. I am delivered from every
satanic trap and plot against my life.

I release the whirlwind to scatter
those who would conspire against me.
Let those who devise my hurt be
turned back and brought to confusion.
Let the nets they have hid catch themselves,
and into that very destruction let them fall.
I bind and rebuke every spirit of Sanballat
and Tobiah in the name of Jesus (Nehemiah 6:1-6).
Hide me from the secret counsel of the wicked
(Psalm 64:2). adapted from Prayers that Rout Demons by D'Blessing A

Saudi Arabia

The people living in darkness have seen a great light; on those living in the land of the shadow of death a light has dawned.
Matthew 4:16

We pray for the political leaders will lead
Saudi Arabia wisely towards peace and justice.

Lord we pray that as Saudi Arabia is undergoing rapid cultural adjustments changes that these new developments would bless citizens with a greater openness to the Gospel. Give Saudis who feel bitter despair the wisdom to not be lured into terrorism, but rather drawn to Christ's hope. Father reach those disillusioned with Islam to abandon Islam and embrace the grace of Christ. Appear to them in dreams and visions. Allow many Christians will come to shine their light in areas where there is no witness now. Encourage, inspire, and sustain local believers who feel alone and are persecuted.

Remove fears of fellow believers about contacting each other and increase fellowship discipleship unity.

Lord of the Harvest send and raise up believers to disciple Saudis so that they in turn will disciple other Saudi believers. Use expat churches that they would live a life fully committed to Christ and receive a vision to reach out to the locals and to intercede for them. May the Truth be presented to Saudis through personal witness breakthroughs, strategic satellite programs, and influential internet sites. Expand teaching the Bible in Arabic through Youtube, mobile apps, and websites. Decimate the ill-fated atheism on the rise throughout the Arab World.

Lord draw lost souls to Yourself who are disillusioned by anemic promise of rigid religion. Make today the time to surrender lives to Jesus for true inner change and fellowship. Miracle Maker miraculously demolish the stronghold of Islam in this nation. May Matthew 4:16 come true.

Dave Davidson

Scripture Prayers

My word...will not return to me empty, but will accomplish what I desire and achieve the purpose for which I sent it. **Isaiah 55:11**

I pray _____ will receive Jesus Christ. (John 1:12 Acts 8:15) I pray that the gospel of the kingdom will be preached in _____ as a witness to all. (Matthew 24:14) Lord, grant Your servants in _____ boldness to proclaim Your word. (Acts 4:29) Stretch out Your hand to heal _____. (Acts 4:30) I pray the light of the glorious gospel of Christ may shine on the people in _____. (2 Corinthians 4:4) Lord, pour out Your Spirit on all flesh in _____. (Acts 2:17) I pray that the eyes of people in _____ would be opened and they would turn from darkness to light. (Acts 26:18) Lord, open the eyes of the people in _____, that they may see wondrous things from Your Word. (Psalm 119:18) I pray that at the name of Jesus every knee would bow in _____, and that every tongue would confess that Jesus Christ is Lord, to God's glory. (Philippians 2:10-11) I pray that _____ will be filled with the knowledge of the Lord, as the waters cover the sea. (Isaiah 11:9; Habakkuk 2:14) Dave Davidson

Scripture Songs

Sing to him a new song; play skillfully, and shout for joy.
Psalms 33:3

Lord thanks for the privilege of your word in verbatim and paraphrased scripture songs we can

hear in ways past generations never had with smart phones, playlists, and apps.

Lord bless and sustain the grassroot ministries of these internet scripture song artists: The Runyons, Sing Through the Bible, PoetTree.com, Wayne Hooper, Jack Wilmore, Integrity's Scripture Memory Songs, Jim Swanson, Buddy Davis, Mark Altrogge, Kirk Gable, Jack Marti, Tim Ewing, Trilogy Scripture Resources, The Verses Project, Pursuing Life Ministries, Abigail Miller, BibleVersing, The Bible Study In Stereo, Hitchcock Family, Oracles of God, Scripture Songs from Alberta Canada, Hidden in my Heart Scripture Memory Bible, Messenger Project, Sing The Bible, Scripture Lady, Seeds Family Worship, New Life Bible Fellowship, Robert Evans, Sons of Korah, Ian White, Calvary Bible Church, Esther Mui, Jumpstart 3, Ben Koch, Dana Dirksen, Jim Thorpe, Tasha Lee, Greg Stultz, Steve Green, Scripture Lullabies, Fighter Verses, Covenant Life Church, Brother X, Heather Clark Band, Joel Turner, Mr. Daniel, NorthCreek Church, Sherri Youngward, Dick Williams, Scripture Lullabies, Allan Hubbard , The Rizers, The Psalm Project, Lantern Music, Bekah Shae, & Caroline Cobb.

Dave Davidson of ScriptureSong.com

Senders

The harvest is plentiful, but the workers are few.
Ask the Lord of the harvest, therefore, to send
out workers into his harvest field.
Luke 10:2

We thank You for those sent out and supported.
We enter this new millennium with hope, excitement
and faith as what You do will be in the midst of much
mystery to fully understand. Lord, encourage
the businessman, the bookseller, the praying
housewife and the microchip maker as a

partner in world missions.

Esteem them as crucial component of the battle.

Give us all more ownership

in Your great commission, Lord, wherever we are,
whoever we are and whatever we do. Raise up an
army of committed senders to serve those willing
to go. Match up these people as teammates in
a victorious partnership for your gospel
to spread worldwide. George Verwer

(Lord give us this mindset...)

It's not God's will to just stand still... By your work or prayer you can go anywhere, by making a living of going by giving.

from the song Going by Giving Dave Davidson

Open our eyes. Feed us from Your word and bless us to be Your men and women, to go where You want us to go and do what You want us to do. George Verwer

Bless, we pray You at this time, the entire church of God in every part of the earth. Prosper the work and service of Christian people, however they endeavor to spread the kingdom of Christ. Convert the heathen; enlighten those that are in any form of error. Bring the entire church back to the original form of Christianity. Make her first pure and then she shall be united. O Savior, let Your kingdom come. Oh! that You would reign and Your will be done on earth as it is in heaven.

Charles Haddon Spurgeon

Sending Churches

*On arriving there, they gathered the church together and
reported all that God had done through them and how
he had opened a door of faith to the Gentiles.*
Acts 14:27

Forgive us Lord that only five pennies out of every
$100 spent on missions goes to this desperately needy
area of the world. Challenge churches to rectify this
unbalance atrocity. Dear God help churches in
America and other countries give a larger proportion
of their tithes and offerings to enable and equip
10/40 window missionary efforts worldwide.

Instill a greater sense of ownership in ministry leaders
in the great commission and less financial allocations
on local church parking lots and fleeting
inflatable bouncy toys.

Dave Davidson

Senegal

*You have persevered and have endured hardships
for my name, and have not grown weary.*
Revelation 2:3

Father we pray for Senegal. Lord, we ask that You
will bring spiritual breakthroughs amidst the Muslim
majority, many of whom are powerful, well-
organized and increasingly aggressive. Lord Jesus,
we pray also for the few evangelical believers to
persevere while boldly living out their faith
and for Muslims to come to Christ as a result.

We pray for indigenous churches to be planted
among many unreached people groups scattered
throughout the nation. We also ask of You, Lord, that
the Church will take hold of its identity in Christ and
powerfully demonstrate its outworking to the nation.
We ask this in the mighty name of Jesus Christ.
Amen. prayer.africa/Senegal

Serbia & Montenegro

Defend the weak and the fatherless;
uphold the cause of the poor and the oppressed.
Psalm 82:3

Lord save Serbia, a place with the second-highest
rate of drug abuse among countries in the world.
With 800,000 children living at or below the poverty
line and youth employment rate at 49.5%, one of the
highest in the world. We pray for more Serbian youth
to receive and interact with the Bible so that they can
come to know God's love. We pray for peace and love
as different expressions of the church join hands to
help these youth. We pray for God to
transform communities in Serbia.

adapted from Nena Podbury

Seychelles

But now that there is no more place for me to work in these regions, and since I have been longing for many years to visit you.
Romans 15:23

We pray for solid partnerships on the Islands that will unite church leaders to reach the lost together until no place is left as Paul mentioned in Romans 15:23. We pray for our youths. There are so many bad things going on in our schools.

We pray for our country.

There is an increase of young people using drugs and pray people will respond to the Gospel of Christ. Praise God for the opportunity to share the Gospel freely. Praise God for the work we are doing as Campus Crusade for Christ in Reunion and Mayotte. We pray for our leadership teams on both islands. We pray they will be spirit-led as they seek God's will to move forward and launch movements. pray4sea.org/seychelles

Shelter

For I was hungry and you gave me something to eat,
I was thirsty and you gave me something to drink,
I was a stranger and you invited me in.
Matthew 25:35

Loving God, you made us in your image and blessed
us with wisdom, creativity, skill, compassion and
love. Give us sight to see your children in need,
ability to hear your call to serve, and willingness to
be your hands and feet. How lovely is your dwelling
place, O Lord Almighty! Even the sparrow has found
a home and the swallow a nest — a place near your
altar, O Lord. Heaven is your throne and the earth
your footstool. Empower us with your strength
and wisdom to build safe dwellings. You have called
us to share our food with the hungry and to provide
the poor wanderer with shelter — when we see the
naked, to clothe him. Give us willing hearts, Lord,
and inspire us to action. When you call upon the
Lord, spend yourselves on behalf of the hungry and
satisfy the needs of the oppressed. The Lord will
always guide you. He will satisfy your needs and
strengthen you. Grant us safety and protect us as we
build your kingdom through building homes and
communities. He has showed you what is good. And
what does the Lord require of you? To act justly and
to love mercy and to walk humbly with our God.
Transform our world and transform our hearts and
minds. Create in me a pure heart, O God, and renew
a steadfast spirit within me. Make us into one people
— your people — like-minded, having the same love,
being one in spirit and purpose. Habitat.org

Short Term Missions

*But since we belong to the day, let us be self-controlled,
putting on faith and love as a breastplate, and
the hope of salvation as a helmet.*
1 Thessalonians 5:8

Lord, thank You for calling many people to have
the experience of a short-term mission trip, whether
a few weeks or several years. Lord, we pray that these
opportunities to serve would help shape Christians
with a global perspective. Encourage them to
continue praying, giving and going. Lord Jesus,
keep these people in tune with Your priority
of missions and daily growth and holiness

before You, O holy Lord.

We pray for those who are planning a trip or an
outreach. Make provision for their financial needs
and organizational planning. Bless the fruit of their
labor. We pray that many of these people would catch
an even deeper vision and become more involved
in and more committed in long-term ministry.

Dave Davidson

Sierra Leone

Guard my life, for I am faithful to you;
save your servant who trusts in you. You are my God;
Psalm 86:2

O LORD, I beseech Thee favourably to hear the prayer of him who wishes to be Thy servant, and pardon him from presuming to address Thee from

this Sacred Place. O God,

I know my own infirmity and unworthiness, and I know Thine abundant mercies to those who wish to be guided by Thy will. Support me, O Lord, with Thy heavenly grace, and so enable me to conduct myself through this earthly life, that my actions may be consistent with the words I have uttered this day. Thou knowest that I am now about to depart from this place, and to leave the people whom it has pleased Thee to entrust to my care. Guide them O merciful God, in the paths of truth and let not a few wicked men among us draw down Thy vengeance upon this Colony.

Ingraft into their hearts a proper sense of duty, and enable them through Thy grace to conduct themselves as Christians, that they may not come to Thy house without that pleasing emotion which every grateful man must feel when paying adoration to the AUTHOR OF LIFE. But I have great reason to fear, O Lord, that many who frequent Thy Church do not approach Thy presence as becomes them, and they may partly be compared to the Scribes, Pharisees and Hypocrites. Pardon, O God, their infirmities; and as Thou knowest their weakness from the manner in which they have formerly been treated and the little opportunity they have had of knowing THY WILL and getting acquainted with the merits of THY SON, OUR SAVIOUR JESUS CHRIST, look down upon them with an eye of mercy and suffer them not to incur THY displeasure, after they have had an opportunity of being instructed in the ways of Thy commandments.

BLESS, O LORD, the inhabitants of this vast Continent, and incline their hearts towards us that they may readily listen to our advice and doctrines, and that we may conduct ourselves towards them so as to convince them of the happiness we enjoy under THY ALMIGHTY protection. Banish from this COLONY, O LORD, all heathenish superstition, and let the inhabitants know that Thou art the ONLY TRUE GOD in whom we live and move and have our being. If these people who profess Thy religion will not be assured of Thy superior power, convince them, O GOD, of Thine anger for their profession without their practice; for Thou knowest I have brought them here in hopes of making them and their families happy, both in this world and all to eternity.

But I fear they may not be governed by my advice, and that they may ruin themselves and their children forever by their perverse and ignorant behavior. I entreat Thee not to let their evil example affect the great cause in which we have embarked, but I would rather see this place in ashes and every wicked person destroyed than that the millions we have now an opportunity of bringing to the light and knowledge of Thy holy religion should, from the wickedness of a few individuals, still continue in their accustomed

darkness and barbarism.

Thou knowest that I have universally talked of Thine apparent virtue and goodness, and have praised Thy name for having permitted me to be the servant employed in so great and glorious a cause. If I have been deceived, I am sorry for it, and may Thy will be done; but I implore Thee to accept the sincerity of my intentions and my best endeavours to improve the talent committed to my care. Only pardon the infirmity of my nature, and I will trust to Thy mercy.

Should any person have a wicked thought in his heart or do anything knowingly to disturb the peace and comfort of this our Colony, let him be rooted out, O GOD, from off the face of the earth; but have mercy upon him hereafter.

Were I to utter all that my heart now indicates, no time would be sufficient for my praise and thanksgiving for all the mercies THOU has vouchsafed to show me, but as Thou art acquainted with every secret of my heart accept my thoughts for thanks. I have no words left to express my gratitude and resignation to THY WILL. I entreat Thee O GOD, if nothing I can say will convince these people of Thy power and goodness, make use of me in anyway Thou pleasest, to make an attonement for their guilt. This is an awful, and I fear too presumptuous a request; yet if it should be Thy will that I should lay down my life for the cause I have embarked in, assist me, O Lord, with Thy support, that I may resign it in such a manner as to convince these unbelieving people that Thou art GOD indeed.

May the heart of this COLONY O LORD, imbibe the spirit of meekness, gentleness and truth; and may they henceforth live in unity and godly love, following as far as the weakness of their mortal natures will admit that most excellent and faultless pattern, which Thou hast given us in Thy Son our Saviour, JESUS CHRIST, to whom with Thee and the HOLY SPIRIT, be all honour and glory, now and forever. - AMEN.

Governor Clarkson's Prayer for Sierra Leone (1787 - 1987)

Sin & Temptation

I made a covenant with my eyes not to look lustfully at a girl.
Job 31:1

Lord, protect the minds of your people from impure and evil thoughts. Thank you for Your Spirit, which shields and protects us. Take captive our thoughts through our obedience to You and give us the holy and righteous mind of Christ. Lord, thank You for providing a way of escape from temptation. We desire to have a clean and pure heart. Help us to walk in your ways and protect us from tempting and sinful situations. Dan Davidson

For many years it has been my prayer, as I pray on the offensive, "Oh, God, if there is a possibility that I may dishonor or disgrace Your name by becoming involved in a moral, financial or any other kind of scandal that you would discredit my ministry and nullify my love and witness for You, I would rather You take my life first before such a thing could happen." Bill Bright

Singapore

*And so I will show my greatness and my holiness,
and I will make myself known in the sight of many nations.
Then they will know that I am the Lord.*
Ezekiel 38:23

O Lord our God, You made all humanity and called
Abraham from all other nations to worship and to
obey you, precisely so that, through Abraham and his
family, all the nations of the earth are to be blessed.

We thank You for Abraham's descendant, our Lord
Jesus Christ, the full and final expression and
fulfilment of Your blessing to the nations of the earth.
We thank You also this day, for this particular nation
that we live in, Singapore. We thank You for your
grace, protection, and provision throughout the 50
years of Singapore's existence as an independent
nation. We thank You especially for the many who
have given of themselves to build this nation.

We Singaporean Christians confess that we have often failed to acknowledge your sovereignty over our national affairs, ascribing our growth and successes solely to our human ingenuity and efforts. We Singaporean Christians confess that we have not always fulfilled our calling and responsibilities as citizens, retreating behind the walls of our church buildings and Christian subculture.

We Singaporean Christians confess that we have sometimes identified our national interests, or the present government's interests, with Your concerns, and in so doing gagged Your voice, and forfeited our prophetic role to our nation. For these sins, we repent.

Lord, we pray that Singapore will truly grow − in the spirit of Jubilee − to be a more just and equal society, where love and righteousness can be found and celebrated, where the poor and the vulnerable are remembered and helped. We pray that Singapore will be good stewards of what You have entrusted to us − wealth, influence, and knowledge − so that in our time of plenty our nation may help other nations and other nationalities who live among us, as we were helped by friendly nations in our time of need.

We pray for Singapore's political and civic leaders to guide our country towards this. As the church in Singapore, we ask for Your Spirit to empower us to be salt and light towards these ends, exposing the idols of our age without fear, and offering the good news of Your Son Jesus Christ with our words and deeds − until Your perfect kingdom comes in its fullness. For this we pray in the Name of Your Son and our Saviour, Jesus Christ. Amen. ZionBishan.org

Slave Children

*And whoever welcomes a little child like this
in my name welcomes me.*
Matthew 18:5

Deliver hope and answered prayers

to violated young hearts. Through Your Spirit,
give them the power of forgiveness and love!

Lord, rescue the nearly 100
million sold, used and
abused children slaves and
the 10 million child
prostitutes. Bring conviction
and compassion to their
masters and set them free.
(Job 3:19) Rescue these children
and adults like them into the
light of Your saving grace,
comfort and provision.
Have mercy on those
bringing destruction on the
children of the world. Let them repent and be
transformed to godly people who minister to children
rather than defile and discourage them. God in
heaven **break my heart** for the lives of these children.
Use me in prayer for the hope of their survival and
salvation. Reveal to these children that
you are their Redeemer! Dave Davidson

Slovenia

After leaving them, he went up on a mountainside to pray.
Mark 6:46

Speckled with Alpine Mountains and bursting
with thick forests, we pray for the Republic of
Slovenia. We pray that nominal, secular believers
to be ignited with Holy Spirit fervor. We pray for
committed Christians to generously support their
churches and ministers. We pray for disillusioned,
materialistic youth to hear and own the truth
of Jesus Christ. adapted from Prayercast.com

Somalia

*"I will save you from the hands of the wicked
and deliver you from the grasp of the cruel."*
Jeremiah 15:21

Father, this morning we remember as your people
that every Somalian is created in your image.
Our hearts break for the suffering so many are
experiencing right now, including those
who have chosen to follow you.

We pray for the economic, social and physical health
of their nation. We ask you to bring order and
stability. Uphold the righteous. Destroy the wicked.
We ask with the prophet Amos that justice would
roll down like waters, and righteousness
like an ever-flowing stream.

We ask you to protect women who are mutilated,
raped, and abandoned. Have mercy on them.
Defend the innocent.

For we know you are a God of justice and we know you see, we know you are mighty to save. Provide medical care and physical health for their children and protect aid workers who are serving in Somalia.

We pray for the ministry of the gospel in their nation. Rescue Somalia from false notions of Christianity. Turn their hearts to you through practical demonstrations of Christ's love in the lives of your people. We ask you to save men who once martyred Christians for their faith just like you did the Apostle Paul. Turn persecutors into pastors, Lord, and fill the Somalian Christians with unstoppable courage even in the face of death. Make them bold and persistent in proclaiming Jesus Christ and him crucified. Cause them to fear you more than they fear man.

We ask you to build and strengthen the underground church. Deliver them from persecution, especially when they meet in groups. Provide religious freedom. Give them more opportunities to make disciples and raise up more pastors to equip them. For those who are trying to follow you in complete isolation from other Christians, we ask that you would join them to a church family.

Give Somalians who have left the country and become Christians a burden to return and spread the gospel in their native land. Raise up an army of missionaries to invade their nation. We pray that your name would be hallowed and Your will would be done in Somalia as it is even now in heaven. Give us hearts of compassion. Make us faithful to pray. We ask these things in the mighty name of Jesus.

Matthew Williams

South Africa

Let us acknowledge the Lord; let us press on to acknowledge him. As surely as the sun rises, he will appear;
Hosea 6:3

Heavenly Father, we thank You for our beautiful country and for all the wonderful people that You have created specifically for South Africa. Today we come before You and stand on Your promise of restoration. Jeremiah 30:17a (NKJV) says:

'"For I will restore health to you and heal your wounds," says the Lord' Just as You promised Israel, Lord, we believe you are promising South Africa.

We give You glory for the rains that have fallen and for the drought has been broken in most of our provinces. We continue to trust You to allow Your rain to fall in the Western Cape and any other areas of our country that needs Your healing rain.

As we see Your rain fall on and cleanse South Africa, we pray that You will wash away all that is not of Your plan for our land. We continue to pray for the leadership of our land and that the needs of the many that have nothing will always be the most important issue of the day.

We pray that as a country, we will take a firm stand against violence, crime, and corruption, and we ask that You, dear God, will restore the health of our country and heal all the wounds, both past and present. Above all, we pray that we will truly have love for one another – regardless of race, colour, or religious belief. We pray that where there is conflict, we will be able to go in and sow your seeds of love and tolerance. Thank you, Father, that you love us. Thank you that You hear our prayers. We ask this all in the almighty name of Jesus, our Lord and Saviour, Amen. Angelique Geeringh

Lord, we present our country South Africa before you. We exalt and bless your name for all the blessings, the graces, and love that you have given to us as a nation. Our country is now weighed down by various social, political and economic problems. We ask you to join us in our boat to calm the storms in our nation. May your grace challenge our nation and its leadership to repent and turn away from the sin of greed and corruption, which is a result of the worship of money (Matthew 6:24). Protect all those who are speaking out against greed, patronage, and corruption. Renew our nation and its leadership by the light of the Gospel. Bless us with the values and the graces of your kingdom. In Jesus' name, we pray. Amen. Tamar SC

South East Asia

Be strong and courageous and do the work. Do not be afraid or be discouraged, for the Lord God, my God, is with you.
1 Chronicles 28:20

Faithful Father, we pray

for continued faithfulness of Chinese believers despite many hardships. Empower Christians to continue in love and perseverance, boldly sharing Christ in their native land. We lift up the Hmong in Vietnam and tribes that are prohibited from having Bibles in their own languages. We pray that the Holy Spirit will burn in the hearts of Indonesian believers, and that they will come to know Christ. We ask that You, God, will change the heart of the Sultan of Brunei to meet the King of kings. Lord, we ask You to provide for workers to translate God's Word for the Dzongkha people of Bhutan and that Bangladesh will be flooded with Christ's love. God, we beseech You to use North Korea's famine to draw many to the Bread of Life and to send many South Koreans there to minister Your Word. We pray for effective ministry of Western Christians living in Malaysia. Lord, rise up Christian leaders in Maldives, in the war-scarred country of Sri Lanka, and share Christ's peace to open hearts of Tibetan Buddhists to Your unfailing love. Powerful God, we pray that abuses by ungodly regimes will cause many to seek Your true and sustaining grace in Afghanistan. We pray for salvation among Communist Party members in Laos and that the church will help to build bridges between different ethnic groups in Myanmar.

Dave Davidson

South Korea

A time to love and a time to hate,
a time for war and a time for peace.
Ecclesiastes 3:8

Dear God we ask for permanent peace on the
Korean Peninsula; the avoidance of military conflict;
and the emergence of conditions on the Korean
Peninsula that allow for flourishing relationships
between each individual and 1) God; 2) others; 3)
oneself; and 4) all of creation. Solve just and peaceful
resolution to current tensions, including wisdom for
our political, diplomatic and military leaders as they
work across differences toward a goal of peace,
security and freedom; wisdom among leaders from
North Korea, South Korea and China that will allow
God's people on the peninsula and in the US might
live peaceful and quiet lives in all godliness and
holiness; and for God's kingdom to come on the
Korean peninsula and His will be done there as it
is in heaven. We ask for mercy from God
over the Korean Peninsula.

Bless Lord on the efforts of citizens who seek to bridge the vast differences between our countries, including American evangelicals pursuing this work;

May the American church to demonstrate empathy toward the people of the Korean Peninsula, praying in a spirit of friendship, noting the image of God in every human being. christianchurchestogether.org

South Sudan

*"No longer will violence be heard in your land,
nor ruin or destruction within your borders,
but you will call your walls Salvation and your gates Praise."*
Isaiah 60:18

We pray for the many casualties of war in South
Sudan for those bereaved or injured by conflict
for those bereft of their homes and livelihoods
for those in need of medical treatment.
We pray for the work of Christian Aid and its
partners, for the distribution of food, fishing gear
and seeds, for soap, mosquito nets and water
for a safe space for children. We pray for the
work of your church in bringing peace
for a listening ear and understanding heart
for productive negotiations and lasting peace
for strength to walk the long road of rebuilding
and reconciliation. Amen.
ChristianAid.org.uk

Spain

It is impossible for the blood of bulls and goats to take away sins.
Hebrews 10:4

Lord, Spain needs You. Its streets flow with busy
people who are completely unaware of your grace.
From its fields come flowers and food, but those who
plant and harvest don't know of the love they can
find through your word. Spain has more brothels and
bars than any country in Europe, and leads in
consumption of cocaine and marijuana.
It desperately lacks the values, purpose and peace
that only You can provide. Don't delay, Lord…
Each day that passes more and more people are
deceived by a religion of guilt, processions and
rituals, that have nothing to do with the redemption
Jesus proclaimed. Speak to them in the cathedrals that
you are alive, and that the anguished images they
venerate are not the end of your story.

From the Cantabrian to the Mediterranean seas, and the beautiful islands, from Extremadura to Catalunya, all creation celebrates your presence. Spain is a land rich in landscapes and scenery, second in the world in Biosphere reserves. Thank you Father for providing spaces to enjoy your creativity. Lord, we cry out to you in all the languages and accents you've given Spain, that you bring peace to its minds and hearts.

Birthplace of internationally renowned poets and artist, scientist and athletes, we ask for wisdom to reach them with your message of hope. Lord, we know that Spain is known as a world class tourist destination, with its bullfights and tapas, and excellent restaurants, and hundreds of castles and palaces, but we also know that we are also known for the small number of people who live with faith in Jesus Christ. Our prayer is for a rich harvest from all the seeds faithfully planted for over a century by your workers. Let this be the time for Spain.

We ask for faith to see what has yet to be seen in Spain: a sea of changed lives who have found in Christ the purpose and light they longed for. We ask for a new chapter in the history of Spain, that your Spirit work and produce spiritual hunger in Spaniards, and that that your church can more effectively communicate that it is only in Christ that our inner thirst is truly quenched. In the name of Jesus, Amen. aprayerforspain.org

Sphere of Influence

*God did this so that men would seek him
and perhaps reach out for him and find him.*
Acts 17:27

God, You are the harvester of souls with your Holy
Spirit. Go ahead and prepare hearts with a hunger for
spiritual truth, an openness to seek it and a readiness
to receive Christ. Go in advance and convict hearts
to become a shining testimony that glorifies You.
Remind us of our confidence in Christ.

Reinforce in us our true identity of boldness found in
You! We pray for those who know us and those who
come into contact with missionaries and Christian
workers, that their witness will be effective. Let us
be mindful of how You can use our lives as spiritual
ripples that bring about godly encouragement and
inspiration to those around us.
Let us redeem the time You have given us and make
the most of our ministry contact opportunities.

Dave Davidson

Spiritual Gifts

...try to excel in gifts that build up the church.
1 Corinthians 14:13

Dear Lord, thank you for creating us as unique creatures, individuals not punched out cookie cutters. Your purposes for Your followers are as varied as our fingerprint. Thank you for planning a unique place of purposeful ministry that fits the way You have crafted us. The spiritual gifts that you have blessed us with, the ministry desires that you placed deep within us, and the unique way that you built our temperament, all point to a place of meaningful service, like a highly complex puzzle piece fitting precisely in place

by the Master's hand.

Help us understand Your divine enablements. Point us to effective service for Your kingdom's sake. Give us the courage to step out on faith and bring spiritual effectiveness beyond human understanding. Our spiritual gifts, our passions, our temperaments, we put before You to use as You will. Thank You my Savior and Leader, Amen. Steve Buchelt

Spiritual Warfare

Finally, be strong in the Lord and in his mighty power.
Ephesians 6:10

We put on the full armor of God so that we can take
our stand against the devil's schemes. For our
struggle is not against flesh and blood, but against the
rulers, against the authorities, against the powers of
this dark world and against the spiritual forces of evil
in the heavenly realms. Therefore we put on the full
armor of God, so that when the day of evil comes, we
may be able to stand our ground, and after we've
done everything, to stand. We will stand firm then,
with the belt of truth buckled around our waist, with
the breastplate of righteousness in place, and with our
feet fitted with the readiness that comes from the
gospel of peace. We take up the shield of faith, with
which we can extinguish all the flaming arrows of the
evil one. We take the helmet of salvation and the
sword of the Spirit, which is the word of God. May
we be faithful, Lord, to wear the full spiritual armor
You have given us. Thank you for the peace You give
me when I trust and follow you. Show me how
to help others find that peace.

Pray Along: Scripture Prayers based on Ephesians 6

Lord give us wisdom from this writing:

Satan: From a memo to his demons -

If Christians doubt that the lost need to hear of Jesus, their urgency for world missions will be seriously dulled. Doubting the uniqueness of Jesus as Savior is the slippery slope that will lead to glorious victory for our evil armies. If Christians believe that God will find another way to save the lost, their efforts in world missions will be reduced to a fashionable activity with no passion. Churches will send missionary candidates who are merely looking for a cross-cultural adventure. There will be little sense of sacrifice. They will only volunteer for locations with a good climate and the best MK schools. They won't go to countries where we have our greatest strongholds.

If churches doubt that unreached people groups are truly lost, they will go through the motions of missions but will spend more and more of their money on their own local programs. Prayer for missionaries will be dignified, but no one will weep for the lost. Be careful if churches realize the importance of their task and how much power they have - if Christians realize their potential to change the world - our cause will be doomed. Sim.org

Sri Lanka

My soul thirsts for God, for the living God.
When can I go and meet with God?
Psalm 42:2

Lord reload revival in Sri Lanka addressing spiritual
and moral decline in church and society. Intercede
over the state of the church and community burdens.
Thrust an urgent thirst and expectation of revival.

adapted from National House of Prayer Sri Lanka

Starvation

*People do not despise a thief if he steals
to satisfy his hunger when he is starving.*
Proverbs 6:30

Let us pray for the starving
men, women and children whose faces and stories fill
our newspapers, televisions and computer screens.

For the millions who are facing starvation,
who are ill or malnourished, and have no access to medical
care, God of love and justice, hear our prayer.

For the hundreds of thousands who have fled their homes,
traveling long distances in search of food and better
conditions, God of love and justice, hear our prayer.

For the mothers and fathers who are watching their
children die of starvation, for those who have lost all hope,
God of love and justice, hear our prayer.

Let's also pray for those who are already at work
responding to the famine. You are invited to respond with
the phrase "grant them strength and wisdom."

For local, national and international agencies
raising awareness and collecting donations,
God of love and justice, grant them strength and wisdom.

For world governments—and our government,
as they decide how best to respond to the crisis,
God of love and justice, grant them strength and wisdom.

For those on the ground, working with the hungry, the
sick, and the dying, those negotiating with local
governments, and arranging shipments of food and
other supplies, God of love and justice, grant
them strength and wisdom.

Let's also pray for ourselves, and our own response.
You are invited to respond with the phrase "open
our hearts and prompt us to action."

For those of us who have far more food than we need, and money and resources that we could share, God of love and justice, open our hearts and prompt us to action.

For those of us who can speak out against injustice and inaction, and encourage our government's quick and generous response, God of love and justice, open our hearts and prompt us to action.

For those who can find creative ways to raise funds, for those who are willing to continue praying, God of love and justice, open our hearts and

prompt us to action.

In Your mercy, Lord, open our eyes and our hearts to the plight of our starving brothers and sisters. Inspire us to greater compassion, love and generosity — the same compassion, love and generosity that You have shown toward us. We pray this in the name of Jesus Christ, who came to bring abundant life for all. Amen.

Christine Longhurst

Stewardship

Every good and perfect gift is from above, coming down from the Father of the heavenly lights, who does not change like shifting shadows.
James 1:17

Loving Father, you alone are the source of every good gift.

We praise you for all your gifts to us, and we thank you for your generosity. Everything we have, and all that we are, comes from you. Help us to be grateful and responsible. You have called us to follow your son, Jesus, without counting the cost. Send us your Holy Spirit to give us courage and wisdom to be faithful disciples. We commit ourselves to being good stewards. Help us to be grateful, accountable, generous, and willing to give back with increase. Help us to make stewardship a way of life. We make this prayer through Jesus Christ, our Lord, who lives and reigns with you and the Holy Spirit, now and forever. Amen.

rcav.org

Strongholds

The weapons we fight with are not the weapons of the world. On the contrary, they have divine power to demolish strongholds.
2 Corinthians 10:4

We pray, Father in the name of Jesus, that You would place a hedgerow of protection around Your children. We pray for peace, the peace that passes all understanding, to overtake their lives today. Let Your presence be heavy and fruitful in their lives today.

 Spirit of strife, anxiety, restlessness, fear, mental bondage, suicide, death, sickness, disease, depression, oppression, sadness, **hopelessness and doubt be bound in the name of Jesus.** Father, we seek the mind of Christ - which is ordered thought, with every thought coming into captivity and subjectivity of the Holy Spirit as Your word says in Isaiah 26:3 "You will keep in perfect peace him whose mind is steadfast, because he trust in you". Father we trust in You today for our healing and deliverance in every area of our lives today. Thank You for Your precious Spirit in out life. Make us whole today in You, Lord! It is in the Holy name of Jesus we pray. Charlie Waltman

Sudan

You, Lord, will keep the needy safe
and will protect us forever from the wicked,
Psalm 12:7

We pray for the many casualties of war in South
Sudan for those bereaved or injured by conflict
for those bereft of their homes and livelihoods
for those in need of medical treatment.

We pray for the work of Christian Aid and its
partners, for the distribution of food, fishing gear
and seeds, for soap, mosquito nets and water
for a safe space for children.

We pray for the work of your church in bringing
peace for a listening ear and understanding heart
for productive negotiations and lasting peace
for strength to walk the long road of rebuilding
and reconciliation. Amen. ChristianAid.org.uk

Suffering

*For just as the sufferings of Christ flow over into our lives,
so also through Christ our comfort overflows.*
2 Corinthians 1:5

O Lord, the suffering in the world is so widespread
and the pain is so great! Have mercy, and waken the
souls of suffering millions to the hope of some relief
and unsurpassed joy in the age to come.
Send your church, O God, with relief and with the
word of the gospel that there is forgiveness of sins
through faith in Christ and that no suffering here is
worth comparing to the glory that will be revealed to
the children of God. Protect your church, Father,
from callous thoughts about calamities that leave
millions destitute, and protect her also from cowing
to critics, like Job's wife, who cannot trust the wisdom
and power and goodness of Christ in the midst
of inexplicable misery...
John Piper

Lord, here's what I believe You're impressing me to pray for, but
whatever You want, I trust You. Not my will, but Yours be done.
Bill Bright

Suicide

Do not be afraid of those who kill the body but cannot kill the soul. Rather, be afraid of the One who can destroy both soul and body in hell.
Matthew 10:28

Lord God, be with all those who have struggled with suicidal thinking, who have lost a loved one to suicide, and those who need support. Be with them. Help them to know that they are not alone, that they are loved, and that they have places to turn when they're in need. Lord in your mercy…hear our prayer.

Dear heavenly father, I pray for my community and surrounding areas that you would wrap your loving arms around each person who struggles with thoughts of suicide or who may be survivors of suicide. Help our community to be more aware of one another's needs and to show more empathy towards others. Please help the community to make others feel welcome and loved so no one feels alone. Thank you, God, for giving me much discernment and for seeing things in people that others don't see. Thank you for putting me where you want me at any given time. It is in your name I pray. Amen.

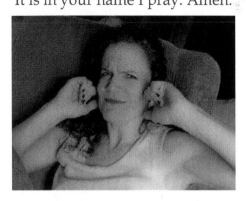

God of grace and forgiveness, strength and healing, we pray for our community, our church, and our families, because we know there are people who are hurting, hopeless, alone, and desperate. We pray for those who are considering suicide as a way to ease their pain because they don't feel that they have any other option. Help them to know your presence and love for them. Help them learn the abounding love, willingness to listen, and graceful gifts that rest in this place. That these gifts, your love, are ready to be shared so that he or she will know that they are not alone. Empower him or her to be open to that love, to seek the person who will listen, to be assured of their purpose and their place in your world, here, and in your kingdom. In the same way, Lord, we pray for those fearful for the safety of a loved one, a family member…give them the courage, grace, mercy, and humbleness to ask, "Are you okay? Have you thought about killing yourself? Guide them…

Dear Lord, I lift up all those having encounters with suicide in any way. I pray for the families and friends who have lost loved ones to suicide. I pray for those who have contemplated it and have lost their desire to live. I ask that You would coat them in Your love, hope, and grace. Encourage them and make Your love and presence known to them. Lord God, I ask that You would raise up people to be support systems to those who are hurting. Help us to be a people full of love and compassion for each other. Bring anything kept in darkness out into the light. Expose it so it can be healed, mended, and restored. Please bring total restoration. Protect us and guard us from any works of the enemy in this area of our lives.

Lord, make us to be a people and place that is life-giving and empowering. Thank You for the work that you have done, are doing, and have yet to do. Be with us in everything we say and do, and in all things help us to abide in you. In Jesus' name, Amen.

Holy and heavenly Father, we come with open hearts and minds to your feet to lay our burdens down. We thank you for your constant, unwavering, and  eternal love, the power of your grace, and the hope we find in your presence. We bring thoughts and prayers this morning for all those affected in any way by suicide. Father, wrap them in your embrace, might they feel your presence, your grace and your love. Make us an instrument of your love, Lord. Might those who are directly affected by suicide know that they are surrounded by a community of those who pray to reflect your love and light on all. We pray for strength for the journey and we pray your will be done. Amen.

Father God thank you for being the God of Life and Love. I lift up those who hear the voice of suicide and ask Father that you will send someone on that they will hear your voice of Life, Love, Hope. May they choose life and not death on this day. Thank you for the Blood of Jesus that covers them even now.
In Jesus name. Amen.
soulshopmovement.org

Suriname

Do not let the floodwaters engulf me or the depths swallow me up or the pit close its mouth over me.
Psalm 69:15

Raise up Suriname named after the Surinen tribe from the northeastern part of South America. Lord bless the 90% population of Suriname living in the coastal areas, of which more than half in the capital city of Paramaribo, which is situated on the left bank of the Suriname River. Bloom the love of Christ Jesus in the capital of Paramaribo meaning 'city of flowers'.

May faith rise higher and farther than actual rising sea waters of potential threatening floods.
Send out effective, culturally sensitive Christian witness to the Hindu population, the young people and Muslims. Increase cooperation and unity among ethnically diverse Christian congregations.

Dave Davidson

Sweden

Discretion will protect you, and understanding will guard you.
Proverbs 2:11

Send sold out servants to the Scandinavian country of forest and mountains, palaces and sea towns, in north of Europe. Train Christian apologists for educational settings. As the now state separated Lutheran Church of Sweden make sense of the Church endorsing same-sex marriage, universalism, and those questioned the divine authority of the Bible. Redirect a repentance revolution from biblical mis-teachings and denying sovereignty. Straighten out Sweden's twisted understanding of love with truth of Christ's perfect power and holiness.

Dave Davidson

_____

_____

_____

_____

Switzerland

*In his hand are the depths of the earth,
and the mountain peaks belong to him.*
Psalm 95:4

Mount upon foundations of historical peace
to cultivate spiritual passion in the church. Awaken
Switzerland from apathy. Return them to the spiritual
fervor as they were during the Protestant
Reformation. Draw the 60% religious, but distant
Swiss to Your heaven welcoming arms O Lord.
Reveal Yourself and the ultimate "higher power".
Answer their prayers and heal complacency.

Dave Davidson

Syria

*Since it was customary for the king to consult experts
in matters of law and justice, he spoke with the wise
men who understood the times.*
Esther 1:13

God of justice, God of peace, we find ourselves
at your mercy seat again; pleading for a nation
we don't really know and interceding for
a situation we don't really understand.

Some call it civil war, some deny it but we, who have
no definition for it are frightened it will have no end.
And you, who see so much more than cameras and
headlines: how much more will you allow?

Please reveal your perfect plan for Syria; deliver her
from her conflict re-establish justice and peace and
protect her people. Give us, like you, a burning fire
that will not leave our hearts until our prayers are
answered and Syria's conflict becomes history.

from The Sanctuary: Where World and Worship Meet

Taiwan

*Look unto me, and be ye saved, all the ends of the earth:
for I am God, and there is none else.*
Isaiah 45:22

Lord what shall we say of Taiwan's 24 million people,
98% of the population has never heard of Jesus
Christ? With hell on the line, may Christ may be
preached! Search out souls to be saved. Transform
lives Lord. Catapult churches. Call the preachers, tug
the teachers, and move the missionaries towards
Taiwan. Dave Davidson

Tajikistan

...persecuted, but not abandoned;
struck down, but not destroyed.
2 Corinthians 4:9

We pray for Christians who are under surveillance by authorities and are beaten and pressured to renounce their faith by their families. We pray that they will stand strong in the face of this persecution. The regime in Tajikistan puts heavy pressure on "deviating" groups, such as Christians.

We pray that this pressure would lessen and that the country would become more open to Christianity. Christians are seen as extremists for their practice of religion outside of state-sanctioned structures. We pray that this view of them would change.

adapted from opendoorua.org

Teenagers

Since my youth, O God, you have taught me,
and to this day I declare your marvelous deeds.
Psalm 71:17

Father, we pray for revival among the millions of lost
and hurting young people of the world. We pray that
these unbelieving young hearts would fall out of love
with the world and would find fulfillment only in
Jesus. Put them in contact with committed Christians
who will love them unconditionally and serve them
radically, setting a great example. For those exposed
to empty or hypocritical "religion" growing up, lead
teenagers to healthy and growing churches where
they can see what authentic Christianity is and model
their life forever. Father, we pray for the countless
young people that are living in places that have little
or no contact with the gospel, that You would
somehow lead them to Your truth and Your
followers, so they experience the way, the truth,
and the life only Jesus offers. Todd Morr

Lord may teenagers gain valuable experience serving
and leading in church matters while they are teens.
Dave Davidson

Tentmakers

Entirely on their own, they pleaded with us for the privilege of sharing in this service.
2 Corinthians 8:3,4

Lord, as the Apostle Paul was a "tent maker", we pray for those who are in some type of professional occupation in a country that is closed or apprehensive to missionaries. We also pray for any Christian, in any country that is a witness for You using their testimony to glorify You by spreading Your gospel of good news. Lord, we pray for the networking and the effectiveness in strategic execution of these ministries. We pray that these people would be encouraged that Your holy word does not return void once it is sent our in Your name.

Lord, we pray that in Your timing, boldness and clarity of Your message would be revealed to these workers and to the people they are ministering to. We pray for tentmakers to draw on the power of Your Holy Spirit to build up houses of faith through their unique skills and specialty ministry efforts.
Dave Davidson

Thailand

It is for freedom that Christ has set us free.
Galatians 5:1

Father God do Your will for the unfinished task in Thailand. We pray that the Thai people would come to know Jesus, the giver of true life and freedom since Thailand means "land of the free,". May Thai people come to know the liberty that Christ gives from sin and that truth of God is crystal clear.

A Thai proverb says, "The truth never dies, but the one who speaks the truth must die." May the Thai come to see how this was fulfilled in the death and resurrection of Jesus, who is the Truth. May the abundant life of Christ grow an eternal harvest in Thailand inspiring the 60% of Thai people make their living in agriculture.

Praise God for moving in Thailand like never before, nevertheless the Thai people are still one of the least evangelised in the world. Equip Thai Christians so they can communicate the gospel in ways that are appropriate to those they are reaching. Let's bring the breakthrough by prayer and the power of God.

Bring Thai people to know the freedom that Christ brings. God equip churches to help people to help people toward the freedom Christ has bought for them. Free up the addicts of drugs, alcohol, gambling, and sex. May God bless the Thai with righteousness. May Thai rulers will govern justly and for the benefit of the whole country and keep genuine religious freedom in Thailand continuing. Bless Thai people with contentment. God free Thai Christians from the love of money and help new Christians break sinful habits and addictions.

Let Thai who have travelled abroad in Korea, Taiwan, Singapore, Australia, the UK and the USA;

hear the gospel and bring it home.

May the blessing of the rule of the king of kings be established in Thailand as we pray for Thai leaders.

May the light of Christ enlighten the hearts of the Thai people. May they come to know the source of life and receive the abundant life that Christ offers them.

Go forth with the gospel communicated imaginatively. May TV and radio programs will bring people to Christ in areas where there are no churches. Grant effective student ministry approaches across all of Thailand's technical and vocational colleges and universities. May the grace of God come to and through the church. Dave Davidson

Thanksgiving

Do not be anxious about anything, but in everything, by prayer and petition, with thanksgiving, present your requests to God.
Philippians 4:6

Heavenly Father, I thank You that You always hear our prayers. I thank You in Jesus' name that You are going to comfort Your children today who read and understand that we absolutely can take You at Your Word as it says in Hebrews 6:12-13.

Mac Gober - Canaan Land Ministries

Thank You, Lord of Hosts,
that You still bring deliverance to Your people!

Pat Daugherty COG World Missions

Thank You, God, for letting me preach the gospel to the poor, to heal the brokenhearted, to preach deliverance to the captives, to set at liberty them that are bruised.

(Isaiah 61:1-3) Billy R. Phillips

Father, I thank You for the Holy Spirit who convicts, teaches, guides and comforts Your church today.

Ray Garner

Lord give us wisdom from this writing:
I can take my telescope and look millions and
millions of miles into space; but I can lay my telescope
aside, go into my room and shut the door, get down
on my knees in earnest prayer, and I see more of
heaven and get closer to God than I can when assisted
by all the telescopes and material agencies on earth.
Isaac Newton

May the great God of this universe
cause us all to leave impressionable footprints
in the sands of many lives. Raymond E. Pedigo

Father, thank You for Spirit-inspired intercession
that brings peace in the midst of trials, hope into
hopelessness, and faith into tragedy.
Mike Cowart

Thank you, Jesus for Your protection, faithfulness and Your powerful Holy Spirit reality in our daily lives.
George Verwer

Third World

...be alert and always keep on praying for all the saints.
Ephesians 6:18

We lift up third world nations such as Haiti, Dominican Republic, Myanmar, Ghana and New Guinea. We come against the spirit of lack, the spirit of poverty, the witchcraft, the idolatry, the sickness,  the exploitation, and the abuse in the Name of Jesus. We bind and rebuke the devourer in Jesus' Name. We lift up the poor, downtrodden, meek outcasts, homeless, forlorn and the hopeless. We speak hope of Jesus into their lives. Hand out peace, shelter and rest as well as food and water. Lord, send wise and loving Christians across their path that can share the good news of Jesus Christ with them. We thank you for Your mercy, grace and love **that stretches beyond the east and the west.** Deliver them from all bondages, from all diseases, giving them the free gift of eternal life. Lord, we pray that they hear the Good News soon Lord. Their very lives, their eternal souls are depending on it. We stand on your Word, Your promises. They will be reached, they will be touched in Jesus' Name. Jorge Parrot - Correll.org

Those Who Have
Heard The Gospel

And even if our gospel is veiled, it is veiled to those who are perishing. The god of this age has blinded the minds of unbelievers, so that they cannot see the light of the gospel of the glory of Christ, who is the image of God…
2 Corinthians 4:3-4

Dear Jesus, for whatever spiritual reason many people have not yet accepted You as their Lord and Savior. We pray specifically to uproot spiritual barriers. In Your Name Lord, and by Your authority we command the devil and his demons to release them and stop blinding them from

Your precious soul saving truth.

We claim salvation for our family members, Lord. By prayer we stand in faith and resist attacks of the devil. We know Lord, it is Your will to save them, so we pray for

Your will to be done.

Thank You Lord, that every believer has authority over demons who attempt to keep people in darkness, instead of receiving eternal life through the Lord Jesus Christ. In the Name of the Lord Jesus Christ, bind the lies of Satan over the life of _____. Jesus with Your power and victory on the cross, break the barriers and demonic strongholds over them. The deceiver can no longer blind them to the Truth. I claim them for the Kingdom of God and command you to loose them now. I claim their salvation and complete deliverance in Jesus' Name. May they now become a trusting believer in Christ today! Open their eyes that they may see clearly Your welcoming arms of redemption. We call upon you by Your authority to turn loose of the loved one we are praying for.

We must claim our loved ones and peoples around the world for Jesus Christ. Lord, bring people to their senses and let them know the truth. May they accept You, Jesus, and escape from the trap of the devil's lies.

Dave Davidson

Those Who Have Not Heard The Gospel

This is good, and pleases God our Savior, who wants all men to be saved and to come to a knowledge of the truth.
1 Timothy 2:3,4

Create a divine encounter where they will hear of Jesus' love for them. Cause them to see their true spiritual condition. Unveil their blindness that hides righteousness. (2 Corinthians 4:3,4)

Give them a distaste for sin.

Replace their lusts with a genuine desire to know God. Expose the futility of their best effort by showing them true Christianity. Let them see the trap they are in. (2 Timothy 2:25,26, Ephesians 2:2) Set them free from the Law of sin and death. (Romans 8:1; Hebrews 2:15) Confirm the freedom and confidence they can have to approach You. (Ephesians 3:12) Build desire within them to be reconciled. (2 Corinthians 5:21) Reveal to them that you are not far off. (Acts 17:27) Place them upon the mind and hearts of Christians who will pray. Prayer Tower

Timor Leste

Whoever aspires to be an overseer desires a noble task.
1 Timothy 3:1

Gracious God, we give you thanks for our partnership with the Protestant Church of Timor Leste. Through this partnership we hear the good news of your presence among the people of Timor and we see how your Spirit is at work bringing faith and hope, nurturing a spirit of service in the search for justice and peace. We pray this day for the people of East Timor. And we pray as well for the land and sea and creatures big and small. We pray for faithful pastors; many serving with very little pay and all striving to bring a word of life, grace and hope to the people. We ask that you give wisdom, guidance and trust to all of us working together to serve the people of Timor. In Jesus' name we pray. Amen.

Tom Liddle

Togo & Tonga

For such people are false apostles,
deceitful workers, masquerading as apostles of Christ.
2 Corinthians 11:13

Father God, when we pray for Togo and Tongo,
we pray for the church to be refined by rooting out
syncretism, false teaching, and idolatry. Lord, we ask
that You will unify the Togolese Church and that
barriers of mistrust and denominationalism
will be broken down.

We pray for indigenous mission agencies to establish
bases which send workers to an increasingly Muslim
population. We also pray, Father, for an end to the
evils of rampant child trafficking, prostitution,
and exploitation of the poor.

Lord, we pray against idolatry and the grip of strong
secret societies in Togo. Father, we ask that you will
shine your light into Togo and that the people will see
your glory. In the name of Jesus Christ we pray.

prayer.africa/togo

Tribal Groups

Go into all the world and preach the good news to all creation.
Mark 16:15

We are grateful many tribal language groups have had the opportunity to hear and respond to the good news of Jesus Christ. For the tribes which have a missionary witness living among them and are close to hearing and learning about the saving work of Christ, send your Holy Spirit to soften hardened hearts and open darkened eyes. Keep them from believing Satan's lies. Lord, give strength to the sick, feeble and old. Reveal your power and glory through miraculous healings so that they will have a chance to hear and respond to Your gospel truth. As village elders and leaders make important decisions, we petition You to work mightily in their hearts. Give each one an open heart and mind to recognize Your truth. May the word of God being preached and taught to these tribal groups go forth with power and conviction. Tom Drost - former New Tribes missionary

Trinidad & Tobago

The voice of the Lord is over the water the God of glory
thunders,   the Lord thunders over the mighty waters.
Psalms 29:3

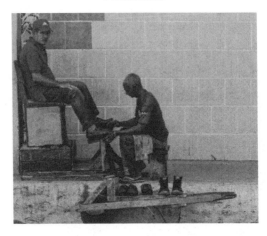

Heavenly Father we come before you today asking for your divine intervention and mercy upon our twin island T&T. Lord we know you spoke in time past with many voices and today you're still speaking the same through waters. Psalm 29:3

We ask for mercy upon Trinidad & Tobago. We ask that through this many will come to the throne room, many will receive salvation, many will repent and give their lives to you. We pray for a spiritual awaking through this in Jesus name. We pray many will see and is seeing your hand and power in Jesus name! We pray for revival and a rebuilding of righteousness and prayer in our Land! We pray hearts will surrender and will be turned back to you in Jesus name! We pray wickedness and innocent blood shed will be abolish in Jesus name!

Pray for Trinidad & Tobago

Tunisia

Seek the LORD and His strength; Seek His face continually.
Psalms 105:4

We pray for Christian youth who are rejected and persecuted for their faith. May young believers who wish to marry, as they face a great deal of opposition and pressure from non-believing family members.

Lord encourage those who are persecuted and who lose hope and lack direction. Reveal Yourself that You're always with them. We pray that the Lord will hinder the plans of Muslim extremists to create chaos in the country. Touch their hearts to bow their knees to Jesus. adapted from opendoorua.org

Turkey

*Now, Lord, consider their threats and enable
your servants to speak your word with great boldness.*
Acts 4:29

Lord have mercy Turkey is gradually enforcing
Islamic influence, and discrimination against
Christians and other religious minorities is increasing.

God enable those experiencing persecution
to fully hope and trust in Him. May converts from
a Muslim background minister graciously and wisely
to their families since often earn heavy pressure from
family, friends and community to return to Islam.

Comfort those who are labeled and treated as traitors
after embracing the Christian faith. While conversion
is not prohibited by Turkish law, it does lead
to heavy social and familial implications.

adapted from opendoorua.org

Turkmenistan

*Therefore I endure everything for the sake of the elect,
that they too may obtain the salvation that is in Christ Jesus,
with eternal glory.*
2 Timothy 2:10

Lord since Turkmenistan is considered to be one of
the most restrictive countries in the world we beseech
You Lord for increased freedoms in this lost land. We
pray for believers from a Muslim background who
are fiercely pressured to return to Islam. Give them
protection and endurance. May the security forces
who are monitoring Christians encounter the gospel.

We pray that their hearts would be softened and that
they might become advocates and protectors of
Christians in Turkmenistan.

adapted from opendoorua.org

Tuvalu

Will you not revive us again, that your people may rejoice in you?
Psalm 85:6

Bless the Polynesian island nation of Tuvalu in the
Pacific Ocean northeast of Australia, the world's
fourth smallest country. Lord reveal Your glory to the
10,00 people who live on the nine islands: Funafuti,
Nanumaga, Niutao, Niulakita, Nanumea, Nui,
Nukufetau, Nukulaelae, and Vaitupu.

We pray that corruption cease, for those suffering
from unemployment/poverty, and that the islands be
protected from flooding and environmental disasters.
May churches experience a revival and show
discernment with sound Biblical teaching.
Bind animistic/occult spirits so the Gospel
spreads all the more. Dave Davidson

Uganda

*Restore to me the joy of your salvation
and grant me a willing spirit, to sustain me.*
Psalm 51:12

Lord, we want to pray for Uganda. First of all we pray for restoration, peace and healing after years of war and conflict. We pray for the 800,000 displaced people who are forced to live in camps amid difficult conditions. We also pray for peaceful

resettlement of these people in the north of Uganda.

We pray for the dissolution of the LRA. Lord, we ask You to demonstrate Your sovereignty in this desperate situation. Father, we pray for the tens of thousands of children, fearing abduction, walking every night from their villages to the safety of larger towns. We ask, Lord, that You will preserve and protect the innocent and that You will teach them Your ways. We also pray for the reintegration of former child soldiers into their families and communities.

Lord Jesus, we pray that you will restore unity among Your church in Uganda and that you will strengthen all the NGO's and mission organizations serving the people of Uganda. We pray also pray that the Church and its leaders will be rooted in truth and unswayed by false teachings and cultural sins. We pray this in Jesus Name. Amen. prayer.africa/Uganda

Ukraine

*Jesus said to him, "Let the dead bury their own dead,
but you go and proclaim the kingdom of God."*
Luke 9:60

We pray for church leaders they would take every
opportunity to proclaim the peace that Jesus offers
and that they would not be limited in their freedoms
to preach the gospel. We pray for the new
government in Kyiv that they would have wisdom
to know how deal a failing economy and with
groups who oppose them in Eastern Ukraine.

We pray for churches, especially in Eastern Ukraine,
that they would exhibit the love of Christ be an
example of how Russians and Ukrainians can coexist!
We pray for the Ukrainian people that there would
be reconciliation and forgiveness between
pro-Russian and pro-Ukrainian groups.

We pray for families as they struggle to provide for basic needs because of a failing economy and high inflation. We pray for Ukrainian soldiers, as many have family and friends in Eastern Ukraine and Russia. Pray that there would be no bloodshed.

We pray for missionaries that God would give them wisdom to best know how to help their brothers and sisters in Christ during this critical time.

adapted from sukofamily.org/praying

United Arab Emirates

For to us a child is born, to us a son is given,
and the government will be on his shoulders.
And he will be called Wonderful Counselor, Mighty God,
Everlasting Father, Prince of Peace.
Isaiah 9:6

We pray for leaders of the UAE to have wisdom and tolerance, allowing citizens to publicly change their faith without fear of persecution. We pray that the government will be able to keep the country safe from insurgent/terrorist groups. We pray for Christian converts who are afraid to reveal their faith in Jesus. We pray for Christian women who convert from Islam and lose their rights to possessions and often, their children.

adapted from opendoorsusa.org

United Kingdom

But whoever is united with the Lord is one with him in spirit.
1 Corinthians 6:17

In the Name of the Father, the Son and the Holy Spirit Great Britain and Northern Ireland we bless you with peace, calm and order. We bless you to know the Lord is sovereign and has all things in His hands. We bless you with patience and trust in Him. We bless you to wait upon the Lord, for His ways are greater and higher than all of our ways. We bless you with shalom – wholeness, well-being and completeness. We bless the people of this nation to wake up and know that Jesus is Lord.

We bless this land with a move of God,
a turning back to Him and His purposes.

We bless the land that the Light of the Gospel will
break through, and no longer will we be in darkness.
We bless the atmosphere over the United Kingdom
of Great Britain and Northern Ireland to be changed;
for love, joy and peace in the Holy Spirit to reign.

In Jesus' name we bless the people of this great nation
to unify, and for a spirit of unity to be poured out.
We bless the people of this land to stand together and
know that the Lord, He is God. We bless the nations
of England, Scotland, Wales and Northern Ireland
to come together and to rejoice in that unity, for
repentance and forgiveness to flow between us.

We bless our Government at this time, for good
strong leadership to emerge. We bless the corridors
of power with righteousness that exalts a nation. We
bless the decisions made at Westminster to reflect the
purposes of God. We bless the Christians in
Parliament to rise up in the will of the Lord, and do
what is right in His sight We bless the law of the land
to come back to its Judeo/Christian foundation.

We bless this nation to fulfil its destiny in God, with
restoration of all that has been robbed. We bless the
call of God, and His irrevocable gifts to emerge at this
time We bless the United Kingdom to rise up once
again in the apostolic calling to take forth the Gospel
of Jesus Christ into the nations. We bless the United
Kingdom to build the Kingdom of God, not empires.

In the Name of Jesus we call back this nation into the
purposes of God, and we bless each and every citizen
of the United Kingdom to live in peace and hope.

We bless the people to love one another and to turn from their wicked ways and worship of idols, and look to the One who can restore all things according to His glorious will. We bless the people of this land with a spirit of humility, and dependence on God.

We bless the people of this nation to be safe and secure and to step into their personal destiny in God We bless this nation to stand on the shoulders of those who went before us, who gave their lives for the sake of the Gospel of Jesus Christ, and those who because of their great faith brought so many changes to this world.

Most of all we bless the Lord our God for the great heritage we have in this land, and the great high calling He placed on it, and we bless Him for His mercy and His grace and His unconditional love. In Jesus' Name AMEN worldprayer.org.uk

USA

Whoever invokes a blessing in the land will do so by
the one true God; whoever takes an oath in the land
will swear by the one true God. For the past troubles
will be forgotten and hidden from my eyes.
Isaiah 65:16

Holy God use the churches

of the United States to spread the ministry of
missions throughout the world via people and
literature. Set aflame, strengthen and bless
the foreign missionary sending churches.

George Verwer

Our Father and Our God,

We praise You for Your goodness to our nation, giving us blessings far beyond what we deserve. Yet we know all is not right… We deeply need a moral and spiritual renewal to help us meet the many problems we face. We pray today for our nation's leaders. Give them the wisdom to know what is right, and the courage to do it. You have said, "Blessed is the nation whose God is the Lord." May this be a new… as we humble ourselves and acknowledge You alone as our Savior and Lord.

Billy Graham, Prayer For National Day Of Prayer 2001

Uruguay

*How long must I see the battle standard
and hear the sound of the trumpet?*
Jeremiah 4:21

Lord we lift up in prayer the 3.3 million people
of Uruguay in southeastern South America.
Despite the highest standards of living in Latin
America, a very literate population, and a large urban
middle class we're compelled pray for the many
abandoned children to find hope and love
in their heavenly Father.

Unveil convincing demonstrations of God's power in the highly secularized society. Unmask false teachings in Afro-Brazilian spiritism. Unfold Your good and perfect will to the 48% of atheists of the population. May Uruguay lay aside their superstitious beliefs and look instead to Jesus and God's Word for spiritual answers and salvation.

Dave Davidson

Uzbekistan

They arrested the apostles and put them in the public jail.
Acts 5:18

Change the hearts of Uzbekistan's
leadership into full acceptance of Christianity.
We pray for Baptists, Evangelicals and Pentecostals
who are threatened, raided, fined and arrested.

Encourage new believers who are placed under house
arrest by their Muslim families to make them recant.
May Christian women forced to marry against their
will trust in God's provision for their lives and faith.

adapted from opendoorua.org

Vanuatu

Have nothing to do with godless myths and old wives' tales;
rather, train yourself to be godly.
1 Timothy 4:7

Praise God the motto of Vanuatu is, 'In God We
Stand'. How awesome it is thousands have turned
to Christ… Though Vanuatu is the third poorest
nation in the Pacific region, over 94% of the
population identify as Christian with thousands
turning to Christ. To God be the glory that this nation
was officially rededicated to the Lord in 2006 with an
outpouring of repentance, celebration, communion
and prayer. Until Christ returns, we ask You God to
solve syncretic beliefs within some churches. We ask
for wisdom concerning Biblical revelation, training,
and teaching for church leaders to grasp of the gospel.
Protect believers from any distracting doctrines in an
influx of other faiths, including Mormonism and
Islam. God also guide government leaders
to lead with righteousness.

Dave Davidson

Venezuela

Let this be written for a future generation,
that a people not yet created may praise the Lord:
Psalm 102:18

Lord it is all about you. Our desire is to serve you.
We want to see the church established in Venezuela.
We pray for the Kingdom of God in Venezuela.
Our greatest longing is to see your will done.
We know you have a perfect plan for Venezuela
and the nations. You have a great destiny.
In you there is a hope and a future.
We pray for your plan for Venezuela.
We ask that your destiny come
forth for this nation.

You have a plan for the present generation in Venezuela. Lord it isn't communism and dictatorship. It isn't injustice but rather life and life more abundantly. Thank you for that. And God you have a plan for the future generation... the children of today. We pray for your protection of the children. And we declare your will done. You have a great harvest of souls. We pray to you, the Lord of the harvest, for that harvest. Bring in the lost. Grow the churches of this nation. In all may you be glorified. Be glorified in the process and in the result. To God be the Glory for the great things He has done!

We declare and decree that the spirit known as negro felipe and all associated spirits and all connected spirits are destroyed and that there hold on Venezuela and the world is lost. All its power is gone, its sheet of deception is lifted and that which is in darkness will be brought forth into the Light of Jesus Christ. This root of African tribalism and shamanism is uprooted and destroyed this day.

We declare and decree that this hidden root of nazism in Venezuela will be uncovered and uprooted in Jesus Name. We declare the defeat and destruction of the presence and influence of the spirits known as elegua, santa barbara, chango, simon bolivar, tamanaco, san juan retornaco, anima ta guapira, negro duarte, ismael, and india tibisae.

We declare and decree that the Bride of Christ will arise. The Body of Christ will come into maturity and into their proper place in Venezuela. A Warrior Cry will come forth in the heart of every believer.

Day 1 & 16 of 40daysofprayerforvenezuela

Vietnam

And everyone who has left houses or brothers or sisters or father
or mother or wife or children or fields for my sake will receive
a hundred times as much and will inherit eternal life.
Matthew 19:29

Lord provide proper discipleship to the ethnic
minorities coming to a saving faith in rural areas.
Strengthen believers with family members pressuring
their relatives to return to traditional faiths and
rituals. We pray that they would come to faith
in Christ through their Christian relatives.

As the Christian minority grows, the government
works hard to monitor churches and curb the growth
of Christianity. Lord loosen of restrictions and
increase freedom in Vietnam one of only five
countries in the world that is still ruled
by a Communist party.

adapted from opendoorua.org

Vision

Without vision the people perish…
Proverbs 29:18

Lord, renew our world vision

and convince us that the faith you have given us
can indeed move mountains. Help us discern how
you are specifically calling us to respond to world
missions. Have us think "wow" for You Lord! Give
us vision for lost souls! Let us know the value of one
soul in your heavenly perspective. May our great
ambitions be aligned with your great commission.
Help us see what we can be for You. Give us
victorious optimism, bold confidence and reachable
goals for the cause of Christ redeeming souls.
Give us dreams that answer the prayers of those
longing to find you Lord. Father God, raise
up godly visionary leaders! Dave Davidson

Exercise our sanctified imagination

that meditates on godly dreams and miracles for
glorifying You and doing Your good and perfect will.
George Verwer

Be Thou my Vision, O Lord of my heart;
Naught be all else to me, save that Thou art
Thou my best Thought, by day or by night,
Waking or sleeping, Thy presence my light.

Be Thou my Wisdom, and Thou my true Word;
I ever with Thee and Thou with me, Lord;
Thou my great Father, I Thy true son;
Thou in me dwelling, and I with Thee one.

Be Thou my battle Shield, Sword for the fight;
Be Thou my Dignity, Thou my Delight;
Thou my soul's Shelter, Thou my high Tower:
Raise Thou me heavenward, O Power of my power.

Riches I heed not, nor man's empty praise,
Thou mine Inheritance, now and always:
Thou and Thou only, first in my heart,
High King of Heaven, my Treasure Thou art.

High King of Heaven, my victory won,
May I reach Heaven's joys, O bright Heaven's Sun!
Heart of my own heart, whatever befall,
Still be my Vision, O Ruler of all.

Dallan Forgaill, 8th Century

Walking in the Spirit

*But the fruit of the Spirit is love, joy, peace, forbearance,
kindness, goodness, faithfulness, 23 gentleness and self-control.
Against such things there is no law.*
Galatians 5:22,23

Heavenly Father, how we pray that our lives would show
forth the beautiful fruit of the Spirit, which is rooted and
grounded in godly love and produced in a life that is
walking in spirit and truth. I pray that the life of Christ
may guard my spirit and rule my life and that I may truly
be submitted to the leading and guidance of Your Holy
Spirit. Teach me I pray, to walk in spirit and truth, to live
as unto the Lord, to depend on Your sufficient grace,
and in Your strength, to fulfil the new commandment
You gave to the Church – to love others as Christ loved us.

My love is weak and poor, but I pray that in Your mercy
You would fan into flame a Christ-like love in my heart,
and develop in me a deep and genuine love for all my
brothers and sisters in Christ. I pray that I would take
every opportunity to demonstrate Your love to others,
in action, attitude, mood and motive.. and to show forth
Your love not only with my lips but in my life, by giving
up myself to Your service, and by walking in holiness and
humility of spirit all the days of my life–to Your praise
and glory. In Jesus name I pray, Amen. Knowing-Jesus.com

War

*You will not have to fight this battle. Take up your positions;
stand firm and see the deliverance the Lord will give you...*
2 Chronicles 20:17

Lord, no doubt the reality of war grieves Your heart in ways we cannot understand. Give us a heart of prayerful compassion for **those engaged in the harsh conflicts of war.** We trust You Lord, that amidst the horror and tragedy of war, in Your sovereign You would use the remnant of war to bring people to a trusting relationship with Jesus.

(Romans 8:28)

Merciful God, save those refugees of war and answer their prayers of restoration, refuge and reconciliation.

Lord, show Your forgiveness to those involved in all aspects of war. Give peace to the many religious based wars going on around the world at any given moment. Protect us Lord from terrorism. Dave Davidson

300,000 children in over 60 countries were involved in armed conflict in 2000.

Widows

*The widow who is really in need and left all alone
puts her hope in God and continues night and day
to pray and to ask God for help.*
1Timothy 5:5

Dear Father, you said, in Isaiah 54:5A, "My maker is my
husband, the Lord of Hosts is His name." Today I need
you to open my heart and make this a living reality for
widows around the world. They are alone, hurting, feeling
a pain and emptiness beyond words. Father, come and
bring new life, vision, hope, and challenge.

Take what seems unbearable

and use it and me to bring Glory to Your name. Help
widows realize that their hopes, dreams, finances, and
security were not in a spouse but in the living Christ.
Be near to them Lord in comfort. Fulfill their unique and
intimate needs that only a spouse is to meet. For You are
the creator, husband, friend, and our God.

Paula K. Leasure, Counselor OMS International

_____

_____

_____

_____

_____

Willingness

Watch and pray so that you will not fall into temptation.
The spirit is willing, but the flesh is weak.
Mark 14:38

Past the host of good intentions
past the burdens of my heart
Past the vows, that men so easily make
Past my psalmic declarations and convictions that I hold
Lord I've come to give myself away

Here am I, send me to the nations
Take my life, and spend me as You will
Break in me, a heart that beats for You
A soul that speaks Your truth, a vessel You can use
So I say, let Your Kingdom come
And I pray, let your will be done
For I am more than willing

There's a fragrance in costly worship
there's an offering I must make
There's a self that must now be denied
There's a purpose worth the living,
there's a world left to save
So I will go as You've commanded in Your name

I am crucified in Christ, and it's no longer just my life
But it's Christ Who is drawing every breath
But I wrestle with the cost, to go and die for the lost
And drink the cup of obedience unto death
So I say, let Your Kingdom come
And I pray, let your will be done
So I say, let Your Kingdom come
For Lord, I am more than willing

Bill Drake from the song More Than Willing
BillDrake.com

Women

We are hard pressed on every side, but not crushed;
perplexed, but not in despair; persecuted, but not
abandoned; struck down, but not destroyed.
2 Corinthians 8,9

Oh, Father God, the treatment of women continues
to be a scandalous tragedy in many parts of the
world. Those fortunate to have a job often work
longer hours for less reward and all too often bear
the greater financial burden to raise their families and
survive in horrendous conditions. Lord, we pray
for countries where female infanticide is widely
practiced, such as China and India. Rescue those
in the growing number of the sex trade and forced
marriages. Lord, we pray those women who are
harassed, persecuted and full of fear. Reveal Your
freedom in Christ and reign in their hearts.

Save those in despicable plots of evil.

Lord, strengthen the plight and hope of women. Raise up godly
courageous leaders who trust You wholeheartedly. Dave Davidson

Lord we pray for the 1.3 billion in deep poverty, 70% are women.

World

For God so loved the world.
John 3:16

Almighty God – Father, Son and Holy Spirit,
We gather with believers all over the world,
to glorify You as Creator of heaven and earth.
You alone are holy and righteous.

We submit to Your authority. We praise and adore You
alone. Father, we honour You Lord Jesus Christ, we
honour You Holy Spirit, we honour You
Our Father in heaven, Thank You for loving the world so
much that You gave Your only Son, Jesus Christ, to die on
the cross for our sins so that we could be reconciled to
You. Fill us with your love as we faithfully intercede for
the lost, the hopeless, the helpless and the world.
Thank You Father, for adopting us into Your family.

Lord Jesus Christ, You died on the cross and redeemed
us to the Father by Your blood. You are Head of the
Church and Lord of all heaven and earth. Let Your
kingdom be established in every nation of the world.
Bring transformation among peoples of all tribes and
languages so that righteousness and justice will prevail.
May Your Name be great, from the rising of the sun
to its setting. Jesus Christ, You are Lord of all.

Father of mercy and grace, We have sinned. Our world
is gripped by the power of sin. Our hearts are grieved
by injustice, hatred and violence. We are shamed by
oppression, racism and bloodshed in our land. We mourn
all loss of life in murder, war and terrorism. Our homes are
broken and our churches are divided by rebellion and
pride. Our lives are polluted by selfishness, greed,
idolatry and sexual sin. God of mercy, forgive our sins.
Pour out Your grace and heal our land. Spirit of the living
God, transform Your Church into the image of Jesus
Christ. Release Your power to bring healing to the sick,
freedom to the oppressed and comfort to those who
mourn. Fill us with compassion for the homeless and the
hungry for orphans, widows and the elderly. Give us
wisdom and insight for our world's problems to use the
resources of the earth for the well-being of all. Holy Spirit,
guide us and lead us. Lord Jesus Christ, You destroyed
sin, conquered death and defeated Satan. Remove the veil
of darkness that covers the peoples.
Restrain the evil that promotes violence and death.
Deliver us from demonic oppression.
Break the hold of slavery, tyranny and disease.
Help us to tear down strongholds and ideologies
that resist the knowledge of God.
Almighty God, deliver us from evil.
King of Glory, Come and finish Your work in our cities,
our peoples and our nations.
From all continents and islands we cry:
Lift up your heads, O you gates!
Be lifted up ancient doors
so that the King of glory may come in!
Come fill the earth with the
knowledge of Your glory
as the waters cover the sea.
The Spirit and the Bride say:
Amen! Come Lord Jesus!
Global Day of Prayer 2015

World Leaders

I urge then, first of all, that requests, prayers, intercession and thanksgiving be made for all those in authority, that we may live peaceful and quiet lives in all godliness and holiness.
1 Timothy 2:1,2

God, guide our leaders in wisdom and compassion. We pray for all the leaders of all governments throughout the world. May they govern in mercy and truth. Bless those who honor and love You, Lord.

Give mercy to those who oppose You. In Your sovereign way Lord, watch and care over their people. May those who rule against the Gospel of Christ be brought to confusion and made ineffective. For leaders who are in spiritual darkness, may they receive Your truth.

May they desire understanding, find it in Your Word and embrace it well! Have leaders living in war-torn nations grow weary of bloodshed and initiate peace and forgiveness. May corrupt leaders recognize their evil ways, repent and lead others to God. Dave Davidson

Wolves in Sheep's Clothing

Watch out for false prophets. They come to you in sheep's clothing, but inwardly they are ferocious wolves.
Matthew 7:15

Lord, there are a lot of ravenous wolves in the world disguised as sheep, just waiting to pounce on the weak, the needy, the helpless, the hopeless and those who lack knowledge of your word.

Lord Jesus, help them. Open their eyes that they would see. Unblock their ears that they would hear. Soften their hearts that they would feel. Grant them your wisdom, that they would understand. Help them to embrace you…

Lord, there are many who pretend

to be your disciples but preach false doctrines. Teach us, your faithful followers, to decipher and recognize these false prophets. They twist the real meaning of your beautiful scriptures to suit what they believe to be right.

Hence, this is where religion comes into play. Oh, loving Father, may we not be religious but be righteous people of your holy land. Religion lists the dos and don's, while your word gives us the key to your kingdom.

May we not be fooled

by these false doctrines and false prophecies, for these are all works of the devil to deceive your people. Send your angels to protect us from all evil.

Cheryce Ramersad

Worship

God is spirit, and his worshipers
must worship in the Spirit and in truth.
John 4:24

Holy Spirit help me live today as a worshipper,
as one who sees every part of life as an great
opportunity to worship and bring glory to God.
Todd Morr

Yemen

*But when you pray, go into your room, close the door
and pray to your Father, who is unseen. Then your Father,
who sees what is done in secret, will reward you.*
Matthew 6:6

The war that Saudi Arabia is fighting in Yemen is
helping extremists from al-Qaeda and IS to move
freely through the country. They are extremely
aggressive towards Christians.

God touch the hearts of extremists so they will
embrace the gospel. We pray that secret gatherings
of believers from Muslim backgrounds would glorify
God, and that Christians would be able to
minister to their fellow Yemenis.

Since 80% of Yemenis depend on aid. Aid is typically
channeled through the tribal and family lines of
which Christians are often disconnected. We petition
You Lord that aid will reach Christians.

adapted from opendoorua.org

You

Teach me your way, O Lord, and I will walk in your truth;
give me an undivided heart, that I may fear your name.
Psalm 86:11

_____
_____
_____
_____
_____
_____
_____
_____
_____
_____
_____
_____
_____
_____
_____
_____
_____
_____
_____
_____
_____
_____
_____
_____
_____
_____
_____
_____
_____
_____
_____
_____
_____
_____
_____
_____

Write out a prayer list of worthy topics not found in this book.

Youth Ministry

Since my youth, O God, you have taught me,
and to this day I declare your marvelous deeds.
Psalm 71:17

Father, for those that claim to be believers, we pray that their lives would be truly transformed and not just be following the religious rituals of their elders. Rise up youth to bear abundant fruit in their lives so that they would have a supernatural influence upon their families, friends, churches, clubs and schools. Father, for those same believers, we pray that they would have a desire to invest themselves in the ministry of the church and the work of the kingdom. Give them Luke 15 compassion for the lost around them and Christlike passion to multiply their lives and to make disciples wherever You would send them. Father, stir secular and Christian universities and schools around the world, that You would bring a radical move of Your Spirit to each of them, exposing life's emptiness without You. Send more youth workers and pastors overseas, out of their comfort zone to be missionary youth workers! Todd Morr

Zambia

Speak up and judge fairly; defend the rights of the poor and needy.
Proverbs 31:9

For Zambia Lord we pray for national unity, the economy, constitution-making process, poverty reduction, general elections, rain and education.

We also seek You Lord about health, mining operations, the media (to be factual and fair), the church and to merely thank God for the stable government. God guide political parties, traditional leaders and the civil society.

adapted from Reverend Pukuta Mwanza

Zimbabwe

*They will be a sign and a wonder
to you and your descendants forever.*
Deuteronomy 28:46

Jehovah-Jireh, Jehovah-Rapha, Jehovah-Shalom,
God of liberty and righteousness, God of peace and
truth, in the glory and wonder of earth, sea, and stars,
in the miracle of all life and form in the whole
universe, in the complexity and confusion of human
experience, we celebrate your loving compassion.

We are called by your name. We seek your face. We
humble ourselves. Hear us from heaven and heal our
world. On this day, in this place and in this moment,
among many other nations, we raise the people of
Zimbabwe in your wondrous presence. We name
their fears and acknowledge their anxieties. We affirm
their aspirations and encourage their expectations.

In the liminal moments of hope and anxiety,
of confusion and clarity, of peace and violence,

Zimbabwe craves your love.
Zimbabwe yearns for your grace.
Zimbabwe cries for your wisdom.
Zimbabwe pants for your discipline.
Zimbabwe thirsts for your freedom.

You are the shepherd of scattered sheep in Zimbabwe.

Where there is impunity, we pray for responsible and accountable leadership. Where there is corruption, we pray for honesty. Where there is abuse of power, we pray for your righteousness. May the leaders of Zimbabwe govern with justice and do what is right. May they defend the poor, protect the weak, and defeat the oppressors.

You feed your people on the mountains, by the watercourses, and in the plains. Where there is hunger in Zimbabwe bring prosperity. Where the economy has been ravaged, bring restoration and recovery. Let there be abundance in Zimbabwe and may all the people flourish.

You are the ultimate physician.

You bind up the injured and strengthen the infirm. Bring recovery to the health sector in Zimbabwe, and may your people be healed and restored.

You are the perfect arbiter.

Where relationships have broken down, bring reconciliation. Where ordinary people have been bullied and silenced, redeem them from tyranny and domination. Their blood is precious and saved.

You seek out your flocks and gather your scattered sheep. Where there are vicious disagreements and turmoil, bring calm conversations and unity of purpose. Where people have been set up against each other, bring discernment of your will and clarity of your mission.

You birthed and mothered your church as your bride on this earth. Where it has been silent give it a voice. May Zimbabwe have a prophetic and courageous church, speaking truth to power, and compassion to ordinary people, in obedience to your command of grace and peace.

God of the cosmos, God of the ordinary, God of small nations, God of powerful states, You are the compass provider, the navigator of wildernesses, Zimbabwe is at a prophetic crossroads. May you guide its people through storm and desert. May this nation join other nations in giving glory to your wondrous name.

collated by Rev Dr Vincent Munyaradzi Jambawo

Afterword Recap

Take a moment to consider this scene from Matthew 25. As we approach the throne of heaven when the Son of Man comes in His glory, we will come face to face with our Creator. Will we regret that we did not spend time in committed prayer for what was important to God's heart? We will have spent more time watching beer commercials than praying for lost souls in Arab countries? Will we miss the opportunity to minister in the name of Jesus through prayer for the lost of the world after all He has done for us?

It would be hard to find an excuse that would ever justify our lack of love and compassion through prayer for orphans, refugees, widows, lost peoples, the hungry and the poor. Here is the super cool thing! We can begin to strengthen our honor of God today with our prayer life for the peoples of the world. We can be part of God's worldwide ministry!

Consider these thoughts about focused prayer by Brother Andrew… "I discovered why Christians don't pray anymore - even though we all feel that we should. The reason is simple: We haven't learned to focus our prayers. Wouldn't you like a real challenge in your prayer life… build your prayer power and discover how to focus on specific needs? Prayer is the basis of everything God is accomplishing in the world, and that is why I consider it so important for us to unlock these hidden reserves of divine power and confront the enemy who is sweeping the earth today. Prayer: It's not the preparation for battle; prayer is the battle."

Jesus taught His disciples this same lesson of focused prayer in the garden of Gethsemane. As Leonard Ravenhill puts it "We must learn to pray, and we must pray to learn to pray."

The work of Operation Mobilization was birthed from one woman praying for a teenager who in turn asked God to make him a man of prayer. Of course, many other ministries attribute their fruit to the promise of God through prayer. God will answer prayer according to His will. We must believe this and stay focused, stay involved and stay in the race!

We have discovered that many of us have different "prayer personalities". We may carry a burden for a certain country, cause or ministry, but find it difficult to know how or what to pray for.

It is our hope that this book will be a supplement and catalyst to your own personal prayer life by including over 100 specific prayers for key ministry needs around the world. We encourage you to add more topics and to share your prayers at PrayAlong.com.

God not only has really big plans, He has really big plans for You in His really big plans. You are invited, commanded and urged to participate in His Great Commission through faithful intercessory prayer.

Consistent prayer is a challenge but also a joyful pursuit in our Christian walk. God has chosen prayer as a powerful agent in accomplishing His will on earth as it is in heaven. What a privilege to be a ministry partner with God Himself, anywhere and anytime for anyone around the globe. Often our prayers and our church prayers are made as supplication for ministries and circumstances that may benefit us. We are indeed called to pray sacrificially beyond our comfort zone to the ends of the earth for the lost and hurting of the world.

Francois Coillard put it this way, "We must remember that it was not by interceding for the world in glory that Jesus saved it. He gave Himself. Our prayers for the evangelization of the world are but a bitter irony so long as we give only of our abundance, and draw back before the sacrifice of ourselves."

Patrick Johnstone wrote "Unless we are utterly convinced of its essentiality and efficacy, we will never make prayer our central ministry as God intended." Corrie Ten Boom wrote "When man listens, God speaks. When man obeys, God acts. When man prays, God empowers."

When man prays for missionaries, lost souls and breakthroughs, God changes the world! We cannot afford to buy the devilish lies that prayer is not a significant endeavor. We must expect a great ambition faith. Now is the time to make world mission prayer vital in your walk with God. Congratulations! If you are reading this,

God is calling you to take action.

Take the spiritual challenge and claim the blessing to make prayers for world missions a higher priority in your life. We pray that God will use this book to change your life and the world.

Dan & Dave Davidson

Andrew Murray once said,
"The man who mobilizes the Christian church to pray will make the greatest contribution to world evangelization in history."

Lord remind us again and again...
"Prayer moves the Hand, which moves the world."
John A. Wallace

...The prayer of a righteous man is powerful and effective. *James 5:16*

Through prayer you can accompany any missionary to remote reaches of the earth.

Through prayer you can walk through crowded bazaars, minister in steaming jungles, feed millions of starving men, women, and children, hungry for bread for their bodies and for the Bread of Life.

Through prayer you can contribute to the ministry of any pastor or evangelist in a church or gospel hall anywhere in the world.

Through prayer you can take a suffering infant in your arms or touch a fevered brow in any hospital, mediating the healing love of Jesus.
Wesley Duewel

We are reaching out in prayer with a supreme purpose of seeing Christ's kingdom ultimately established throughout the earth – and to that end, we must persist. All God's promises must be taken at face value. Dick Eastman

Prayer is not bondage
to a ritual we have to do --
It is the outflow of a loving
relationship with our God!

In my study of God's Word and in my travels
throughout the world, I have become absolutely
convinced that wherever people really pray according
to biblical principles, God works in their lives and
through them in the lives of others in a special way.

Show me a church

or a Christian organization that emphasizes prayer,
and I'll show you a ministry where people are excited
about Jesus Christ and are witnessing for Him. On the
other hand, show me a church or Christian cause
where there is little emphasis on prayer, and I will
show you worldly Christians who have little interest
in the souls of men and women. Their lives can best
be described by the experience of the Church of
Ephesus and the Church of Laodicea
in Revelation 2 and 3.

Bill Bright

GeorgeVerwer.com
George@GeorgeVerwer.com

George Verwer lives his passion recruiting and encouraging churches to follow the Acts 13 example of sending out missionaries into the harvest fields. He is the founder of Operation Mobilisation, a ministry of evangelism, discipleship training and church planting he led for 40 years. He and his wife, Drena, have three adult children and are now involved in Special Projects Ministries full-time. George's mission work has taken him all over the world both in travel and through prayer. When not using his mobile phone you can find him speaking to thousands of young people. God uses 80-year-old + George to stretch once preconceived notions about missions and God's priority of reaching the world for Christ.

Upon his teenager conversion he said, 'Only one thing I want in life – I want to learn to pray, to love you, I want to know you and commune with you.' He has not moved from that principle. George shares the Christian revolution of love and balance right around the world. He starts at home emphasizing the need to worship God, live in fellowship with one another by walking in the light, and live a disciplined life of victory as forgiven, repentant, Cross-centered Christians.

As the author of several inspiring books, his staple book, "Out of The Comfort Zone" is challenging people all over God's globe. His recent titles include "Messiology" and "Drops From A Leaking Tap". He also co-wrote "God's Great Ambition" and "Surviving Temptation Island" with brothers Dan and Dave Davidson.

BillDrake.com
Bill@BillDrake.com

Abused and unwanted as a child and young teenager, Bill Drake knows what it is to feel hurt, rejected and without hope. At the age of 19 he was playing piano in bars and nightclubs in his native America and was on the brink of ending what he describes as his "unlovely life." Only by the grace of God, did he not commit suicide. God radically changed his life and began to use his musical gifting to challenge and encourage others.

Several years later George Verwer, founder of Operation Mobilization, heard Bill lead worship at Biola University in California and threw out a challenge: "How can you play and sing songs like that if you are not willing to back it up with your lifestyle?" George went on to challenge Bill to live the commitment he was singing about and join OM as International Music Minister. Since then, Bill has been privileged to minister in over 50 countries.

Bill is fond of saying, "If the purpose of your life is not wrapped up in God's purpose for the world, you will miss the reason you're alive." Bill is also fond of saying, "Friends, don't be afraid of failure. But be very afraid of being successful at things that don't matter." Most recently Bill has been asked to lead a new Division in OM Internationally, called Catalytic Ministries. He has produced thirteen albums of original music and two books. Bill's fourteenth album project, Legacy, contains 75 of Bill's songs recorded over 30 years.

DanDavidson.com
Dan@DanDavidson.com

Dr. Dan Davidson is a chiropractor and founder of The Back Resort & Rejuvenation Health Center since 1984. He is the author gobs of books and half the brother duo of Dan & Dave.

Todd Morr
toddcmorr@gmail.com

Todd has been a missionary his entire adult life mobilizing leaders throughout eastern Europe with various agencies with his wife Hanna and gobs of kids.

DaveDavidson.com
Dave@DaveDavidson.com

Brothers **Dan & Dave Davidson**
share the same mission statement in the acronym
T.I.M.E. Teach, Inspire, Motivate and Encourage.
Train. Influence, Mentor & Equip.

Dave has written, designed, and published over 200 books...
His comedy pen name is Hugh Myrrh with over dozen titles.
Cyrano D (a.k.a. Cyrano De Words-u-lac) with over 2 dozen
titles is a combined pen name shared with brother Dan.
He has over a dozen poetry books in print and just as many
motivational business & inspirational quote books.

Dave is also a founder of the Verse Rehearse, Pray Along,
ScriptureSong.com & Teenager Church part of Surge Up
Ministry efforts. As a scripture songwriter he has recorded
over 350 songs, all found for FREE at PoetTree.com.

He has published political books from photographing
Iowa presidential politics for over a decade for Prezography.
With experience of over 200 weddings, he compiled his best
images for the Artsy Bride Guides for the Picture Perfect
Wedding, Phoday and other photography collections.

He is a perennial youth pastor, missionary, speaker and
photographer. Dave and his wife Joan, (1991) have 8 children.

Photo of Dave by Glen Cornell

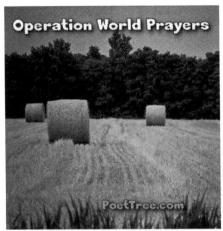

You've read the book,
"Pray Along World Mission Prayers"
now hear the scripture songs soundtrack entitled…

"Operation World Prayers"
available FREE at **PoetTree.com**
Free scripture songs soundtrack with
prayers for the world to 'Pray Along" with.

More Pray Along resources
at Amazon & PrayAlong.com

SurgeUp.com

Verse Rehearse

Verse Memes

Books of the Bible

VerseRehearse.com

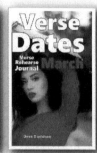

Verse Rehearse
Verse Dates

VerseRehearse.com

Pray Along with the entire 10/40 Prayer Bucket List Library

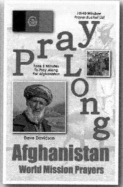

PrayAlong.com

Pray Along with the entire 10/40 Prayer Bucket List Library

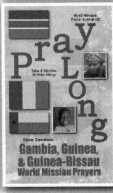

PrayAlong.com

Pray Along with the entire 10/40 Prayer Bucket List Library

PrayAlong.com

Pray Along with the entire 10/40 Prayer Bucket List Library

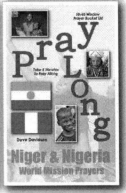

PrayAlong.com

Pray Along with the entire 10/40 Prayer Bucket List Library

PrayAlong.com

Pray Along with the entire 10/40 Prayer Bucket List Library

PrayAlong.com

Take the dare
to share the FREE
full color ebook
version of this title at
PrayAlong.com with
every believer you
know in life.

Be resolute in prayer.
Make any sacrifice to maintain it.
Consider that time is short and that business
and company must not be allowed
to rob these of thy God.

Adoniram Judson

43526638R00273

Made in the USA
Lexington, KY
30 June 2019